Pete Dice
Quick Boot

Pete Dice

Quick Boot

A Guide for Embedded Firmware Developers

2nd edition

ISBN 978-1-5015-1538-5
e-ISBN (PDF) 978-1-5015-0681-9
e-ISBN (EPUB) 978-1-5015-0672-7

Library of Congress Cataloging-in-Publication Data
A CIP catalog record for this book has been applied for at the Library of Congress.

Bibliographic information published by the Deutsche Nationalbibliothek
The Deutsche Nationalbibliothek lists this publication in the Deutsche Nationalbibliografie;
detailed bibliographic data are available on the Internet at http://dnb.dnb.de.

© 2018 Pete Dice
Published by Walter de Gruyter Inc., Boston/Berlin
Printing and binding: CPI books GmbH, Leck
♾ Printed on acid-free paper
Printed in Germany

www.degruyter.com

MIX
Papier aus verantwor-
tungsvollen Quellen
FSC
www.fsc.org
FSC® C083411

Acknowledgments

The studies, data, results, and guidelines compiled in the book are the result of many talented engineers at Intel who have a strong passion for BIOS and firmware. The contributions they have made and the time they have spent, much of it outside their normal duties, deserve to be acknowledged.

For significant contributions to this book for analyses, cases studies, and written content, I'd like to thank these talented engineers:

- Jim Pelner—who crafted the original white paper that echoes the main themes of this book and for contributing to several chapters early on.
- Jaben Carsey—who wrote the shell chapter in the book above and beyond his many contributions to the UEFI shells in general.
- Sam Fleming—who created Appendix A and has been one of my mentors in BIOS from the beginning.
- Mike Rothman, Anton Cheng, Linda Weyhing, Rob Gough, Siddharth Shah, and Chee Keong Sim—for their exquisite multiyear collaboration around the fast boot concept and multiple case studies over the year.
- BIOS vendor Insyde Software for donating feedback and volunteering for the foreword.

Thanks to my program manager, Stuart Douglas, for getting me through the writing phase and then on to the finish line (are we there yet?).

Reviewer comments and suggestions were extremely valuable for both editions of this work. I deeply appreciate those who took the time to provide indispensable feedback, including Drew Jensen, Mark Doran, Jeff Griffen, John Mitkowski, and Dong Wei and at my publisher, Jeff Pepper, Megan Lester, Mark Watanabe and Angie MacAllister for her work on fixing the art and tables.

I would also like to acknowledge my peers in the BIOS/FW engineering and architecture teams within the computer industry for their drive to make this technology an ever more valuable (and less obtrusive) part of people's everyday lives. Lastly, I want to thank my wife, Anita, for her patience and everything she's done to allow me time to complete this.

Contents

Foreword from the First Edition

How do you explain what BIOS is? I generally explain it as the code that runs when you first turn on the computer. It creates a level playing field so that the operating system has a known state to start from. If the other person has some programming knowledge, he or she generally says something like, "Oh. You're one of *those* guys!" Let's face it. BIOS isn't sexy. The hardware engineers will always blame the BIOS engineers if the system fails to POST. It's generally up to BIOS engineers to prove it isn't their code that is the problem.

When I first started as a lowly BIOS Engineer II, the BIOS codebase was pure x86 assembly code—thousands of files across almost as many directories with lots of cryptic comments like, "I don't know why this is here, but it breaks if I remove or modify it! Beware!" It took 45 minutes to do a clean compile. Comments would commonly refer to specifications that no longer existed. To say a BIOS is filled with some secret, arcane algorithms is like saying driving a Formula 1 car is just like driving on the freeway, only faster! There are no college courses that teach BIOS programming. There are no trade schools to go to. A few software and electronic engineers will be able to make it as BIOS engineers because it takes a bit of both to be successful.

This book is the first one I'm aware of that attempts to shine light onto the esoteric field of BIOS engineering. A field that makes everything from the big-iron servers to the lowly smartphone turn on. This book has combined two fundamental concepts. What you need to know to make a BIOS that works and what you need to know to make a BIOS that works fast! It wasn't that long ago that a POST in under ten seconds was considered pretty fast. Today's standard is now under two seconds. There are topics outlined in this book that will help get you to that sub-2-second goal. I am currently working on a quasi-embedded system that is in the sub-1-second range with full measured boot using these concepts!

This book has something for the recent college graduate as well as the seasoned BIOS engineer. There are nuggets of tribal knowledge scattered throughout. Help yourself become better acquainted with the BIOS industry and read it.

–Kelly Steele,
Former BIOS Architect, Insyde Software, Inc.,
Now at Intel Corporation

This book has something for the recent college graduate as well as the seasoned BIOS engineer. There are nuggets of tribal knowledge scattered throughout. Help yourself become better acquainted with the BIOS industry and read it.

Chapter 1
System Firmware's Missing Link

Hardware: the parts of a computer that can be kicked.

—Jeff Pesis

Booting an Intel architecture platform should be easy. Anyone who thinks that writing an all-purpose Intel® architecture Basic Input Output System (BIOS) and/or an operating system (OS) boot loader from scratch is easy has yet to try it. The complexity and sheer number of documents and undocumented details about the motherboard and hardware components, operating system requirements, industry standards and exceptions, silicon-specific eccentricities beyond the standards, little-known tribal knowledge, basic configuration, compiler nuances, linker details, and variety of applicable debug tools are enormous. While it can be difficult, it doesn't have to be.

This book is designed to give a background in the basic architecture and details of a typical boot sequence to the beginner firmware developer. Various specifications provide the basics of both the code bases and the standards. While a summary is provided in the chapters below, there is no substitute for reading and comprehending the specifications and developer's manuals first-hand. This book also provides insights into optimization techniques to the more advanced developers. With the background information, the required specifications on hand, and diligence, many developers can create quality boot solutions. Even if they choose not to create, but to purchase the solution from a vendor, the right information about boot options makes the decision making easier.

Start by Gathering Data

First you must 'know the ground'; obtaining and using the right data are essential to success. To begin to gather the appropriate documents at the start of the project requires research. Full system initialization is like a large puzzle where someone has hidden some of the pieces:

- Motherboard schematics are an absolute must. If you are designing the board, then that is not a problem. If you are reusing an off-the-shelf solution, there is a high likelihood that the vendor who created the board is unwilling to release schematics readily. You can reverse-engineer some of the data, like system management bus addresses, but things like IRQs and GPIOs will be very difficult. If there is an embedded controller in the picture, the number of unknowns increases.
- A standard system BIOS today covers at least 70 industry standard specifications alone that can apply to the mainstream client and server boxes commercially

DOI 10.1515/9781501506819-001

available. For application specifications, there could be dozens for a given market segment. If it is a new or emerging type of system, there will be no mature standard and you will be chasing a moving target. Obtaining the list of industry standards that apply is a daunting task and may require some registering and joining to gain access to specifications and/or forums to get your questions answered. Some older specifications are not published and not available today on the Internet.

– There are many long-in-the-tooth legacy devices that may need to be initialized, and finding documentation on them is challenging. They may exist only in the dusty drawers of a senior engineer who retired five years ago.

– In some cases, nondisclosure agreements (NDAs) must be signed with the various silicon, BIOS, or motherboard vendors. The NDAs can take precious time to obtain and will require some level of legal advice.

– UEFI provides a handy API for interfacing to the OS. It has a modular framework and is a viable starting place supporting many industry standards such as ACPI and PCI.

– Until now, no single reference manual has documented the required steps needed to boot an Intel architecture system in one place. Nor has anyone detailed the order of initialization to get someone started.

Those who have been exposed to system firmware at a coding level and the inner workings of the black art that is system BIOS understand that it is difficult to explain everything it does, how it does it, or why it should be done in exactly that way. Not many people in the world would have all theanswers to every step in the sequence. Most people who work in the code will want to know just enough to make necessary changes and press on with development or call up their BIOS vendor.

Fortunately, there are many options available when choosing a firmware solution, which we will examine in the next few pages. The more you know about the options, the key players, their history, and the variables, the better decision you can make for your design. The decision will be a combination of arbitrary thought, low-hanging fruit, economies of scale, technical politics, and, of course, money vs. time.

Intel has created an open-source-based system, known as Intel® Boot Loader Development Kit (Intel® BLDK), which provides a turnkey solution without a huge learning curve. Developers can go to www.intel.com and download Intel BLDK for various embedded platforms.

Intel® Quark processor also has a UEFI implementation that is entirely open source and is built using the UEFI framework. This can be found online by searching for Galileo UEFI firmware.

Initialization Roles and Responsibilities

First, let's get our definitions straight; understand what the industry has been up to, and how we can move forward to make the best decision we can make. Traditionally, a platform based on Intel architecture boots in three steps: system firmware, OS loader, and finally the operating system itself.

System Firmware

The system firmware is a layer between the hardware and the OS that maintains data for the OS about the hardware. As part of the power on self-test (POST), the system firmware begins to execute out of flash to initialize all the necessary silicon components, including the CPU itself and the memory subsystem. Once main memory is initialized, the system firmware is shadowed from ROM into the RAM and the initialization continues. As part of the advanced initialization stages, the system firmware creates tables of hardware information in main memory for the operating system to utilization during its installation, loading, and runtime execution. During POST, hardware workarounds are often implemented to avoid changing silicon or hardware during later design phases. There may be an element of the system firmware that remains active during latter stages to allow for responses to various operating system function calls. The system firmware is customized for the specific hardware needs of the platform and perhaps for a given application. The last thing the system firmware does is hand off control to the OS loader.

System firmware can be constructed in a proprietary legacy code base and/or in a Unified Extensible Firmware Interface (UEFI) framework. Legacy BIOS incorporates a legacy OS interface and follows legacy software interrupt protocols that have been evolving organically since the IBM PC (circa 1981). UEFI is a specification detailing an interface that helps hand off control of the system for the preboot environment—that is, after the system is powered on, but before the operating system starts—to an operating system, such as Microsoft Windows or Linux. UEFI provides an interface between operating systems and platform firmware at boot time, and supports an architecture-independent mechanism for initializing add-in cards (option ROM). We will dig in to the story of how and why legacy BIOS has been converted to UEFI in a minute. A key takeaway is that the system initialization code is either going to be UEFI-based, or legacy-based, or try to support elements of both depending on the operating system requirements.

OS Loader

The OS loader does exactly what its name implies. It is customized with knowledge about the specific operating system, how it is ordered, and what blocks of the OS to pull from the OS storage location. A long list of OS loaders is available in the market today for Linux. We will examine a few of these in later chapters. Microsoft Windows and real-time custom operating systems also have their own flavors. It is possible that the OS loader may be enabled or configured to extend the platform initialization beyond the system firmware's scope to allow for more boot options than was originally planned.

It is possible, depending on the system architecture and the firmware solutions that you work on, that the OS loader and the system firmware are part of the same binary image located in the same component on the system, or it may be separated.

Operating System

The operating system completes, or in some cases repeats, the initialization of the hardware as it loads and executes the software kernel, services, and device drivers. It potentially loads the human/machine interface (HMI) and finally begins to run the applications. Depending on the application, there are various ways that the OS can be initiated. We will dig into this more in future chapters.

Care should be taken when considering combining elements of various components together as proprietary, and public licenses may prohibit linking the objects together in various ways.

Legacy BIOS Interface, UEFI, and the Conversion

For the three elements to communicate effectively, they share a common set of interfaces. The interfaces have undergone a dramatic change in the past decade. This conversion from legacy BIOS interfaces to UEFI interfaces has not been without some major challenges. During the past ten years, much has been said in industry forums about the platform innovation Framework for EFI, also known as the Tiano code base. When selecting a starting point for development it is important to know the legacy, limitations, and benefits of various solutions.

Tiano Benefits

There are several benefits to UEFI over legacy BIOS:

- *Location of option ROMs.* Legacy option ROMs have been constrained for many years by having to reside below the 1-MB boundary of 16- bit code. Between C0000h and FFFFFh in system memory, all option ROMs including required components like Video BIOS, LAN, SCSI/RAID, manageability, and the system firmware runtime code all had to coexist. In server platforms, this limited the number of add-in cards that could be plugged in. Each of the legacy option ROMs had to do unnatural things to keep their code sizes minimized. A native UEFI system can move the option ROMs above 1 MB, enhancing their capabilities and size. The benefit has real value, especially in larger systems with many add-in devices.
- *UEFI option ROMs themselves have many benefits over legacy option ROMs.* They can be created without the 16-bit code interface, which adds substantial overhead to a legacy option ROM. There is also a UEFI-defined interface to allow for a cohesive user interface instead of creating and maintaining a unique/proprietary command line UI or inventing a GUI, which saves a great deal of size and development overhead in UEFI option ROMs.

  Lastly, UEFI option ROMs can also utilize EFI Byte Code (EBC), which allows a single binary to be executed by 64-bit or 32-bit system firmware, thereby reducing validation and inventory issues.
- *Potential for faster boot.* Another advantage of UEFI option ROMs is the ability to initialize only those needed to boot the OS and load the rest later through UEFI function calls from the OS, which speeds the boot process. It requires that the OS utilize a native UEFI interface and that the OS loaders used are also UEFI capable. This benefit has been proved on complex systems between legacy and UEFI solutions, taking the boot speeds from 40 seconds down to 15 seconds in one case.
- *The modularity of the PEI and DXE modules allows for faster integration of differing code modules.* In some cases, this allows for the faster adoption of the code bases' newer technologies into the platform. It is believed that legacy system BIOS would be unable to integrate new and complex concepts such as Intel® Trusted Execution Technology (Intel® TXT) without extended time in development and validation. Quickly integrating new bus support and in turn new system firmware and OS storage solutions are also a benefit of UEFI. It has been proved that legacy code bases can have difficulty integrating newer technologies.
- *UEFI Shell.* The shell was designed to support features from DOS or UNIX environments in order to be a potential replacement for these older OS. Many of the same commands are supported. Simple native applications similar to older OS applications can be created to run single function operations for the platform or provide diagnostics or a flash upgrade path. UEFI shells have become standardized in the past few years. For more information on shells, please refer to "Harnessing the UEFI Shell" or proceed to Chapter 9.

- *Scalability.* Having an open-source system-firmware offering supported by a community of many computing companies, including BIOS vendors, OEMs, motherboard manufacturers, add-in card vendors, OS vendors, and silicon vendors, can be very advantageous when starting and maintaining your own development in the long term. If you're using a legacy proprietary code base, the learning curve exists as with any code base, and there are continuous improvements and maintenance costs/time. The solution may not scale quite so easily between computing segments.
- *Security.* In the most recent updates of the UEFI development kit (UDK2015), Internet Protocol v6 is supported. UEFI variables can be securely stored and easily authenticated. A new UEFI security binary can be added to allow for hashing. UEFI option ROMs that are added in can be signed and the signatures checked before execution. As new operating systems come online, security will be a vital requirement across most market segments. UEFI is ready for the tasks.
- *Longevity.* UEFI has legs for the foreseeable future. Legacy is legacy for a reason, and continuing to support that legacy adds costs and complexity.

There are some clear advantages to UEFI: faster boot, modularity, DOS replacement, scalability, security, overcoming the limitations of legacy PC AT interfaces, and longevity.

Previous UEFI Challenges

In the past, there have been some challenges early in the adoption of UEFI. While these challenges have been discussed and dealt with at an industry level, some still see the need to address bringing up these points of debate. As embedded architecture moves forward into new segments, it is vital that open and honest dialogue can occur about the firmware solutions that exist and their pros and cons. As these perceptions may still exist, let's review the points and discuss how they have been eliminated or minimized over time.

- Maturity: Like any new code base, UEFI source initially lacked 20 years of industry validation and experience. It did not consider every known add-in card workaround or industry standard. It was not ported to many environments. It was not yet validated over the long term across multiple generations of products (and developers). Over the past decades, this has changed. The solution is now well validated by many industry teams and groups. Workarounds have been included, the industry standards have been adhered to, and new environments have been adapted.
- Some tend to adapt to any new technology slowly. Despite the benefits of a new standard, a new code base takes time to adopt and adapt to, in part due to NIH (not invented here) syndrome. In other cases, it has been a matter of having to

support a code-base change while maintaining the legacy one. It takes several cycles to convert before the technology is broadly embraced.

– One common belief of early adopters has been that handwritten assembly code would always outperform C code. Intel and other maintainers of compilers have advanced their craft, and these compilers can now surpass and put to rest the ASM-only ideology.

– The original Tiano code base was not constructed like a traditional system BIOS in the core-to-platform-to-motherboard architecture. Instead, it was constructed as an OS might be, with a core-to-bus-to-device- driver model, which proved difficult to adapt to some new segments. The newer version of the code base, EDK II, has evolved to facilitate development with input from major BIOS vendors and OEMs.

Persistence of Change

In the end, what started out as an idea exclusive to Itanium® began to see early UEFI projects started in mainstream computing. First in the mobile-computing segments, where UEFI was designed into many laptop computers starting around 2002. It then spread to adjacent segments in desktop machines, and is now implemented in a broad range of products from high-end servers to embedded devices. And not just Intel Architecture, but ARM architecture as well.

The Next Generation

As with any first-generation product, changes and improvements to the design were made to meet the industry needs. Working together within the UEFI forum, where most major players in the computing business are working on the next-generation firmware architectures and implementations of UEFI open source code base, the team has produced the EDK II. It has taken many years to work through and prioritize some of the improvements and changes required to help the industry to evolve and remain vibrant. Major computing manufacturing companies and BIOS vendors are ready to ship products on this new code base, which promises more flexibility and streamlined features, including GCC (GNU Compiler Collection) compatibility.

Also, while being deep in complexity, the documentation of the newer versions of the code is unsurpassed within the industry. The API today is more robust and usable than in previous generations and more easily adapted to new and upcoming operating systems.

This was the history of the major conversion and some of the reasons you can decide to select a standard UEFI implementation or a different firmware technology to start on for development. Strategically, EDK II easily makes the best long-term solution. Let's look at the state of the commercial BIOS business that has emerged from the transition.

Commercial BIOS Business

Looking at commercial independent BIOS vendors (IBVs), it's evident the industry has been evolving since 1983, when Phoenix Technologies Limited (Phoenix) shipped its first BIOS. Like any industry, it has grown and shrunk, and new companies have started while major competitive players have merged.

Award

Award BIOS was started in Taiwan and with its unique per-unit license quickly took advantage of local tax loopholes to gain the edge at local motherboard vendors. The simplicity and affinity of the Award code base has kept the product entrenched in various motherboard manufacturers years after Phoenix had discontinued the product.

General Software

Formed in 1989 by former Windows NT architect Steve Jones, General Software created unique and dynamic solutions for the embedded segment. General Software has in the past been one of the major players in the embedded space but did not penetrate much into the mainstream markets.

Phoenix Technologies Limited

Phoenix, headquartered in Milpitas, CA, was founded in 1979 (pre-BIOS). In 1998, Phoenix purchased the Award BIOS, and in 2007 acquired General Software. By combining the code bases and resources of the three original companies, Phoenix BIOS has a large amount of intellectual property to draw from as it moves forward. Phoenix has gone through great changes in the past few years, including branching out into adjacent software ventures.

American Megatrends Inc.

AMI was founded in 1985 by Subramanian Shankar and has created a large variety of solutions, including BIOS, software diagnostics, RAID technology, and hardware platforms. Beyond having a broad base of products, AMI is the only consistently privately owned commercial BIOS company. Its products today include the AMI 8 legacy core and the AMI Aptio core (a UEFI base first demonstrated in 2004) and AMI-Diags, all focused on system firmware.

Insyde Software

Insyde is a Taiwanese BIOS vendor formed in 1998, brought forth from the ashes of SystemSoft. Insyde was the first to launch a UEFI solution in the BIOS industry, Insyde H2O. They have expanded to include offerings in multiple segments and are today the only vendor in the Itanium segment. Besides UEFI Framework base BIOS, Insyde also offers UEFI applications and keyboard firmware.

ByoSoft

In early 2006, Nanjing ByoSoft Co., Ltd. (ByoSoft), was established in China. In 2008, ByoSoft became one of the four independent BIOS vendors in the world providing professional UEFI BIOS products and service and the only one based in mainland China. While they are the new kid on the block, they have many long-time BIOS engineers working for them and major companies signed up.

Value of BIOS

The bill of material (BOM) impact of a system BIOS from segment to segment can differ greatly depending on a variety of factors. The business model can be based on a combination of non-recurrent engineering (NRE) and/or royalty per motherboard. Depending on:
– Original innovation
– Porting cost
– Source level access
– Support need
– Expected volume
– Customization requirements
– Vendor/supplier history

This is not unlike many other free market dynamics. If volume pricing can apply, royalties per board could be a relatively low percentage of the bill of materials (BOM) cost. When volumes do not apply, then royalties per board can rise to affect the BOM. Embedded systems customers often must pay a much higher cost per board because of the diverse nature of the business segments, limited volume, and high-touch model for adapting the mainstream products for custom applications.

Proprietary Solutions

Beyond the four commercial BIOS companies mentioned above, it is possible that many name-brand computer manufacturers have teams that can and/or do write their own proprietary BIOS. Over the years, many have created their own BIOS, starting with IBM and the IBM PC. In some cases, separate business units within very large companies have even created their own solutions.

- At IBM, a team of developers created a boot firmware for its new desktop machine in August, 1981, which became known as a BIOS. Today, IBM has a choice of who they use for which product, internal or external.
- In 1982, Compaq wrote the first BIOS specification by reverse- engineering the IBM BIOS with one team that wrote the specification and then handing the specification to another team, which in turn wrote the Compaq portable PC firmware from scratch.
- Today, HP does their own BIOS and utilizes BIOS vendors depending on the product lines.
- While Intel currently employs the maintainers of the UEFI solutions at www.tianocore.org, it does not produce commercially available BIOS, not counting Intel-branded motherboards.
- Other large computer and motherboard manufacturers around the world have the capability to develop their own solutions, and often opt to employ their favorite BIOS vendors for core and tool maintenance.
- Apart from front-end system firmware, server manufacturers in particular have extensive value-add firmware-based solutions for baseboard management controllers (BMCs), which are embedded controllers that control the back-end subsystem to enhance a server board's ability to be remotely managed and for increased fault tolerance.

Making a Decision on Boot Firmware

Whether a company works in the private, public, or academic space, the firmware make-or-buy decision can be difficult without proper insight. In the embedded space, many smaller OEMs maintain a small staff to manage and/or develop their system firmware. Depending on the level of experience and number of designs they have to support, they may decide to implement a commercial BIOS product or they may try to create their own.

When a BIOS vendor is not an option, they must roll up their sleeves and search for alternatives. In the education arena, software engineering, computer engineering, and electrical engineering students all learn a certain level of low-level firmware coding as part of just a few of their classes, but most curriculums don't include a class that takes the student through the full experience of system firmware development. Except for some graduate level projects, most students do not get to develop their own solutions from scratch.

There are three basic options: BIOS vendor, reuse/borrow from open source, from scratch.

Consider Using a BIOS Vendor

Talking to a BIOS vendor is a great idea when the situation demands product-ready solutions, and the return on investment merits it. To get starter code from a BIOS vendor normally requires various levels of licenses and agreements for evaluation, production, and follow-on support. The business and legal negotiations can take time, so if you want to implement this, you should start early. A commercial BIOS comes with a varying amount of nonrecurring engineering (NRE) and/or royalties per unit or subscription costs. If you choose this route, there is a very high likelihood that you are getting exactly what you need to get started and get to a successful production cycle. You can outsource the duties and responsibilities entirely if you choose to. First-generation products often have hiccups and, even if you are not inclined to take the easy way out on a regular basis, you should consider what BIOS vendors can offer. Many successful and established computer OEM development teams employ BIOS vendors to provide a base level of software core competency, basic OS support, tools, and on-call support while the in-house developers focus at the finer details and ensure that the job is done on schedule. BIOS vendors may offer starter kits with a lesser number of features and limited support, which smaller companies or individuals can take advantage of if they do not have the time to dive deep into the firmware realm. As everyone's concept of what constitutes cheap versus expensive varies, product teams should weigh their options and the return on investment levels and make the right decision for them for a given project. The next project or another parallel project in the pipeline may require another solution with entirely different requirement sets. Scalability may be something that internal teams cannot meet on their own due to a tight production cycle.

Some say that BIOS vendors (and BIOS) are becoming obsolete, especially considering silicon vendors supporting boot loaders, but this is not true. People said the same thing when Tiano originally came out 10 years ago—"say goodbye to BIOS." Some thought it would come true when Linux BIOS started, but they too have been disappointed. If the Linux multiverse is anything to go by, commercial distribution houses such as Red Hat, offering commercially, prepackaged products and support, continue to thrive even when parallel royalty-free and subscription-free alternatives exist on the same kernel and with many of the same products. Why? Because Linux isn't free—people must roll up their sleeves and do the work upfront and continue to maintain it. The same thing can be said about system firmware. Commercial BIOS vendors like Insyde, Phoenix BIOS, AMI, ByoSoft, and others will continue to provide turn-key product quality and services to the computing industry in the future, regardless of the codebase being used. They provide value-added products, plain and simple.

Consider Open-Source Alternatives

For those who choose to take the plunge to create their own solution in whole or in part, free and open-source alternatives can be downloaded from the Web that offer a starting point and/or reference. Two of the well-known open-source products available to the market are Coreboot and Tiano.

Tiano

The Tiano core uses a BSD license and provides a flexible framework. Developers normally must get certain initialization codes from the silicon vendor individually, or they must reverse-engineer code that already exists on other platforms. Tiano, by default, also lacks the needed legacy interfaces to allow many older operating systems or PCI device option ROMs to be used. Developers can choose to create a Compatibility Support Module for legacy operating system based on the IBM BIOS specification. Tiano does have enough documentation, as well as the UEFI API, which replaces the legacy interface, and the UEFI drivers, which replace legacy option ROMs; overall more robust.

Coreboot

Formerly Linux BIOS, Coreboot provides source code under a GPL license. It has grown and evolved since starting out at Cluster Research Lab at the Advanced Computing Laboratory at Los Alamos National Laboratory. It got a lift from Google in the last 5 years as a few of the leads joined the company.

Uboot

Also known as Das Universal Boot, or Das U-boot, Uboot is owned by DENX software and is distributed under a GPL license. Uboot is broadly used in embedded devices.

For more information about these and other alternatives, like Aboot, please explore the web.

Consider Creating Something from Scratch

Regardless of the challenges, it is possible to start coding from 0s and 1s, in assembly, or in C, or PERL, and so on. The language doesn't matter. You would have had to take on the tasks of initialization one at a time, and likely have a tightly bundled RTOS or native-mode application. It is possible to boot Intel architecture completely from scratch. You can also use the open sources as reference code (licenses included). It may take an NDA with a few companies to get the necessary details of secret sauce bits to toggle on more advanced machines. Having other options available with the benefits of some of these have already been outlined above. Starting fresh is not the best option once you step back and look at the alternatives and trade-offs. But there are more options out there. . . .

Consider a Native Boot Loader for Intel ® Architecture

When market needs precipitated a native boot loader, Intel created the Intel Boot Loader Development Kit (Intel BLDK) to provide a way to bootstrap firmware developers new to Intel architecture. It was a good experiment and provided support for a few Atom-based embedded platforms. Providing a combination of source, binary, tools, and documentation, BLDK allows embedded firmware developers to not only debug and boot their platform, but customize and optimize it for their basic production needs. It is designed to do the basic silicon initialization required to bring the processor out of Reset, enable the system's main memory, enable the device path to the target OS storage device, fetch the initial sector of the OS, and hand control to the OS. It provides a great reference for people new to the firmware and BIOS industry.

It is for system firmware developers working on platforms for embedded devices based on Intel® Atom™ Processors. Students can gain an insight into what happens before the OS takes over and in the background while the OS runs. System firmware and hardware designers can grasp the level of work required to perform Intel architecture initialization.

Intel BLDK lacks extended features that would allow the user to run many standard off-the-shelf operating systems. As BLDK is an extendable kit, system developers are free to make their own additions and modifications to take advantage of all the latest and greatest technologies coming from Intel. It however doesn't have enough platform support to be considered universal.

Just Add Silicon Initialization

The Intel® Firmware Support Package (FSP) provides chipset and processor initialization in a format that can easily be incorporated into many existing boot loaders. FSP will perform all the base initialization steps for Intel silicon, including initialization of the CPU, memory controller, chipset and certain bus interfaces, if necessary. The initialization will enable enough hardware to allow the boot loader to load an operating system. FSP is not a stand-alone boot loader as it does not initialize non-Intel components, conduct broad bus enumeration, discover devices in the system, or support all industry standard initialization. FSP must be integrated into a host boot loader, such as those open-source solutions mentioned above, to carry out full boot loader functions.

Summary

Booting Intel architecture should be easy. While open source provides many advances in case you need to know the nuts and bolts, this book provides that background. Most of the basics in the system firmware space are not something taught in college; they are learned through on-the-job training.

Options are available when choosing a firmware solution as a starting point. The more that you know about them, as well as about the key players, their history, and the variables, the better decision you can make for your current and future designs. The decision will be a combination of arbitrary thought, low-hanging fruit, economies of scale, technical politics, and, of course, money versus time.

In the following chapters, we describe details of the typical Intel architecture boot flow and then detail how to port and debug an Intel architecture motherboard and add custom initialization for your own design. We will examine different OS loader support for typical use cases. Hopefully this gives you an appreciation of the scope involved and gives you some ideas.

As the title implies, this book is a supplement for embedded developers. We will use Intel BLDK as an example, but the following chapters apply to all initialization solutions. The Intel® Galileo board also has full UEFI source, which is available on GitHub if developers want to play with these concepts and develop their own bootloaders.

Chapter 2
Intel Architecture Basics

Architecture is a visual art, and the buildings speak for themselves.

—Julia Morgan

Architecture begins where engineering ends.

—Walter Gropius

Intel Architecture has been evolving since before the PC AT computer. It has ridden along with and contributed to many industry standards or become a de facto standard over the years. What used to be the IBM or a "clone," or IBM-compatible, is now simply a PC motherboard most likely with Intel's CPU and chipsets.

Most people didn't really begin to understand this until the Intel® Pentium® Processor with MMX technology and the bunny-suited fab workers dancing to Wild Cherry's *Play That Funky Music* commercials. The accompanying five-tone melody reminds you from across the room, in a crowded sports bar, whose chips are in the computer they just ran an ad for, even when you cannot see the TV. And then there was the Blue Man Group commercials for the Intel® Pentium® III processors. Which did it? I'm not sure...you pick. Likely it was all the stickers on the machines that gave it away.

To understand the why and how of the current designs, you should go back and study history a little, maybe not quite as far back as the systems based on the AT bus (also known as the Industry Standard Architecture, or ISA bus), but it would help. We then can understand how the different advancements in bus technology and capabilities of add-in cards, from ISA to PCI to PCI-X to PCIe, have gone along and how popular and mature functions have been integrated into the Intel chipsets. Today most of the Intel architecture revolves around PCI devices in the chipset. You can specifically look at graphics and how it has individually adapted over the years to take advantage of the location in the system and proximity to CPU, memory, and I/O. Each step along the path of this evolution has gone toward increasing bandwidth and reducing bottlenecks, putting the next key technology in the best possible position to show the extensibility, modularity and speed of the platform. This is a universal truth in building the better mouse trap year after year.

In communicating with software and the evolution of the platform, there are multiple angles to consider: the BIOS or firmware, the operating system, the applications, and how these interact with each other. The hardware interfaces are built into the BIOS, and the OS kernel, and the device drivers. The applications and software interfaces can change dramatically, but one cannot talk about hardware architecture without also talking about the instruction set architecture, (ISA), not to be confused with the older platform bus of choice. While the rest of the platform

DOI 10.1515/9781501506819-002

has had the benefit of fundamental revision (gradually leaving legacy behind), BIOS has grown through accretion on the same architecture. Table 2.1 illustrates some example advances.

Table 2.1:

Advancement	1980s	1990s	2000s	2010s
CPU	16 bit internal 8 bit 3xternal	32bit Virtual memory, Pentium, P6, Dual Processors	64b extensions Pentium®4, Intel® Xeon, bigger caches, multi threading	64b processing, 128b extensions Intel® Atom, intel® Core, multiple cores, little cores (again)
Buses	8 bit ISA	Microchannel†, XT, EISA, PCI†, USB†	PCI-X†, PCI Express†, USB2	USB3, Light Peak
Memory	16–64 KB down, 196 KB expansion PROMs, EEPROMs	EDO, BEDO, SDRAM, RDRAM, DDR, NOR, FWH	DDR2, DDR3, NAND, SPI	Lower power DDR, DDR4, SSDs, PCIe NVMe
Video	MDA for text, EGA	Color, VGA, SVGA, XVGA	DVI, HDMI, DP	eDP, 4K and soon 8K
Graphics	CGA to TV	2D, 3D	3D enhancements	GPUs
Audio	PC speaker, 1 Ch. PWM	SoundBlaster†, AC'97	Intel® HD Audio	Lower power and codec enhancements
Storage	Cassette tape, KB with 5¼-inch floppy drives	HDDs, megabytes, with IDE and UDMA, PATA	USB, SATA, SATA2, SSDs, gigabytes	Terabytes, SDIO, MMC, SATA3, ONFI NAND
OS	PC-DOS 1.0 and above	Windows† 3.1, Windows 95 Windows 98 Windows NT	Linux† Windows 2000 Windows XP, Windows 7,	Windows 8, 81., Windows 10, full protected mode operating systems, Linux 2.6.18 and above
Firmware	8 KB ASM BIOS 32 KB BASIC	Up to 1 MB EFI and legacy	4 MB and 8 MB UEFI and legacy	16 MB, offload engines

The Big Blocks of Intel Architecture

If you are reading this book, you are probably familiar with a computer's basic parts: chassis, motherboard, power supply, CPU, and hard drives. To understand how to adapt Intel architecture to a variety of embedded usage models that will work with today's system on a chip (SoC) and be ready to program and debug the devices, we really need go several layers deeper.

As features are added to the platform, chipset, and processor, several new definitions have been added to the memory maps of Intel architecture machines. The definition and usage of these regions are vital to understand whether, when, and how to initialize the system properly for a given use case. We will start with a look back. While some may be bored to tears by history, much legacy is built up over time and if we intend to advance or move beyond it, we have to understand why it was done to properly utilized it for embedded designs (or ignore it).

We will skip past the first two decades of computer technology and start with the basic Intel processor and Intel chipset combinations of the 1990s and then point ahead at what we are looking at in the present (at least to when this book was written). In the 1990s, Intel discrete processors used a front side bus connection to a north bridge of the chipset, PCIset, or AGPset, where a PCI host controller is combined with a memory controller. While the system architecture has changed dramatically since, it is here that you should start understanding what the architecture is and why it works and why you may or may not need to include or exclude something (see Figure 2.1).

This is where you start when debugging most computer problems. Essentially, the two-chip chipsets are the key integrated parts on the motherboard. Each part is generally connected to one other part via a bus, link, or interconnect, which is just a series of wires (or cables, traces, lanes, fabric, or backbone). It is through these buses and interconnects that the various components talk to one another.

The CPU

For most basic computing, the processor is the engine that makes everything work. The addition of hyper threading, multiple threading, multiple cores complicates the programming and the debug scene for parallel or concurrent computing, but hasn't made that big of a difference to the BIOS or bootloader, which is normally, but not necessarily, single threaded. After 2010, processors have multiple processor cores, integrated memory controllers and a variety on interconnect combinations, including PCIe, DMI, Intel® QuickPath Interconnect (Intel® QPI), and ESI. The integration of the "uncore," or system agent, which includes the memory controller and graphics interface (if not a graphics engine itself) present challenges when dealing with multisocketed designs and making sure they the performance software stacks are made Non-Uniform Memory Access (NUMA) aware. But the BIOS and bootloader isn't that affected by making sure that the processor booting the system is close to the memory where the pieces got shadowed.

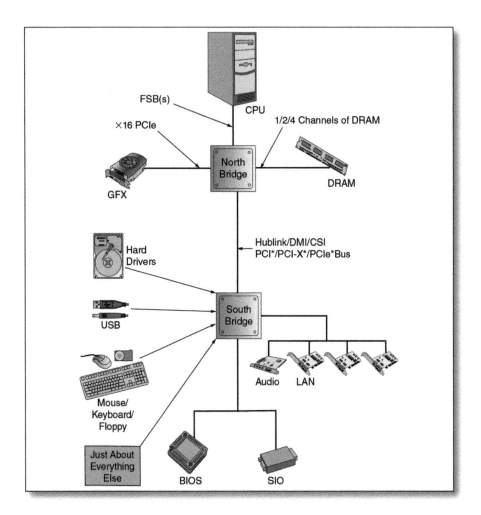

Figure 2. 1: Intel® Pentium® Pro Architecture

Several technologies in the CPU have initialization impact:
- Multi-core architecture separates real-time and non-real-time tasks to improve response time. There are different implementations of "multi-core," both shared and non-shared caches, shared and separate front side buses, and so on.
- Intel® Hyper-Threading Technology (Intel® HT Technology) enables one physical processor to appear and behave as two virtual processors to the operating system.

Intel HT Technology means more efficient use of processor resources, greater throughput, and improved performance.

– Intel® Virtualization Technology (Intel® VT) combines with software-based virtualization solutions to provide maximum system utilization by consolidating multiple environments into a single server or PC. By abstracting the software away from the underlying hardware, a world of new usage models opens up that reduce costs, increase management efficiency, and strengthen security, while making your computing infrastructure more resilient in the event of a disaster.

All these technologies are enabled by system firmware and add real value to performance and platform capabilities.

One of the keys to the many flavors and brands of Intel processors is that they have been produced with a common Instruction Set Architecture (ISA), Itanium being an exception to a unified ISA. Today the cores for Intel Xeon, Intel Core, Intel Atom, and Intel Quark are the same root instruction set with some minor additions every generation. The key decision that remains to be made by system firmware is whether you will run in 32-bit or 64-bit mode, which is done with a compiler switch if the code is correctly designed.

The Front Side Bus

The front side bus (FSB), which had been between the CPU and the North Bridge, was a proprietary parallel bus that normally linked to the PCI host controller in the north bridge, or the memory controller hub (MCH), as it is sometimes referred to in documentation. With the integration of the north bridge into the processor on the Nehalem processor, the front side bus is no longer visible externally, and its functionality has been replaced with invisible fabric internal to the chip. Instead of the FSB being the connection between the CPU and the rest of the system, it is now via one of a few serial interfaces. Intel QPI is the new name for interprocessor connections and to IOH and PCH components; it is the DMI or ESI link, or similar.

The North Bridge, PCIset, AGPset, MCH, Uncore, System Agent

It has had a string of names over the years, but the primary interface to the processor on older chipsets contains the PCI host controller (PCI Bus0, Dev0, Func0), the memory controller, a graphics port, and/or integrated graphics.

As part of the North Bridge, the *PCI Host Controller* converts FSB signals to the appropriate PCI bus traffic. It has been the home of the PCI configuration space, which controls the memory controller. For that reason, people seem to consider them one in the same, which we can grant if it is known that the memory controller hub (MCH) serves other important purposes.

Another part of the North Bridge, the *Memory Controller* is kind of self-explanatory. Memory has been evolving steadily every product generation or so. The general rule is: the faster the access times and the larger the memory the better. There are limitations as far as address lines of the memory controller, speed of the bus, number of memory channels, the memory technology, and the thermal envelope, especially in larger sizes and densities, which tend to limit the size available to the system.

The days of Fast Page, EDO, BEDO, and SDRAM are long over. RDRAM is dead, and for good reason (electrically way too sensitive and an expensive nightmare to debug). These days a form of Dual Data Rate (DDR) memory is the de jure standard. In the past, there have been memory translation hubs (MTHs) and Memory Repeater Hubs (MRHs), but these are no longer on the Intel roadmaps. Other not-quite-straight-memory devices do exist, including the fully buffered DIMMs and other devices that allow for a memory riser scenario. We may still be waiting for a nonvolatile form of main memory, such as phase change memory (PCM), to come along and remove the need for reinitialization of this key component on every boot; 3D XPoint is not claimed to be PCM, and has not replaced DDR.

The *Graphics* (GFX) engine is normally located as close to the physical memory and processor as the architecture allows for maximum graphics performance. In the old days, cards had their own private memory devices for rendering locally. While that is still the case for add-in cards, any integrated graphics today utilizes a piece of main system memory for its local memory. The killer add-in graphic cards for PCI have been replaced, first with the Accelerated Graphics Port (AGP), and now that has been replaced over time by the PCI Express Graphics (PEG) port as the pole sitter of add-in devices. On some embedded and server designs, the PEG port can be used at a x16 PCIe channel for increased I/O capacity.

The Transparent Link (Hublink, DMI, ESI)

The link between the north and south bridges has been updated from the Hub link to the DMI link. Now with up to 2 GB/s concurrent bandwidth, DMI provides up to 4x faster I/O bandwidth compared with the previous Intel proprietary Hub link I/O interface. A similar enterprise south bridge interconnect (ESI) is available that supports speeds of 2.5 Gb/s and connects to an Intel ICH south bridge or be configured as a x4 PCIe Gen 1 port. In the past, these links have been referred to as virtual bridges because they are transparent to any PCI transactions that may be sent across them. With PCI bus 0 devices both in the north and south complexes, there is no change in PCI bus numbers when you cross the border between chips. So, the software doesn't need to know that it is dealing with a two-chip or a one-chip (SoC) solution. The link not only handles PCI transitions, but also several proprietary chip-to-chip messages, or die-to-die messages if on a SoC.

The South Bridge, Also Known as the PIIX, I/O Controller Hub (ICH), I/O Hub (IOH), Enterprise South Bridge (ESB), and Platform Controller Hub (PCH)

The south bridge in the past has taken on various forms, including the PIIX, the ICH, the ESB (enterprise south bridge), the SCH (system controller hub), the IOH (I/O controller hub), and now the PCH. All basically equate to the main I/O channels to the outside world. If you want full documentation on the older corners of the newest integrated component, you may want to go all the way back to the PIIX documentation, which can still be downloaded from www.intel.com. While you may be able to avoid the terror of threading through fifteen years of change to a particular interface to build a holistic I/O "driver" for your firmware, you may need to make changes to some very old code and wonder "why did they do this; it doesn't say it in the this datasheet." This is where legacy gets to some very deep layers in the code. As the parts have morphed over time, the code to support them has as well.

Formally known as the 82371FB (PIIX) PCI/ISA/IDE Xcelerators are multifunction PCI devices implementing a PCI-to-ISA bridge function and a PCI IDE function. As a PCI-to-ISA bridge, the PIIX integrates many common I/O functions found in ISA-based PC systems—a seven-channel DMA controller, two 8259 interrupt controllers, an 8254 timer/counter, and power management support. In addition to compatible transfers, each DMA channel supports type F transfers. Programmable chip select decoding is provided for the BIOS chip, real time clock, and keyboard controller. Edge/Level interrupts and interrupt steering are supported for PCI plug and play compatibility. The PIIX supports two IDE connectors for up to four IDE devices providing an interface for IDE hard disks and CD ROMs. The PIIX provides motherboard plug and play compatibility. PIIX implements two steerable DMA channels (including type F transfers) and up to two steerable interrupt lines. Even with the oldest device you'd realistically want to examine, that's a lot of programming in the BIOS to get the I/O setup to run "anything." Perhaps the coolest BIOS-centric pieces it had was the SMM interrupt controller, used back then for advanced power management (APM).

The PIIX generations of south bridges continued to expand its list of integrated devices and expansion buses:

- The PIIX3 added IOAPIC, USB UHCI, PCI 2.1, and upgraded DMA and IDE capabilities. There was a PIIX2 in between which supported PIO Mode 4, but it didn't have the legs of the PIIX3 and was soon overtaken.
- The PIIX4 added ACPI and DMA to the IDE controllers. Prior to this, the CPU was involved in all PIO mode transfers. Another important advancement was the addition of the RealTime Clock, SMBus controller to talk to things like thermal chips, embedded controllers, and so on. There was an enhanced version of the

PIIX4 where something kind of important was fixed. And there was a mobile version of the component where extra power management features were added for helping keep your laps cooler in a remarkably deep green way.

- PIIX5 never left the starting line.
- PIIX6 was gearing up for adding IEEE1394, but was shelved for bigger and better platform architecture advances.
  - o With the first ICH, ICH0, Intel added many basics, each with system firmware impact:
- DMI to PCI bridge—external PCI bus.
- Serial ATA (SATA) for hard drives and SSDs.
- USB 1.1, USB 2.0, and soon USB 3.0—up to 14 ports and 2 integrated hubs.
- Intel® High Definition Audio (more bits, less noise).
- Serial Presence Interface (SPI) to connect to the NOR based NVRAM.
- Low Pin Count (LPC) Interface to get to the Super IO or Embedded Controllers and replace the ISA bus from a software point of view.
- PCI Express Root Ports to get to PCIe bus(es). These can be configured in a variety of different combinations from x1 to x16 lane widths.
- 1-Gigabit Ethernet (GbE) controller and now 10-Gigabit Ethernet (Xbe) functionality.
- High Performance Event Timers (HPETs), which offer very high granularity event capability.
- Power management capabilities—most of the clocks and control of the platform power rails run though the PCH.
- General purpose I/O and assorted native functionality—pins can be configured for either input, output, or some other native function for the platform. The datasheet will detail which of the 70-some GPIOs do which function.
- Direct Memory Access (DMA).
- Real Time Clock (RTC).
- Total Cost of Ownership features (TCO).
- Manageability Engine (ME), which provides many backside capabilities and can continue to run even when the front side system is asleep. This is like baseboard management controllers (BMCs) on larger server designs.

With each subsequent ICH or PCH generation, each I/O subsystem has changed slightly, and a major I/O interface or other key feature has been added. Register changes may have taken place and depending on the I/O needs of the platforms, the system firmware will have to consider these requirements. It is best to review the latest datasheets at developer.intel.com to understand how the systems have expanded. In recent years, the system on a chip, a combination of north bridge, south bridge, and processor, has been in vogue. While the names of a device's internal interconnects have changed and we talk about fabrics and other nonsensical abstractions for silicon, the same principles spelled out for CPU, memory, and IO still apply, as do the standards contained therein.

Data Movement Is Fundamental

So...now what have we learned? Nothing but the basics. But we now start to understand which components are on the platform and which buses and perhaps bridges and buffers lie between the processor and the NVRAM part where the BIOS hides. We can use this to begin to take that high-level block diagram abstract and make some sense out of why the transactions take so long to get from point A to point B and back, which is the execute-in-place latency times we need to avoid.

As shown in Figure 2.2, with Execute in place (XIP),

1. The CPU wants to read memory from the BIOS (probably an OP code instruction at boot time, let's say). It starts the MEMORY READ cycle on the CPU bus.
2. The north bridge sees the cycles and claims it. It says, "Mine!" and then tells the CPU to wait for me to get the data (it inserts wait states). CPU is stuck waiting for the north bridge to return the data (a small lie—pipelining can affect this).
3. North bridge "ADDRESS DECODES" this memory cycle. It has to figure out where to send it. Memory? Hublink? AGP Bus? Since the address is not memory or AGP, it forwards it to Hublink bus. You can insert new terms.
4. The south bridge will grab the cycle, and since it's not directed at an internal resource, forwards it out on the PCI bus, depending on the south bridge.
5. None of the devices on the PCI bus claims the cycle (network/sound card is shown). Therefore, since nobody else wants it, the south bridge figures that somebody 'down below' on the LPC bus wants it. This is called *subtractive decoding*. In the past, the ISA bridge in the system was the only subtractive decoding agent, but these days the LPC's job is to make sure that we do not get an Abort.
6. South bridge sends the cycle down to the LPC bus. The BIOS SPI chip knows this memory address is for him and claims it.
7. Since BIOS is slow, it will have to tell south bridge to wait a minute for it to get data (wait states).
8. BIOS returns data via LPC Memory Read Cycle.
9. LPC bus is now freed (STOP sign removed). LPC Memory Read Cycle over.
10. South bridge returns data to north bridge via Hublin.
11. North bridge returns data to CPU via end of CPU Memory Read Cycle.
12. CPU Bus now freed. Remove stop sign.

This entire process is repeated until we have partial cache enabled or we finally have memory ready to shadow our remaining BIOS code and data into. There are ways around some of the delays that may be incurred on the way to and from the CPU and the SPI NVRAM chip such as PCI Delayed transactions, pipelining, or prefetching. But this isn't the fast-boot chapter.

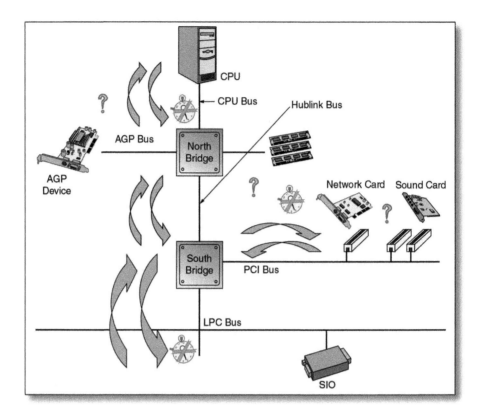

Figure 2.2: Data Movement across Buses between Components

It's a Multiprocessing System Architecture

There is a further thought to be made here outside of "that's nice." When we look at even a single-processor, single-core, single-threaded system, you should realize that we have a multiprocessing environment even if there is just one CPU. Typically, several of these data flows are happening concurrently:

- The CPU is "reading" code from DRAM (and probably writing back data structures).
- The GFX is bitmapping data from DRAM to its own memory.
- The LAN controller is bus-mastering incoming streams to DRAM.
- The CPU is writing sound data to DRAM; the audio chip is sending this data down to itself via direct memory access (DMA).
- The USB, mouse, keyboard, floppy, and so on are sending interrupts to the CPU; the CPU is performing minor reads/writes to controller registers. Some memory is used here depending on the specific interface.
- All of this is happening at the same time.

We can encounter posting of transactions in buffers at most levels of the architecture. Buffers exist in north bridge, south bridge, LAN cards, and so on. In the course of debug, we can run into deferred cycles, as well as bus- mastering devices, especially with respect to GFX.

As an example: the CPU was sending data to the GFX. The GFX was locking up (not returning read data). Further debug discovered by monitoring *both* the FSB and the PCIe bus that a certain type of cycle was *not* being forwarded through the MCH to the PCIe. After studying the bus/interconnects, the workaround was a simple bit flip to ensure that the data was passed correctly and in a timely manner. The buses have settings that allow traffic to flow more efficiently for a particular use case or for a particular time when you are trying to execute something. This may not be a runtime setting, but it may be an init-only setting.

The Memory Map

Intel processors can access two different address ranges, memory and I/O, using different CPU op codes to access each range. Figure 2.3 shows the classic IA32 memory map.
–   The top of physical memory limit is specific to CPU and chipset.
–   The bottom 1 MB has all the backward compatibility legacy baggage from the original IBM PC.
–   Below 4 GB there is a variety of ranges required to support newer technology platform-specific memory ranges needed to make the system work. Four gigabytes were chosen when 32-bit hardware and operating systems were the norm, and there weren't any systems on the mainstream market that could hold 4 GB of physical memory. It was all virtual at the time. Times have changed.
–   Similarly, below the platform-specific ranges are the PCI memory ranges for prefetchable and non-prefetchable. Again, when PCI was the ultimate in standard buses, there was plenty of virtual space below the top of the 4-GB boundary that was free to use virtually.
–   DRAM occupies the lower region, from 0 GB to however much memory you have (called Top of Lower Memory = TOLM), 3 GB in this example. Note: this is why a Windows XP system with 4 GB usually reports about 3 GB.
–   It is possible that memory exists above 4 GB and that DRAM will be accessible. This would be the top of memory or top of upper memory.
–   Also, there is a way to recover the physical memory, which used to hide behind the former virtual ranges lost to PCI memory by remapping that physical memory above the top of upper memory. This is done with a trick in the memory-controller addressing.

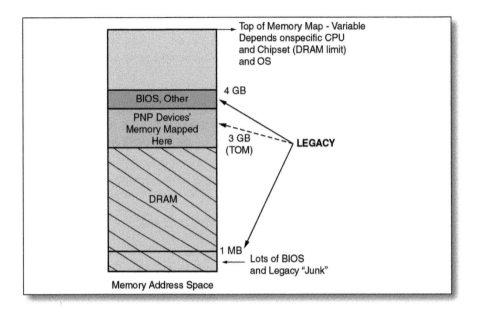

Figure 2.3: Classic IA32 Memory Map

I/O Address Range

The Intel architecture full I/O range is 0–64 KB and is intended for register mapping of hardware devices. Just as legacy hardware and software was handled years ago—and for the universal good—you have to keep maintaining backward compatibility if you want to ensure the hardware and software from years ago still works with modern machines. The PCIe specification supports I/O Space for compatibility with legacy devices which require their use because it requires the ability to support existing I/O device drivers with no modifications.

Besides the simple fixed legacy I/O ranges (see Figure 2.4), there are Base Address Registers per device that are enumerated by the BIOS and/or the operating system to suit their idea of perfection. PCI-to-PCI (P2P) bridges also requires a 4-KB minimum between them.

Alternatively, the term *Memory Mapped I/O* has nothing to do with actual I/O space. It is memory space used by hardware (usually, register space) that is accessed from a configurable base address register. While this mechanism is similar to that of I/O access from a high level, the transactions are routed very differently and are fundamentally different beasts to the platform with different rules.

Address	Internal Unit	Address	Internal Unit	Address	Internal Unit
00h-08h	DMA Controller	70h	RESERVED	Coh-D1h	DMA Controller
09h-0Eh	DMA Controller	71h	RTC Controller	D2h-DDh	RESERVED
0Fh	DMA Controller	72h	RTC Controller	DEh-DFh	DMA Controller
10h-18h	DMA Controller	73h	RTC Controller	F0h	FERR#IGNNE#
19h-1Eh	RESERVED (DMA Controller)	74h	RTC Controller	170h-177h	IDE Controller2
1Fh	DMA Controller	75h	RTC Controller	1F0h-1F7h	IDE Controller1
20h-21h	Interrupt Controller	76h	RTC Controller	376h IDE	IDE Controller2
24h-25h	Interrupt Controller	77h	RTC Controller	3F6h IDE	IDE Controller1
28h-29h	Interrupt Controller	80h	DMA Controller	4D0h-4D1h	Interrupt Controller
2Ch-2Dh	Interrupt Controller	81h-83h	DMA Controller	CF8	PCI Address
2E-2Fh	LPC SIO	84h-86h	DMA Controller	CF9h	Reset Generator
30h-31h	Interrupt Controller	87h	DMA Controller	CFC	PCI Data
34h-35h	Interrupt Controller	88h	DMA Controller		
38h-39h	Interrupt Controller	89h-8Bh	DMA Controller		
3Ch-3Dh	Interrupt Controller	8Ch-8Eh	DMA Controller		
40h-42h	Timer/Counter	08Fh	DMA Controller		
43h	RESERVED	90h-91h	DMA Controller		
4E-4Fh	LPC SIO	92h	Reset Generator		
50h-52h	Timer/Counter	93h-9Fh	DMA Controller		
53h	RESERVED	A0h-A1h	Interrupt Controller		
60h	Micro controller	A4h-A5h	Interrupt Controller		
61h	NMI Controller	A8h-A9h	Interrupt Controller		
62h	Micro controller	Ach-ADh	Interrupt Controller		
63h	NMI Controller	B0h-B1h	Interrupt Controller		
64h	Micro controller	B2h-B3h	Power Management		
65h	NMI Controller	B4h-B5h	Interrupt Controller		
66h	Micro controller	B8h-B9h	Interrupt Controller		
67h	NMI Controller	BCh-BDh	Interrupt Controller		

Figure 2.4: I/O Ranges

The Operating System

To Intel architecture, the key requirements for the OS can be boiled down to a few standards. The OS communicates to the BIOS via one interface or the other. There are three key interfaces between the BIOS and the OS:

1. ACPI (Advanced Configuration and Power Interface). This specification defines how the BIOS passes the "reserved memory ranges" and other PnP interfacing between the BIOS and the OS. It also covers a lot of interface information on power management, interrupts, and multiple CPUs that the operating systems require.

2. PCI (Peripheral Component Interface). This is the quintessential internal plug-and-play specification. It has evolved and remains a central computing industry tenet. If you are designing an add-in device, or even an integrated device, having it utilize this standard interface can be a make-or-break hinge factor. If you don't have this interface, then everything on the part is custom, and your OS will not understand how to interpret the hardware. Yes, other interfaces can be run, including USB which is plug and play, but to talk to the internals of the chipset/CPU, the IO has to go through PCI.

3. UEFI (Unified Extensible Firmware Interface). This is an industry specification defining BIOS and BIOS-to-OS interfaces, which change from boot phase to boot phase. It is like what Buddhism is to religion; it can encompass all, and it does encompass ACPI and several legacy table components. It has been designed to reduce cost in development and time to market for new technologies and platforms. Its real purpose is to replace the Legacy BIOS-to-OS interface, to potentially abstract and replace legacy hardware (82xx) from the platform.

4. Legacy Interface code (16-bit code), which I am not counting as we're trying to remove it. It is basically the runtime handlers (INT 10, INT 16, INT 13, INT 19, and so on) as defined by IBM AT Technical Reference Manual. In modern system firmware, the legacy interface has been placed into a lifeboat called the Compatibility Segment Module. The interface that communicates between 32-bit/64-bit code (EFI/UEFI) and CSM 16-bit code is implemented per CSM Specification Version 0.97. No additional document is required because it follows the specification. The newer EFI interface should be preferred for newer designs; however, if the requirements of the platform/applications spell out the need for an older operating system to be supported, then the legacy interface will remain a key part of the overall firmware landscape.

Summary

Intel architecture has grown to become the industry standard. Understanding how it has been developed, what the basic subsystems entail, and how they interact and advance the system, help to provide a foundation of how or why systems operate the way they do.

Chapter 3
System Firmware Terms and Concepts

For anyone new to Intel® architecture, the concepts behind three-letter acronyms can be a bit overwhelming. This chapter explains numerous concepts that should help set up the basic terminology used in future chapters. Many concepts are introduced, and it is best to refer to this chapter as you progress through the book.

Typical PC/Intel® Architecture Overview

By design, Intel architecture is unique and somewhat complicated. To boot, firmware must initialize the hardware by using either a Basic Input Output System (BIOS) or a custom boot loader solution. Certain subsystems, either integrated in silicon or added as a peripheral, may require additional firmware, which is obtained from that vendor.

Figure 3.1 illustrates the hardware components that typically make up a PC. The BIOS or boot loader is typically kept in flash.

Memory Types

Traditionally, there is ROM and RAM. We will define them for the purist, but today most people get the concepts.

ROM. Read-only memory (ROM) is locked memory that is not updatable without an external ROM burner. It never loses its context once it is programmed. Logistically it makes development and bug fixes in the field much costlier. It is hard to find true ROMs today, as flash technology has provided programmability during runtime. Of course, you can have things like EEPROMs, which have ROM in the name and are programmable, but see NVRAM below.

It is possible for silicon to have embedded ROM inside of it to enable must-have interfaces, such as a NAND controller interface, if your required boot firmware solution is sitting behind it.

RAM. Random access memory (RAM) does not retain its contents once power is removed. This type of memory is also referred to as *volatile*. There are many types of RAM, such as static RAM (SRAM) and dynamic RAM (DRAM). In the context of this book, system memory and sometimes memory refer to any of the available types of RAM.

DOI 10.1515/9781501506819-003

NVRAM. Flash technologies have improved since the time of the dinosaur PC AT. Instead of ROMs, which store things like system BIOS, or RAM, which loses its mind when you power down, most systems today contain a piece of programmable and nonvolatile RAM known as NVRAM. If you have a flash upgrade utility for a device, it is likely to be nonvolatile RAM, not formal ROM.

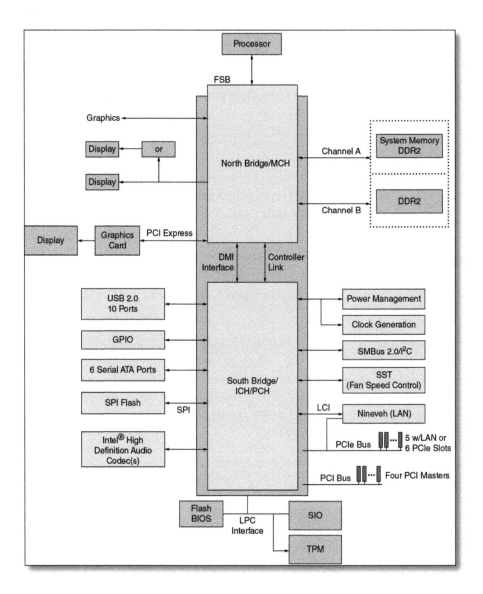

Figure 3.1: The Hardware Components of an Intel® Architecture PC

Two basic technologies cover NVRAM types—NAND and NOR.

NAND stands for "Not AND" technology. NAND flash, which resembles traditional NAND gates, has become prevalent with the advent of USB sticks in the market and flash cards for cameras. Now they have grown up into full-blown solid-state drives. NAND flash requires a controller to be located between the bus and the memory itself. The controller manages and maintains the NAND flash, which is a black art unto itself. That controller must be configured before accessing the memory behind it. A database and maintenance algorithms must be loaded before accessing memory behind it. The flash cells are good only for so many read/write cycles, so there are wear- leveling algorithms to keep things "good." If you keep asking experts questions, eventually someone says, "I don't know how it works." While the technology is more metastable than magnetic media, it is so fast, and so big for the price, that nobody notices. Chances are you will upgrade your drives long before the NAND flash drive decides to wear out.

NOR stands for "Not OR" technology. Firmware hubs and SPI devices are examples of NOR flash.

Besides the NAND controller initialization, the two technologies differ in two main ways that we care about as firmware developers:

1. *Access*: NAND reads require access in pages of data, while NOR can be read by byte. If you are reading pages of data, you will have to have somewhere to store that (SRAM or cache). NOR can be executed in place, which makes it slower and cheaper to implement for little tasks.
2. *Size*: NAND tends to be much larger than NOR. While NOR flash is in the order of megabytes, NAND is on the order of gigabytes.

Other platform design considerations need to be handled because of the differences between the technologies, but that could fill another book.

Several types of memory are used in system firmware: processor cache, system main memory, CMOS, small NVRAM flash chips, and large disk drives.

Processor Cache

Processors have local memory on them. While not normally thought about as memory, it is akin to "short-term memory" for the system. During runtime, the processor manages the cache per ranges that the system BIOS or operating system configure. Caching of information provides the best access times you can get. Cache used to be disabled by default, but these days, cache is enabled when the processor is powered.

During early system BIOS phases, the cache can be configured to provide a small stack space for firmware to execute as soon as possible. Cache must be set to avoid evictions and then disabled after main memory is up, but for a short time using more advanced algorithms. More on this "cache as RAM" potential later.

System Memory

When you buy memory for a computer or other expandable device, people think about modular DIMMs. There have been many technology changes over the years, from EDO to BEDO to SDRAM to RDRAM and back to SDRAM in the form of DDR, DDR2, DDR3, and, coming soon, DDR4. In the future, there is a roadmap of memory that will make today's best seem like EDO or ROM. On a scale of fastest to slowest in the system, main system memory is in the middle.

Access time to this memory is typically faster than from NVRAM (disk- or SPI-based), but slower than CPU cache. It is sized for the platform market to be ideal for execution of operating system and applications during runtime. Memory DIMMs required a memory controller, formerly in the north bridge of the chipset, now integrated into the processor. Memory initialization can take between several milliseconds to several seconds, depending on the transition state of the system (coming from off or a sleep state). During the normal boot flow, once main memory is initialized by the system BIOS, the shadowing of the "rest of the BIOS" can take place. The memory is divided into a memory map for various usages by different subsystems; not all memory is used or available by the operating system. Eventually, the OS is loaded into main memory and the system is then "booted" from a BIOS point of view. Of course, the OS may need to load the drivers and applications ... but that is its own book.

Complementary Metal-Oxide Semiconductor (CMOS)

In a BIOS context, the 512 bytes of CMOS is RTC battery-backed SRAM that is in the south bridge of the chipset. Although it is not NVRAM, it is used to store the setup menu and other user-dependent or board data that needs to be retained across power state transitions (when the system is off). Depending on the system BIOS implementation, CMOS may not be used except for clock data storage. Over time, the setup menu data became too complex, and the bitmap of 512 bytes got too tight. Tiano-based iterations started use of flash memory storage that is not limited by SRAM sizes.

System BIOS Flash Memory (NVRAM, FWH, or SPI)

A small nonvolatile RAM (NVRAM) chip is used for storing BIOS code data. *Flash Memory* is used to store the BIOS or boot loader. One advantage of flash memory is that it can be written to as the system powers up. This allows either the BIOS or boot loader to be stored in flash, as well as any data that the BIOS or boot loader may need during the boot process. Flash memory may also be used to store an OS as well, but depending on the technology of flash used, it may be cost prohibitive to do so. The packages that the flashes have come in over the years have been in the form of firm-ware hubs (FWH) and Serial Presence.

Real-Time Clock (RTC)

The RTC is available in most PC systems, and the RTC's internal registers and RAM are organized as two banks of 128 bytes each. The RTC contains the CMOS, as well as a real-time clock. The RTC consists of 14 bytes that are used to set the time and date.

The backup battery and the RAM is referred to as the CMOS battery and CMOS, respectively.

System Memory Map

A 32-bit Intel architecture system has up to 4 GB of address space. If the Physical Address Extensions (PAE) feature is available in the processor, up to 36 address bits are available, however, increasing the possible addressable memory space. The address space for the Intel® System Controller Hub is illustrated in Figure 3.2 as an example for this section.

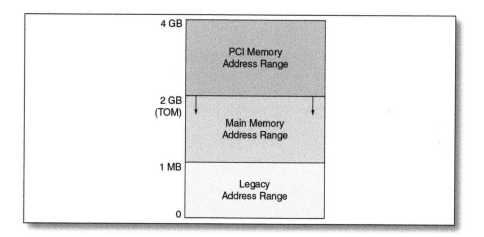

Figure 3.2: System Memory Map for the Intel® IO Controller Hub, TOM is variable

The memory map contains specific regions used for specific purposes.

Legacy Address Range

The Legacy Address Range is used for multiple things in legacy systems. The Interrupt Vector Table (IVT) is located at physical address 0. Interrupts were discussed in depth in Chapter 2. The video BIOS gets loaded at 0xC000:0 and the video buffer resides in the 0xA000 segment. The 0xC800:0 through 0xD000 segments can be used for option ROMs. The 0xE000 and 0xF000 segments are typically reserved for any runtime BIOS or boot loader code or data.

Main Memory Address Range

The Main Memory Address Range, referred to earlier as system memory, is the memory available to the OS. Parts of the Main Memory Address Range may not be available for the OS to use, such as Stolen Memory or ACPI tables. This will be discussed in more detail in Chapter 8, which describes OS handoff structures.

PCI Memory Address Range

The PCI Memory Address Range is used during PCI enumeration to assign any requested memory-mapped input/output (MMIO). This memory is used to access registers in a specific PCI device.

For systems that have 4 GB or greater of system memory, the PCI Memory Address Range still resides just below 4 GB. In order to avoid losing access to the system memory in the location of the PCI MMIO, the memory is remapped just above 4 GB. Figure 3.3 illustrates how memory remapping works.

Splash Screen

Today, most system firmware hides the diagnostic information behind a bitmap with the company logo or any other image that the PC vendor deems suitable. These bitmaps are also known as splash screens—screens that keep the user's eyes occupied until the OS can load. They serve no other purpose normally than a bit of marketing/brainwashing. It is common for BIOS or boot loaders to use splash screens to hide the boot process from users and to give them something to look at.

They are popular for embedded systems where the user is accustomed to some type of feedback as soon as they turn on the system. A set-top box is an example of this; if users do not get visual feedback almost immediately, they would assume that something was wrong.

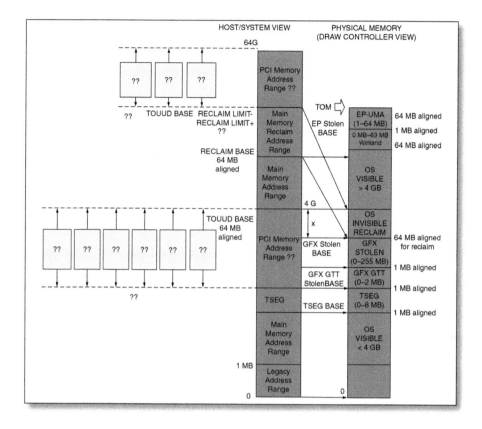

Figure 3.3: System Memory Map for the Intel® 4 Series Chipset Family

Status and Error Messages

The following are types of status and error messages that provide information during the initialization process.

Display Messages

The diagnostic information hidden by splash screens can prove very useful in determining the state of the machine, should there be problems caused by an initialization issue, such as the inability to boot the PC to an OS.

These status and error messages are communicated to the user in different ways. The most obvious is by printing messages on the screen. Typically, the BIOS has an option for turning off the splash screen in order to display these diagnostic messages.

Most people have seen the memory test performed by the BIOS in much older systems where you see the message count to the size of memory in the system before printing that the memory test passed.

Beep Codes

There are times when a hardware failure occurs before the graphics device is initialized so that messages printed to the display device are useless. In this case, the BIOS or boot loader displays beep codes in order to help the user determine what has gone wrong. Of course, beep codes are not at all obvious but can be referenced in the BIOS documentation.

POST Codes

For firmware developers working on a motherboard, processor, or chipset power-on, a POST code display is used to indicate the last code that is executed. This method helps the developer determine where the failure occurred, regardless of whether it was caused in the hardware or in the firmware.

POST codes are typically displayed on two seven-segment displays. The displays are written to I/O port 0x80. Almost all BIOS or boot loaders use this method for debugging. Debug methods will be covered in depth in a later chapter.

Master Boot Record

The Master Boot Record (MBR) is on the first sector of a partitioned mass storage device. It contains the partition table, as well as boot code. The boot code is OS-dependent code whose primary purpose is to load the OS into memory. Once the BIOS, firmware, or boot loader reads the MBR, it will verify that "0xAA55", the MBR signature, is present, as shown in Table 3.1. The BIOS or boot loader will then load the boot code to memory location 0x7C0:0 and will jump to that location.

Table 3.1: Master Boot Record

Address (in hex)	Description
0	Boot code
0x1B8	Optional signature
0x1BC	0x0
0x1BE	Partition table
0x1FE	0xAA55

GUID Partition Table

The GUID Partition Table (GPT), part of the UEFI specification, has replaced the Master Boot Record (MBR) in part because MBR is limited in size to 2.2TB. As drives have grown in size, the GPT allows for a maximum disk and partition size of 9.4 zettabytes. Most modern operating systems support and/or require a GPT above and beyond a legacy MBR. The Legacy MBR is located in LBA0, and the GPT header is located in LBA1, followed by the partition table itself.

Real Mode

Real Mode is 16-bit code created to work with 16-bit registers. Real Mode allows the accessing of only 1 MB of memory. Memory is accessed in the following format: **segment : offset**. The physical address is calculated by shifting the segment left by four bits and adding the offset to it. Figure 3.4 shows an example of calculating the physical address.

```
Segment   0xF000
Offset    0x5432
Physical address   0xF0000   0x5432
Physical address    0xF5432
```

Figure 3.4: Example Physical Address Calculation in Real Mode

Protected Mode

Protected mode was introduced to address memory above 1 MB. Protected mode also allows 32-bit code to execute. Protected mode uses the segment register content as selectors or pointers into descriptor tables. Descriptors provide 24-bit base addresses with a physical memory size of up to 16 MB, support for virtual memory management on a segment swapping basis, and several protection mechanisms. The descriptors referred to are part of the Interrupt Descriptor Table (IDT) and Global Descriptor Tables (GDT). They are beyond the scope of this book. For more details on the GDT/IDT refer to the Intel® 64 and IA-32 Architectures Software Developer's Manual online.

Logical Addressing

The segment selector identifies the segment to be accessed, and the offset identifies the offset in that segment. The logical address is formed by adding the base of the segment selector to the offset. The processor translates the logical address to a physical address, making the conversion transparent to software.

Flat Protected Mode

The preferred mode for system firmware is flat protected mode. This mode allows addressing memory above 1 MB, but does not require a logical-to-physical conversion. The GDT is set up so that the memory maps 1:1, meaning that the logical and physical addresses are identical.

Reset Vector

When an Intel architecture boot-strap processor (BSP) powers on, the first address fetched and executed is at physical address 0xFFFFFFF0, also known as the reset vector. This accesses the ROM or flash device at the top of the ROM: 0x10. The boot loader must always contain a jump to the initialization code in these top 16 bytes.

Programmable Interrupt Controller

The Programmable Interrupt Controller (PIC), or 8259, contains two cascaded 8259s with sixteen available IRQs. The PIC provides ISA-compatible interrupts and can support PCI-based interrupts by mapping the PCI interrupt onto the compatible ISA interrupt line. Table 3.2 shows the ISA compatible IRQ assignments.

   The priority of the interrupts available in the 8259 is defined by the IRQ number itself, with 0 being the highest priority. The timer interrupt, or IRQ0, has the highest.

Advanced Programmable Interrupt Controller

There are two types of Advanced Programmable Interrupt Controllers (APIC), the I/OxAPIC, and the Local APIC.

The I/OxAPIC

The I/OxAPIC is contained in the south bridge, or ICH. It expands the number of IRQs available and allows an interrupt priority scheme that is independent of the interrupt number. For example, interrupt 9 can have a higher priority than interrupt 4.

Each IRQ has an associated redirection table entry that can be enabled or disabled and selects the IDT vector for the associated IRQ. The I/O APIC is only available when running in protected mode.

Table 3.2: PIC ISA-Compatible IRQ Assignments

8259	IRQ number	ISA Interrupt Function
Master	0	Internal Timer (PIT)
Master	1	Keyboard
Master	2	Cascade interrupt to slave 8259
Master	3	Serial Port A
Master	4	Serial Port B
Master	5	Parallel Port
Master	6	Floppy
Master	7	Parallel Port
Slave	8	RTC
Slave	9	Generic
Slave	10	Generic
Slave	11	Generic
Slave	12	PS2 mouse
Slave	13	Coprocessor
Slave	14	Hard disk
Slave	15	Hard disk

The Local APIC

The local APIC is contained inside the processor and controls the interrupt delivery to the processor. Each local APIC contains its own set of associated registers, as well as a Local Vector Table (LVT). The LVT specifies the way the interrupts are delivered to each processor core.

Summary

Now that the basic terminology is clear, we can discuss more advanced items.

Chapter 4
Silicon-Specific Initialization

> Since when has the world of computer software design been about what people want? This is a simple question of evolution. The day is quickly coming when every knee will bow down to a silicon fist, and you will all beg your binary gods for mercy.
>
> —Bill Gates

So if developers strive to be binary gods, as Bill Gates puts it, then they really need to know what they are doing when it comes to silicon initialization. Hopefully they have more than a binary to start from. They are going to need code and proper documentation.

When initializing silicon should be easy: "It's a few rdmsrs, and a wrmsr for the processor. It is a 0xCFC here and a 0xCF8 there with the standard config space for PCI device, a peek and a poke to some special-sauce registers. Then just glob on the expansion ROMs or blobs for the add-in devices and voila you are done, right?" Such would be the case in a perfect world.

While silicon initialization is a process in which the BIOS or system firmware must set a few bits and enable the system in the correct sequence, the nuances of the silicon and the recent changes must be updated every design cycle.

Listen to the Designer, Then Experiment, and Fix It

Regardless of the language used to program the firmware or the BIOS or the bootloader, the outcomes still needs to match up to what the silicon design engineer (Si DE) is expecting. Or what the Si DE thought should happen before the first parts were powered on and debugging started. During a power-on, the BIOS toggles the state machines, sets the bits, and, in many cases, is the first test software to run on the product. When this process happens for the first time, bringing silicon to life, it can find silicon bugs, and the ideal initialization algorithms may need to change, sometimes drastically. It may be a case where the default bit settings are no good and have to be programmed to new values through I/O, PCI, or memory-mapped I/O programming. There may be a toggle of a bit to increase or decrease the frequency or decrease the frequency of a clock or add cycles to the data paths to eliminate a potential race condition for a buffer to fill or clear. It's a lot of very methodical and deliberate step-by-step work to do that debug! Or it may just be flipping a few bits or changing some strapping values and the entire system just starts right up. More on this in Chapter 6.

Silicon programming for Intel architecture really means needing to understand the individual controller's nuances. When done properly it can be fantastic, making a system come to life and run faster than anything else on the planet. When done without proper preparation, and if the board designer has not followed the prescribed

DOI 10.1515/9781501506819-004

hardware design guidelines, it can be a ferocious nightmare where the board sputters and grinds and makes magic blue smoke. As the first chapter indicated, this is where it is vital to have the right level of data about the component.

Chipsets

For a chipset, the firmware developer has to consider several features:
— Flash programming (NOR, NAND, or integrated)
— Reset controls
— I/O and MMIO base address locations and ranges
— Standard PCI header details
— Timers and clock routing
— General purpose I/Os and bells and whistles.
— Thermal management
— Power management, APM, ACPI tables and ASL code support
— Interrupts
— Bus support per major interface (DMI, PCIe, audio, Ethernet, SMBus, USB, SATA).

The chipset comprises a series of integrated PCI devices connected to a fabric, backbone, or bus, which connects to an interface (such as DMI) to the processor. Each device/function on the component will get PCI BIOS standard initialization, but also some amount of proprietary bit twiddling. Most of these bits will be detailed in the datasheet, but it is best to get the BIOS specification for the particular chipset, which may require a special NDA with the manufacturer. There are also industry standards to follow, depending on the type of controller (SATA, USB, and so on). There may be exceptions to industry standards per component. In the end, we need to keep it all straight and avoid conflicting memory, I/O, ranges, IRQ and interrupt settings, for all of the components to come alive and start talking to one another before the OS takes over with its set of device drivers, settings, industry standards and exceptions, and additional capabilities.

Processors

For a processor, there is much more than a few rdmsrs and wrmsrs. Today we have no less than:
— CPUID and branding strings
— More than 100 model-specific registers, some specific to package, core, or thread.
— Bus-to-core ratios
— Overclocking controls
— Turbo mode

- Intel® Speed Step technology
- Cache controls
- CPU RESETs
- Microcode updates
- Multithreading and multicore initialization
- The xAPIC
- System management mode
- CPU ACPI Power states (P-, C-, S-, and T-states)
- System management BIOS
- Thermal management
- Power management
- Intel EM64T
- Intel® Trusted Execution Technology (Intel TXT)
- Intel® Virtualization Technology (Intel VT)
- Machine check architecture
- Security features

For supplemental information regarding MSRs or other processor features, refer to the *Intel® 64 and IA-32 Architecture Software Developer's Manual, Volume 3B, System Programming Guide, Part 2*. However, for chip-specific data needed to program an Intel CPU successfully, there is a processor BIOS writer's guide, which may require an NDA to get to the detailed bits and algorithms.

Basic Types of Initialization

For BIOS, there are four types of programming:
1. Bit setting, per industry specification or per designer
2. Standard algorithms, per specification
3. Custom routines, per designer
4. Expansion ROMs, per vendor

Simple Bits

"Bit banging" is slang for the sequence of reading/modifying/writing to registers in the silicon. This can be to CPU model-specific registers (MSRs) or to PCI or I/O or memory-mapped I/O. The register/bit settings are normally done in a priority order as dictated by logic to speed up the system initialization, or it is done out of simple fear in doing a workaround as early as possible to avoid the errata condition, but the order may not matter. Normally these bits are set once at boot time and never looked at again. It is possible that the bits are also locked when set to avoid tampering by malware during runtime.

Standard Algorithms, Minding the Ps and Qs

Standard routines are programmed to follow industry specifications, such as PCI, ACPI, USB, JEDEC, or others. This is done with the assumption that the silicon being programmed is designed exactly per the specification. If this is the case, then the algorithms should never change once written and that standard easily can go from component to component, device to device, year over year. If this is not the case, then you will have to create the exception and determine the trigger for that exception—a vendor ID and device ID combination in the case of PCI headers perhaps? A revision ID, or is that for a specific CPUID? Or is it form factor or board-specific condition that it will have to be read from a GPIO? There are many standards and when something needs to ship and it is not quite in line with the standard, a quick exception and/or workaround is created and the product ships.

Custom Algorithms: It's All About Me

Custom routines are just that: custom. It is up to the developer and/or the designer to make the calls as to what needs to happen with initialization of a device beyond the standard PCI base address registers, IRQ routing, and so forth. A custom routine can provide the flexibility to do what is needed apart from the industry standards, such as PCI, USB, SATA, or others. Custom routines mean that they could be one-off implementations for specific applications and will need to be redone for the next component design, such as ASICs. Often, custom routines provide the best efficiency in boot speeds overall, as standard implementations typically mean slowing down to detect and meet any unusual scenarios. The algorithms and bit settings could be entirely memory mapped and have absolutely no standard to program to, such as PCI or ACPI. Most OSes, though, do not match up easily to that lack of standards; custom OS-level drivers would also be needed, and that OS driver may be very different from the initialization drivers in a UEFI system firmware.

An interesting example is USB initialization. Per the specification, one needs to use USB protocols to interact with each controller and identify whether any devices are attached to those ports that need further initialization. One alternative mechanism that can be utilized is the access to this information through memory-mapped I/O (MMIO) instead. Such an enhancement would need silicon changes to create the mappings in memory space, but could achieve potentially a much faster and leaner initialization mechanism. Alternatively, beyond the USB specification requirements, study of the actual timing of the silicon and shortening of the "standard" delays down to what is actually required by the component can yield great benefits. Results may vary by the controller and device manufacturers, but the potential time savings are dramatic. More on this in Chapter 12.

Embedded controllers are custom programmable hardware that can interface with and extend the abilities of the system, as well as provide a back-end solution to some interesting design problems. These controllers come with their own firmware and control interfaces to the system BIOS, besides embedding keyboard controllers and other super IO functionality.

Field Programmable Grid Arrays (FPGAs) are examples that provide fixed functionality until they get reprogrammed. Their sizes can vary and their applicability depends on the market segment in which they are found. Like CMOS, they need battery backup to maintain their NV status ... along these lines. The usage can follow standard programming needs, like PCI or USB, ACPI, and so on, or it can be completely custom or need no additional programming at all. FPGAs are normally used to provide feature augmentation to a design or early development phases of new silicon.

Option ROMs

Formerly ISA-expansion ROMs, PCI-option ROMs such as video BIOS and now UEFI drivers such as graphics output protocols provide another mechanism for taking things one step beyond industry standards. These objects do so, though, in a very standard way that can be easily implemented either though binary or source or mixture. Expansion ROM code extends the BIOS capabilities beyond what the standard CPU and chipset programming requirements provide.

They can be used for add-in cards or with integrated components. Option ROMs get loaded and executed by the system firmware during initialization and, if needed, shadowed during runtime. Newer capabilities of UEFI option ROMs offer the developers a driver model where the ROM can be loaded but not executed unless it is needed to be enabled via the boot path. There are some other advantages to UEFI option ROMs:

– Prior to EFI capabilities, all legacy option ROMs are located below 1 MB between 0xC0000 and 0xFFFFF and carry around a good deal of 16-bit code.
– Newer option ROMs can be called by various names, including DXE drivers in the Tiano realm and can be relocated above 1 MB, which eliminates the crunch on size requirements of most option ROMs and alleviates the expansion limitation of larger server systems.

Devices such as LAN, SCSI, SATA, RAID, and video often have option ROMs initialize key low-level requirements of proprietary designs. It is possible to embed or integrate the code into the main BIOS ROMs. Sometimes the intellectual property of the various silicon integrated into the design may not allow access to that code or knowledge of the exact registers. There is a positive aspect to binary code: As a developer, you don't have to fix what cannot be fixed. And as the black box, a legacy option ROM binary gives an excellent chance to innovate along alternative lines when the opportunity presents itself.

Summary

This chapter contained a high-level overview of some of the programming requirements of basic components. For complete details on a particular chip, go to the silicon provider and obtain the required documentation, such as the data sheet and programmer's reference manual.

Chapter 5
Industry Standard Initialization

Beware of geeks bearing formulas.

—Warren Buffett

As the previous chapter begins to highlight, the industry standards that can be applied to today's computing systems are vast and varied. Understanding their impact on systems and devices is key to creating a robust and stable pre-OS firmware. By some counts, it can be up to 70 specifications that apply:

1. UEFI
   a. UEFI Specification Unified Extensible Firmware Interface Specification v2.7
   b. Platform Initialization Specification v1.2 (for UEFI)
2. PCI
   a. PCI Express Base Specification
   b. PCI Local Bus Specification
   c. PCI-to-PCI Bridge Architecture Specification
   d. PCI Hot-Plug Specification
   e. PCI Bus Power Management Interface Specification
   f. PCI BIOS Specification
   g. PCI Firmware Specification
   h. PCI Standard Hot-Plug Controller and Subsystem Specification
   i. PCI-X Addendum to the PCI Local Bus Specification
   j. PCI Express to PCI/PCI-X Bridge Specification
3. IDE
   a. ATA/ATAPI 6
   b. ATA/ATAPI 7
   c. Programming Interface for Bus Master IDE Controller
   d. PCI IDE Controller Specification
   e. Serial ATA: High Speed Serialized AT Attachment
   f. Serial ATA International Organization: Serial ATA
   g. Serial ATA Advanced Host Controller Interface (AHCI)
   h. ATAPI Removable Media Device BIOS Specification
   i. El Torito Bootable CD-ROM Format Specification
4. USB
   a. Universal Serial Bus Specification
   b. Universal Host Controller Interface (UHCI) Design Guide
   c. Universal Serial Bus (USB) Device Class Definition for Human Interface Devices (HID)
   d. Universal Serial Bus (USB) HID Points of Sale Usage Tables Version 1.01

DOI 10.1515/9781501506819-005

    e.   Universal Serial Bus (USB) HID Usage Tables

    f.   Universal Serial Bus Mass Storage Class Specification Overview

    g.   Universal Serial Bus (USB) Device Class Definition for Physical Interface Devices (PID)

    h.   Universal Serial Bus Mass Storage Class Bulk-Only Transport

    i.   Universal Serial Bus Mass Storage Class Control/Bulk/Interrupt (CBI) Transport

    j.   Universal Serial Bus Mass Storage Class UFI Command Specification

    k.   Enhanced Host Controller Interface (EHCI) Specification for Universal Serial Bus

5. Advanced Configuration and Power Interface (ACPI)

    a.   ACPI Specification 2.0

    b.   ACPI Specification 3.0

    c.   ACPI Specification 4.0

    d.   ACPI Specification 5.0

    e.   ACPI Specification 6.0 (and 6.1 and 6.2)

6. Small Computer System Interface (SCSI)

7. BIOS Boot Specification

8. System Management Bus (SMBus) Specification (not related to SMBIOS)

9. Formatting

    a.   FAT: General Overview of On-Disk Format Version 1.03

    b.   PE-COFF Specification

10. Unicode Standard Version 4.0.0

11. POST Memory Manager Specification

12. Debug Port Table Spec

13. TPM Specification

14. PC Client Specific TPM Interface Specification (TIS)

15. Watchdog Timer Description Table Specification

16. IA-PC HPET (High Precision Event Timers) Specification

17. Serial Port Console Redirection Table Specification

18. Static Resource Affinity Table Specification

19. Hardware Watchdog Timers Design Specification

20. System Management BIOS (SMBIOS) Reference Specification

21. Alert Standard Format (ASF) Specification

22. IPMI Specification

23. Intel® Virtualization Technology for Directed I/O Architecture Specification

24. Intel® 64 and IA-32 Architectures Software Developer's Manual

25. Intel® Itanium® Architecture Software Developer's Manual

26. EISA Specification

27. VESA - BIOS Extension (VBE) Core Functions Standard

28. VESA - Enhanced EDID Implementation Guide

29. Boot Integrity Services (BIS) Application Programming Interface

30. Preboot Execution Environment (PXE) Specification
31. BIOS Enhanced Disk Drive Specification
32. Multi-Processor Specification
33. PCMCIA
34. SD Card
35. IPv4, IPv6, and TCP
36. PC SDRAM Serial Presence Detect (SPD) Specification 37. RFC 791, 792, 768, 793, 862, 1122, 1122, 1323, 1350,
37. 1531, 1783, 1784, 2090, 2131, 2581, 2988, 3782
38. 38. AC'97

Let's take a high-level look at the four most important industry specifications beyond UEFI from a system firmware and BIOS perspective:
1. PCI
2. SATA (formerly known as ATA, IDE)
3. USB
4. ACPI

PCI

PCI is the single strongest hardware standard of the Intel-architecture-based platform. All the key I/O controllers on the platform, including the embedded memory controllers, system agents, and the graphics ports on Intel CPUs, are either PCI or PCI Express (PCIe) devices.

The PCI standard is divided into several generations of key specifications. The latter generations are, for the most part, backward compatible with previous generations. If you join the PCI Special Interest Group (SIG) at www.pcisig.com, you will have access to all the latest PCI industry standard specifications. The following paragraphs highlight some of the PCI pre-OS key points, but are by no means exhaustive (please download and read/memorize these specifications). Also, it should be well understood that exceptions will occur for specific devices, as with any standard.

Understanding the PCI Local Bus Specification is the first step to understanding the bus transactions and protocols necessary to communicate with hardware or software driver designers and help debug platform level issues. There are several PCI standard configuration header registers listed in the specification that are key to PCI enumeration, which must be completed prior to a common off-the-shelf OS to load properly on the platform. Several devices are PCI enumerated in the OS.

Some real-time operating systems may have enough a priori knowledge of the PCI subsystem to hard code the needed values in order to boot and load drivers and may not require full PCI enumeration. While some of off- the-shelf operating systems repeat some of the PCI enumeration during OS load time, without a basic level PCI enumeration, none of the devices on the Intel architecture platform will function, including the OS storage device. Full enumeration on today's components only takes 20 milliseconds (ms) and the flexibility it provides outweighs hardcoding of values per board/system.

Besides the main PCI Local specification, there are also PCI Bridge specifications, PCI Hot Plug specifications, and PCI Power Management specifications that play roles in pre-OS PCI programming and compatibility. Up to a point in PCI history, most of the pre-OS required details are outlined in the PCI BIOS Specification 2.1.

Here are some of the basic requirements from the PCI-SIG specifications for pre-OS firmware and BIOS.

Note: Again, this laundry list does not replace the PCI specification. Please get the specifications and read copiously! Read The Friendly Manual!

PCI Device Enumeration

For dynamic PCI enumeration, the pre-OS firmware must scan the PCI bus for devices and bridges. To do this, the BIOS must start looking for devices at the host to PCI bridge (PCI Bus 0, PCI Device 0, PCI function 0), and start scanning or "walking through" the devices, methodically looking for PCI devices and PCI bridges. When function 0 is not present in the system, it is assumed that the functions 1 through 7 of that device are not incorporated. For each PCI device/function found, the BIOS must:
- Examine the header type register to determine if the device is a PCI- to-PCI bridge. The Header Type field at register offset 0x0A will indicate type 0 for devices and type 1 for bridges.
- For Type 0 headers:
    - Assign Standard Base Address Registers
        - Prefetchable Memory
        - Non-Prefetchable Memory
        - Legacy I/O ranges to device
    - Enable Bus Mastering, memory, and I/O ranges as needed in the configuration register
    - Program Master Latency Timer Register
    - Program Cache Line size
    - Program Min Grant and Max Latency values (not used for PCI Express)
    - Program Subsystem Vendor and Device IDs
    - Assign PCI IRQs and INTA, INTB, INTC, or INTD lines. Care should be taken to read the schematics on down PCI devices and PCI slots,

as the IRQs are board-specific. Internal PCI controller devices in the PCH or CPU have programmable IRQs assignments as well.

o Flag any PCI Expansion option ROMs (or UEFI driver) that needs to be executed for initialization or shadowed and programming the Expansion ROM BAR. These may not be executed during PCI enumeration, but will likely be dealt with in a later stage of the BIOS.

o Program any Error registers to trigger the proper error handler response

- For Type 1 Headers, when a PCI bridge is found, several registers' programming is similar to that of any other device, but there are marked differences:

o Local Memory BARs for the bridge device itself

o Configuration register for the bridge

o Primary and secondary bus latency timers

o Cache line size

o Primary bus register, secondary bus register, subordinate bus assignments must be made, and then the devices behind the bridge(s) must be discovered and enumerated.

o After the PCI bus/device network under a bridge is completely enumerated, assigning of nested Memory, and I/O ranges must be made to PCI bridges

o Bridge Control Register

While there are up to 256 buses on PCI, the minimum granularity of the I/O base and limit registers of 4 KB really limit that to approximately 16 bridges possible (assuming each has some amount of I/O required).

When configuring the PCI devices of the chipset and CPU, there will be several private registers above 0x3F in PCI and in the PCI Express ranges that will need to be programmed for specific purposes. Also, in the chipset, memory-mapped I/O configuration spaces are mapped by the Root Complex Base Address register at Bus 0, Device 31, Function 0, Offset 0xF0. It specifies the physical address of Chipset Configuration space. Also used in "RCBA xxxxh," where xxxxh is the offset of a particular register location in the Chipset Configuration space.

For static PCI enumeration, a designer can define a specific mapping and hard-code the standard registers for a particular system. But that is not the right way. While some believe that this saves time in walking the buses dynamically, the entire bus scan should take on the order of 20 ms. The benefits of doing it dynamically will likely outweigh the return of saving 20 ms and hand-coding the map statically for every closed-box configuration. If there are any expansion slots on PCIe buses on the system, then static enumeration is really not an option.

PCI BIOS

PCI BIOS Specification v2.1 spells out PCI BIOS calls via legacy software interrupt Int 1Ah; however, legacy calls are fast becoming obsolete in the modern world of UEFI. PCI BIOS (Int 1Ah) function calls are listed in Table 5.1.

Table 5.1: PCI BIOS (Int 1Ah) Function Calls

Function	AH	AL
PCI_FUNCTION_ID	B1h	
PCI_BIOS_PRESENT		01h
FIND_PCI_DEVICE		02h
FIND_PCI_CLASS_CODE		03h
GENERATE_SPECIAL_CYCLE		06h
READ_CONFIG_BYTE		08h
READ_CONFIG_WORD		09h
READ_CONFIG_DWORD		0Ah
WRITE_CONFIG_BYTE		0Bh
WRITE_CONFIG_WORD		0Ch
WRITE_CONFIG_DWORD		0Dh
GET_IRQ_ROUTING_OPTIONS		0Eh
SET_PCI_IRQ		0Fh

Most operating systems today can access PCI devices directly with their own class driver. As the PCI bus is completely discoverable (unless hidden by the BIOS for a board-specific reason), then through that class driver they can access PCI devices, class codes, as well as read and write configuration registers as needed.

The more useful calls are Get_IRQ_Routing_Options and Set_PCI_IRQ, which some operating systems still use.

Get PCI Interrupt Routing Options

This routine returns the PCI interrupt routing options available on the system motherboard and the current state of what interrupts are currently exclusively assigned to PCI. Routing information is returned in a data buffer that contains an IRQ routing for each PCI device or slot. The format of an entry in the IRQ routing table is shown in Table 5.2.

Table 5.2: Format of an Entry in the IRQ Routing Table

Offset	Size	Description
0	Byte	PCI Bus Number – The bus number of the slot.
1	Byte	PCI Device Number (in upper five bits) – The device number of the slot (shifted left 3 bits)
2	Byte	Link Value for INTA# – A value of zero means this interrupt pin is not connected to any other interrupt pins and is not connected to any of the Interrupt Router's interrupt pins. The nonzero link values are specific to a chipset and decided by the chipset vendor. A value of 1 through the number of interrupt pins on the Interrupt Router means the pin is connected to that PIRQn# pin of the Interrupt Router. A value larger than the number of interrupt pins on the Interrupt Router means the pin is wire OR'd together with other slot interrupt pins, but the group is not connected to any PIRQn# pin on the Interrupt Router.
3	Word	IRQ Bitmap for INTA# – This value shows which of the standard AT IRQs this PCI's interrupts can be routed to. This provides the routing options for one particular PCI interrupt pin. In this bitmap, bit 0 corresponds to IRQ0, bit 1 to IRQ1, and so on. A 1 bit in this bitmap indicates that routing is possible; a 0 bit indicates that no routing is possible. This bitmap must be the same for all pins that have the same link number.
5	Byte	Link Value for INTB#
6	Word	IRQ Bitmap for INTB#
8	Byte	Link Value for INTC#
9	Word	IRQ Bitmap for INTC#
11	Byte	Link Value for INTD#
12	Word	IRQ Bitmap for INTD#
14	Byte	Slot Number – This value is used to communicate whether the table entry is for a system-board device or an add-in slot. For system-board devices, the slot number should be set to zero. For add-in slots, the slot number should be set to a value that corresponds with the physical placement of the slot on the system board. This provides a way to correlate physical slots with PCI device numbers.
15	Byte	Reserved

Set PCI Hardware Interrupt

Set PCI hardware is intended to be used by a configuration utility or a Plug-N-Play operating system like Windows* 98 or higher. It can assign a specific IRQ to an interrupt pin on a particular Bus and Device number.

$PIR Table

Per Microsoft's PCI IRQ Routing Table Specification 1.0, the PCI IRQ Routing Table is in system memory from F0000h to FFFFFh on a 16-byte boundary. It begins with a signature of $PIR, and the resulting table output is compatible with the formatting of the buffer pointing to Int 1Ah Get_PCI_interupt_routing_options call above.

The PCI IRQ Routing Table ($PIR) has the header structure shown in Table 5.3.

Table 5.3: Header Structure of the PCI IRQ Routing Table ($PIR)

Byte Offset	Size in Bytes	Name
0	4	Signature - The signature for this table is the ASCII string "$PIR". Byte 0 is a 24h, byte 1 a 50h, byte 2 is a 49h, and byte 3 is 52h.
4	2	Version - The version consists of a Minor version byte followed by a Major version byte. Has to be 0x0100.
6	2	Table Size holds the size of the PCI IRQ Routing Table in bytes. If there were five slot entries in the table, this value would be 32 1 (5 3 16) = 112.
8	1	PCI Interrupt Router's Bus
9	1	PCI Interrupt Router's DevFunc - The Device is in the upper five bits, the Function in the lower three.
10	2	PCI Exclusive IRQs - This is an IRQ bitmap that indicates which IRQs are devoted exclusively to PCI usage. For example, if IRQ11 is devoted exclusively to PCI and cannot be assigned to an ISA device, then bit 11 of this 16-bit field should be set to 1. If there are no IRQs devoted exclusively to PCI, then this value should be 0.
12	4	Compatible PCI Interrupt Router - This field contains the Vendor ID (bytes 10 and 11) and Device ID (byes 12 and 13) of a compatible PCI Interrupt Router, or zero (0) if there is none. A compatible PCI Interrupt Router is one that uses the same method for mapping PIRQn# links to IRQs, and uses the same method for controlling the edge/level triggering of IRQs. This field allows an operating system to load an existing IRQ driver on a new PCI chipset without updating any drivers and without any user interaction.
16	4	Miniport Data - This DWORD is passed directly to the IRQ Miniport's Initialize() function. If an IRQ Miniport does not need any additional information, this field should be set to zero (0).

Byte Offset	Size in Bytes	Name
20	11	Reserved (Zero)
31	1	Checksum - This byte should be set such that the sum of all of the bytes in the PCI IRQ Routing Table, including the checksum, and all of the slot entries, modulo 256, is zero.
32	16	First of N Slot Entries. Each slot entry is 16-bytes long and describes how a slot's PCI interrupt pins are wire OR'd to other slot interrupt pins and to the chipset's IRQ pins.
(N 1 1) 3 16	16	Nth Slot Entry

Figure 5.1 is an example of the $PIR table.

Entry	Location	Bus	Device	Pin	Link	TRQs							
0	embedded	0	2	A	0x60	3	4	5	6	10	11	14	15
1	embedded	1	0	A	0x60	3	4	5	6	10	11	14	15
1	embedded	1	0	B	0x61	3	4	5	6	10	11	14	15
1	embedded	1	0	C	0x62	3	4	5	6	10	11	14	15
1	embedded	1	0	D	0x63	3	4	5	6	10	11	14	15
2	embedded	0	29	A	0x60	3	4	5	6	10	11	14	15
2	embedded	0	29	B	0x63	3	4	5	6	10	11	14	15
2	embedded	0	29	C	0x62	3	4	5	6	10	11	14	15
2	embedded	0	29	D	0x6b	3	4	5	6	10	11	14	15
3	embedded	0	31	A	0x62	3	4	5	6	10	11	14	15
4	embedded	4	13	A	0x61	3	4	5	6	10	11	14	15
5	embedded	2	4	A	0x60	3	4	5	6	10	11	14	15
6	embedded	4	3	A	0x68	3	4	5	6	10	11	14	15
7	slot 1	3	7	A	0x62	3	4	5	6	10	11	14	15
7	slot 1	3	7	B	0x63	3	4	5	6	10	11	14	15
7	slot 1	3	7	C	0x60	3	4	5	6	10	11	14	15
7	slot 1	3	7	D	0x61	3	4	5	6	10	11	14	15

Figure 5.1: An Example of the $PIR Table

The $PIR table is not the only way to describe the IRQ routing to the operating system. Microsoft Windows 2000 and later versions of Windows use ACPI tables and methods to determine the IRQ mapping supported per PCI devices. The ACPI table FADT will show which mode.

PCI IRQ Routing with ACPI Methods

As multiprocessor systems introduced APICs, starting with *ACPI Specification, Revision 1.0b, Multiprocessor Specification, Version 1.4,* was superseded. The table information contained in the MP specification was carried over into the ACPI Specification. The interrupt routing to IOxAPICs is now described in the ACPI namespace using ASL. For details, please refer to the latest ACPI specification online.

PCI Recommendation

As the PCI specifications have progressed, the PCI Express Specification and the PCI Firmware Specification have become supersets of previous PCI local bus specification and PCI BIOS specifications. The PCI Express Specification is similar and has backward compatibility to the PCI Bus Specification. For this reason, developers should implement section 7 of the latest PCIe Specification. Several implementation notes are also included in the PCIe specification to avoid common pitfalls.

PCI Power Management

PCIe ASPM – Active State Power Management
- a. PCI Express Base Specification
- b. PCI Local Bus Specification
- c. PCI-to-PCI Bridge Architecture Specification
- d. PCI Hot-Plug Specification
- e. PCI Bus Power Management Interface Specification
- f. PCI BIOS Specification
- g. PCI Firmware Specification
- h. PCI Standard Hot-Plug Controller and Subsystem Specification
- i. PCI-X Addendum to the PCI Local Bus Specification
- j. PCI Express to PCI/PCI-X Bridge Specification

USB Enumeration and Initialization

In the USB world, there has been a progression from UHCI to ECHI to XHCI as speeds have gotten faster, smarter, and USB devices are now ubiquitous. OHCI exists but is not widely supported on Intel architecture. There are varying degrees of support to handle USB pre-OS. In order, the BIOS must:

1. Supply PCI resources for onboard USB controllers and wait for the OS drivers to load and enumerate the USB devices before they are usable. The USB controllers or devices may also be armed to wake the system via ACPI.
2. Add a USB stack in the firmware to enumerate the USB bus and allow for limited functionality pre-OS for such things as HID devices (keyboard/mouse) or storage devices (boot to USB).
3. Add an SMI handler to allow for OS Bootloader and OS runtime support on OSes that do not have a native USB driver stack. This is also known as "legacy USB support."

These are the basics that have existed since USB started in the 1990s. Adding this USB pre-OS support to a firmware stack is a substantial effort (multiple-man months). The additional boot times involved can also be inhibitive, several hundred milliseconds to several seconds depending on the number of USB ports/devices/usages enabled.

In addition to the USB pre-OS support listed above, there are a few other areas of USB that can be explored for additional value to the platform:

1. Pre-boot authentication (PBA) may also require USB support and that is an additional concern that must worked out with the PBA vendors and the OEM of the system.
2. Trusted USB, where there is an established root of trust from the boot vector and where a USB device is not allowed to function unless it is authenticated and/or secured in some manner in either the BIOS hardened firmware and/or the operating system.

PBA devices and Trusted USB share some common and interesting traits, but we will focus on the non-secure USB enumeration and initialization in this book.

There are different versions of USB controllers implemented in the Intel chipsets and systems on chips. Here we will focus on the PCH.

PCI Enumeration and Initialization of USB Controllers

The simplest form of USB support is basic PCI support with no additional USB network initialization. During the PCI enumeration in the BIOS flow, the USB controllers' BARS are assigned, IRQs are provided, and memory and I/O space may be enabled. Additionally, the system firmware can also hide controllers, disable ports, and arm for ACPI wake events.

Hiding USB Controllers' PCI Space

Depending on the number of ports routed and utilized on the platform, some number or types of USB controllers may be hidden or disabled to save PCI resources and, depending on the chip, for power savings. When a device is hidden, an OS is incapable of both discovering and using the hidden device via PCI configuration space. To hide a host controller, the BIOS must program the Function Disable register at (RCBA + 3418h). See the PCH datasheet for a description of the register.

When disabling UHCI host controllers, the USB 2.0 EHCI Structural Parameters Registers must be updated by the system BIOS with coherent information in "Number of Companion Controllers" and "N_Ports" fields, which are:

- (Device26)/(Device29):F0:04h[15:12]
- D26/29:F0:04h[3:0], respectively.

It is important to note a quirk here that the BIOS cannot configure the device to provide UHCI support only in the Intel USB controllers on the PCH. This configuration is prevented per the PCI Specification requirements; that is, PCI devices must always implement function 0. Therefore, the UHCI host controller support must always be accompanied by support by at least one EHCI host controller (D29/26 Function #0).

To ensure that a disabled USB function cannot initiate transactions for USB transfers or be the target of memory or I/O requests, the system BIOS must also ensure the controller memory, and I/O control bits are disabled prior to hiding the function. Also, the USB functionality is disabled in the controller's registers:

- Clear the Run/Stop bit and verify that the HCHalted bit becomes set (EHCI and UHCI)
- Set the Interrupt disable bit, PCI Cfg offset 04h[10] (EHCI and UHCI)
- Clear Asynchronous schedule enable bit, USB20 MEM_BASE 20h[5], and Periodic schedule enable bit, USB20 MEM_BASE 20h[4]
- Wake capabilities (UHCI, GPE0_EN, and EHCI, D26/D29:F0:62h)

Once set, the device will be disabled until the next platform reset occurs. The policy to disable the EHCI functionality is not a dynamic one. This restriction also applies to subsequent warm boots.

Disabling USB Ports

System BIOS may choose to disable individual USB ports to save power or for security purposes. Each of the USB ports has a corresponding bit within the PCH USB Port Disable Override Register (RCBA + 359Ch). The PCH USB Port Disable Override Register can be locked by setting the Write Enable bit of the PCH USB Per-Port Register Write Control Register, PMBASE + 3Ch[1]. Refer to the PCH datasheet for more details on these registers.

USB Wake from ACPI Sx (S3, S4, S5 to S0)

The EHCI host controllers may generate the wake from the internally routed PME signal. An enable/disable bit (PME_B0_EN) is provided to support the resume events from Bus#0 using the PME signal. For supporting EHCI host controller wake in an ACPI environment the _PRW ACPI method package to describe the "Wake from USB 2.0" functionality should also be present under PCI Bus#0 for each of the EHCI host controllers.

```
Device  (USB7) {
Name    (_ADR,   1D0000)
Name    (_PRW,   Package  (  ){0D, 03})
}
Device  (USB8) {
Name    (_ADR,   1A0000)
Name    (_PRW,   Package  (  ){0D, 03})
}
```

USB Enumeration

The system BIOS initializes the EHCI hardware in two phases, PCI enumeration as outlined above and EHCI initialization outlined next.

EHCI initialization places the EHCI in a fully functional state. While the operating system USB driver will repeat these steps for its own stack, it is required for the BIOS to perform for any pre-OS USB functional support.

1. Program Port Routing and ModPhy settings.
2. Perform a Host Controller (HC) Reset.
3. Delay required (X ms).
4. EHCI requires detection for companion controller (UHCI) initialization.
5. Check number of ports, scan connection status.
   a. If devices/hubs are connected, do a root port reset.
   b. Root port reset is driven for a required time. This short duration is needed to suppress any possible resume signals from the devices during initialization. Per the EHCI version, the BIOS needs to track duration and clear the bit at the proper time. (XHCI version will clear the bit by itself and the BIOS only needs to poll.)
6. The BIOS must poll for port enable bit to be set. While the specification says 2 ms, the completion will happen sooner than that for Intel PCHs.
7. Perform speed detection.
8. Perform a reset; recovery timing is 10 ms.

9. EHCI version – proceed to get a descriptor to know what is connected to root port. Two potential answers:
    -   Hub – if Hub, configure it for address, wait 10 ms per specification (may not need to for Intel component). Get delay needed for power on delay. Wait for that delay then configure each of the ports
    -   Root port 0 index – ID as hub. Then configure USB network downstream

It is recommended that the BIOS enable all the root ports in parallel, to avoid the otherwise additive serial time delays and then go deeper into the hub/ device layer as required for the platform. This is in some ways a platform policy decision.

If the BIOS finds a USB Device—get the ID from the descriptor, then set the address. Depending on the device type, we may need to get a further descriptor and configure as needed. What interface to query is next.

These steps are repeated for each root port.

SATA

Intel components have supported ATA controllers in one form or another since early 1990s chipsets. These have converted over time from Parallel ATA to Serial ATA. Today most Intel platforms support only SATA controllers, up to a maximum of six SATA ports. It is possible to still find PATA-supported chips in the market either as integrated controllers or as discrete PCI devices. Intel datasheets have complete details on number and types of controllers, number of ports, and available configurations and SATA-generation support per component, as well as complete set of registers.

SATA controllers support the ATA/IDE programming interface and may support Advanced Host Controller Interface (AHCI), not available on all chips. In this section, the term "ATA-IDE Mode" refers to the ATA/IDE programming interface that uses standard task file I/O registers or PCI IDE Bus Master I/O block registers. The term "AHCI Mode" refers to the AHCI programming interface that uses memory-mapped register/buffer space and a command-list-based model.

SATA Controller Initialization

The general guidelines for initializing the SATA controller during POST (S4/S5) and S3 resume are described below. Upon resuming from S3, System BIOS is responsible for restoring all registers that it initialized during POST.

Setting the SATA Controller Mode

The system BIOS must program the SATA controller mode prior to beginning any other initialization steps or attempting to communicate to the drives. The SATA controller mode is set on mainstream PCHs by programming the SATA Mode Select (SMS) field of the Port Mapping register (Device31: Function 2: offset 90h, bit[7:6]).

There are three modes that software could be operating in:
- AHCI
- RAID
- IDE (compatible) modes

Not every mode is supported on every component. Depending on which version of the component (mobile or desktop, RAID or non-RAID), the allowed configurations vary.

RAID and AHCI modes require specific OS driver support and are identical except for differences in PI and CC.SCC values. IDE mode does not have any special OS requirements and is sometimes termed compatible mode. In addition to the three operation modes above, software can choose to operate SATA ports under a single controller mode or dual controller mode.

Software, typically the BIOS, decides up front which controller mode the system should be operating in before handing over the control to the OS.

If system BIOS is enabling AHCI Mode or RAID Mode, then it must disable the second SATA controller on the part (Device 31, Function 5) by setting the SAD2 bit, RCBA 1 3418h[25]. System BIOS must ensure that memory space, I/O space, and interrupts for this device are also disabled prior to disabling the device in PCI configuration space.

IDE (Compatible) Mode
IDE mode is selected by programming the SMS field, D31:F2:90h[7:6] to 00b. In this mode, the SATA controller is set up to use the ATA/IDE programming interface. In this mode, the SATA ports are controlled by two SATA functions. One function routes up to four SATA ports, D31:F2, and the other routes up to two SATA ports, D31:F5 (this is for desktop SKUs only). In IDE mode, the Sub Class Code, D31:F2:0Ah and D31:F5:0Ah will be set to 01h. This mode may also be referred to as compatibility mode as it does not have any special OS driver requirements.

AHCI Mode
AHCI mode is selected by programming the SMS field, D31:F2:90h[7:6], to 01b. In this mode, the SATA controller is set up to use the AHCI programming interface. The six SATA ports are controlled by a single SATA function, D31:F2. In AHCI mode, the Sub

Class Code, D31:F2:0Ah, will be set to 06h. This mode does require specific OS driver support.

RAID Mode

RAID mode is enabled only on certain SKUs of the Intel components and requires an additional option ROM, available from Intel.

When supported, RAID mode is selected by programming the SMS field, D31:F2:90h[7:6] to 10b. In this mode, the SATA controller is set up to use the AHCI programming interface. The SATA ports are controlled by a single SATA function, D31:F2. In RAID mode, the Sub Class Code, D31:F2:0Ah, will be set to 04h. This mode does require specific OS driver support.

In order for the RAID option ROM to access all 6/4 SATA ports, the RAID option ROM enables and uses the AHCI programming interface by setting the AE bit, ABAR 04h[31]. One consequence is that all register settings applicable to AHCI mode set by the BIOS must be set in RAID as well. The other consequence is that the BIOS is required to provide AHCI support to ATAPI SATA devices, which the RAID option ROM does not handle.

PCH supports stable image compatible ID. When the alternative ID enable, D31 :F2 :9Ch [7] is not set, PCH SATA controller will report Device ID as 2822h for desktop SKU.

SATA Mode Default Settings

The system BIOS may implement a setup option that provides the user with the ability to select the SATA controller mode. This ensures that the operating system can be loaded and made operational on the platform if the required device driver support is not available. For embedded devices, of course, this is unlikely, but can be implemented via a tool-tunable NVRAM variable.

Enabling SATA Ports

SATA drives cannot start to spin-up or start to become data-ready until the SATA port is enabled by the controller. In order to reduce drive detection time, and hence the total boot time, system BIOS should enable the SATA port early during POST (for example, immediately before memory initialization) by setting the Port x Enable (PxE) bits of the Port Control and Status registers, D31:F2:92h and D31:F5:92h, to initiate spin-up of such drive(s).

In IDE mode, the system BIOS must program D31:F2:92h[3:0] to 0Fh and D31:F5:92h[1:0] to 3 for a SKU with six ports to enable all ports. If no drive is present, the system BIOS may then disable the ports.

In AHCI and RAID modes, the system BIOS must program D31:F2:92h[5:0] to 3Fh for six ports and 0Fh for four ports. In AHCI-enabled systems, the PCS register must always be set this way. The status of the port is controlled through AHCI memory space.

If Staggered Spin Up support is desired on the platform due to system power load concerns, the BIOS should enable one port at a time, poll the Port Present bit of the PCS register and Drive Ready bit of task file status register before enabling the next port.

The ATA/ATAPI-7 specification recommends a 31-second timeout before assuming a device is not functioning properly. Intel recommends implementing a ten-second timeout and if the device fails to respond within the first ten seconds, then the system BIOS should reinitiate the detection sequence. If the device fails to respond within an additional ten seconds, the system BIOS should reinitiate the detection sequence again. If the device fails to respond within ten more seconds, the system BIOS can assume the device is not functioning properly.

It is recommended that software or system BIOS clear Serial ATA Error Register (PxSERR) after port reset happens by writing 1 to each implemented bit location.

Setting the Programming Interface

The SATA controller supports three combinations of programming interfaces to access the maximum number of 6/4 SATA ports: a combination of legacy and native IDE, native IDE only, and AHCI.

Using the combination of the legacy and native IDE is possible only when the SATA controller is operating in IDE mode. The programming interface is selected by setting the PCI standard programming interface register, D31:F2:09h, appropriately. There are two native mode enable bits in the PI register to control the primary and secondary channels of SATA1, D31:F2:09h[2,0]; these bits must always be programmed identically. The PI register is found in both the SATA functions, but only SATA1 can be set to use legacy IDE, SATA2 supports native IDE only, and the PI register is read-only. If legacy IDE use is intended, the system BIOS must set the decode-enable bits in the IDE Timing Registers (D31:F2:40h[15] and D31:F5:42h[15]).

When the SATA controller is configured as RAID or AHCI mode, the PI register becomes read-only and the controller can use native IDE access mechanisms until the AE bit, ABAR 04h[31] is set. It is important to realize that in RAID and AHCI mode, native IDE will allow access only to the first four ports of the controller; to access the maximum of six ports, AHCI access mechanisms must be used.

Initializing Registers in AHCI Memory-Mapped Space

When the SATA controller is configured to operate in RAID or AHCI mode, the system BIOS must initialize the following memory-mapped AHCI registers specified by ABAR, D31:F2:24h:

- CAP register, Host Capabilities register (ABAR + 00h).
    - o Set SSS (ABAR 00h[27]) to enable SATA controller supports staggered spin-up on its ports, for use in balancing power spikes.
- Clear ABAR A0h [2][0] to 0b
- Clear ABAR 24h [1] to 0b
- PxCMD register (ABAR 118h, 198h, 218h, 298h, 318h, 398h).

After the BIOS issues the initial write to AHCI Ports Implemented (PI), ABAR 0Ch, register (after any PLTRST#), there is a request for the BIOS to issue two reads to the AHCI Ports Implemented (PI) register.

Some of the bits in these registers are platform specific and must be programmed in accordance with the requirements of the platform. The details regarding how these registers must be programmed can be found in the Serial ATA Advanced Host Controller Interface (AHCI) specification.

Some of the bits in these registers are implemented as read/write-once (R/WO). It is a requirement that the system BIOS programs each bit at least once, even if the default setting of the bit is the desired value (that is, system BIOS must write 0 to a bit, even if the hardware reset value is 0). Doing so will ensure that the bit is unchangeable by software that is not system BIOS. Please refer to the PCH EDS to determine which bits are R/WO.

Registers containing multiple R/WO bits must be programmed in a single atomic write. Failure to do so will result in nonprogrammable bits.

RAID Mode Initialization

When the SATA controller is initialized in RAID mode, the system BIOS needs to initialize the SATA controller and attached SATA devices as stated in the previous sections, with the following exceptions:

- The system BIOS does not need to initialize DMA mode for hard disk drives (HDDs) discovered behind the SATA controller when in RAID mode. The RAID option ROM will provide the initialization.
- SATA HDDs discovered by the system BIOS behind the SATA controller in RAID mode must *not* be added to the hard drive count at 40h:75h. The RAID option ROM will enumerate those drives and update the 40h:75h value accordingly. Updating the drive count at 40h:75h by the BIOS will make it appear that more drives are attached to the system than are actually available.

- System BIOS must *not* install INT 13h support for the SATA HDD devices discovered, nor may it treat such devices as BAID (BIOS-Aware Initial Program Load) devices, as the RAID option ROM implements the necessary INT 13h support for them.
- ATAPI devices attached to the SATA controller must be under the full control of the system BIOS and treated as BAID as they are in non-RAID mode.
- The system BIOS must load the RAID option ROM when the controller's SCC (D31:F2:0Ah) returns 04h and VenderID/DeviceID match that of PCHR RAID SKU (refer to the PCH EDS or EDS specification update for DID/VID information).

RAID Option ROM

The Intel® Rapid Storage Technology RAID option ROM is a PnP option ROM that adds the Int13h services and provides a pre-OS user interface for the RAID implementation. The option ROM's Int13h services are used up to the point where the PCH RAID OS driver takes over.

The RAID option ROM is delivered as a single uncompressed binary image compiled for the 16-bit real mode environment. To conserve system flash space, the integrator may compress the image for inclusion into the system BIOS. System memory is taken from conventional DOS memory, attached to the EBDA, and is not returned.

The RAID option ROM will first attempt to rely on the interrupt-driven mechanism handled by system BIOS and then will fall back to the polling mechanism if the system BIOS does not support the interrupt-driven mechanism. The determination is made via a memory semaphore at location 40:8E in the BIOS Data Area (BDA).

Initialization

RAID mode initialization occurs as follows:
- System BIOS configures the SATA controller for RAID mode, initializes IO BARs and ABAR, and assigns an IRQ to the controller. System BIOS optionally sets up an ISR for the SATA controller and enables interrupts for the SATA controller.
- System BIOS loads the RAID option ROM (OROM).

Int13h Drive Access to an ATA Device. System BIOS control flow: if the system BIOS uses the interrupt mechanism, then the system BIOS ISR gets control.
- If this is an unexpected interrupt, the system BIOS assumes this is a RAID request.
- The system BIOS clears the Interrupt status in the SATA/RAID controller.
- The system BIOS does *not* mask the IRQ in the PIC.
- The system BIOS sets byte 40h:8Eh to a nonzero byte value.
- The system BIOS issues an EOI and IRET.

If the system BIOS does not use the interrupt mechanism, then the system BIOS does not receive this INT13h request; therefore, it does nothing.

Int13h Drive Access to a SATA ATAPI Device. System BIOS control flow: system BIOS can choose any method to access the ATAPI drive (interrupt or polling).
- System BIOS completes the INT13h service request.
- Contact your Intel Representative to get the RAID option ROM.

Enable Flexible RAID OROM Features

Panther Point with RAID-capable SKU can customize the RAID features through setting the Intel® RST Feature Capabilities (RSTF) register before loading the RAID option ROM. The RAID OROM will enable the desired features based on the setting in that register; please refer to the Panther Point EDS for more details.

For example, if the platform-desired features are RAID0, RAID1, RAID5 and RAID10, system BIOS should set RSTF (ABAR + C8h [15:0]) to 002Fh before loading RAID OROM.

Additional Programming Requirements During SATA Initialization

System BIOS must execute several other part-specific steps as part of system BIOS initialization of the SATA controller on both cold boot (G3/S5) and S3/S4 resume path. The bit settings are required for basic operation. Please refer to the PCH datasheet for the SATA initialization settings and the actual register indexes/values to be programmed.

External SATA Programming

If an external SATA port is implemented in the system, there are additional steps that need to be followed.
- Follow steps in 13.1.6 for additional programming to external SATA port.
- Enable the port through the corresponding bits (example: D31:F2:92[5:0]).
- Put the port into Listen Mode (refer to AHCI specification for Listen Mode information), which achieves similar power savings as if the port is in SATA Slumber power state.

Compliance with Industry Specifications

To ensure a satisfactory user experience and to provide the RAID option ROM implementation with a "well-known" framework under which it can operate, the system BIOS and option ROM need to be implemented in accordance with the following specifications:

- Enhanced Disk Drive Specification, v3.0, rev0.8.
- BIOS Boot Specification, v1.01.
- PCI BIOS Specification, v2.1. POST Memory Manager Specification, v1.01.
- Plug and Play BIOS Specification, v1.0A.
- SATA AHCI Revision 1.1 specification.

Advanced Configuration and Power Interface (ACPI)

ACPI consists of tables and namespace. While many people equate this with simple power management descriptions of system and device power management features, ACPI as an industry standard has usurped several other legacy system tables over time to become the unified method for describing the platform capabilities to the operating system.

ACPI Tables

There are ACPI tables to describe every aspect of the system hardware and its preferred capabilities to an ACPI-aware OS. The ACPI tables that matter are:
- *Root System Description Pointer (RSDP)*. The Main ACPI table that points to all the other tables, the Root System Descriptor Table (RSDP) is located either at E0000-FFFFF in legacy BIOS or can be located elsewhere as specified in the UEFI system table.
- *System Description Table Header*. Common structure that is at the top of every table, except FACS.
- *Root System Description Table (RSDT)*. A 32-bit table that is becoming obsolete and may no longer be used in modern systems. It still can be used to point to many of the other tables listed below, but the system may lack certain feature compatibility. Older ACPI-aware operating systems may require this for functionality.
- *Extended System Description Table (XSDT)*. Replaces RSDT and supports both 32/64-bit systems. It points to all other tables (see below).
- *Fixed ACPT Description Table (FADT)*. Provides fixed addresses for key ACPI hardware registers, including GPE block, PM block, and ACPI Timer. It also provides I/O port details to access or enable SMI ports, which turns on ACPI mode (and the value written), and the Port address and value to reset the system.

The FADT was previously known as FACP and is pointed to by the XSDT, and in turn the FADT points to the DSDT and FACS tables.

- *Firmware ACPI Control Structure (FACS).* Hardware signature, waking vector of the 32-bit real mode, and 64-bit physical address resume vectors and global lock support.
- *Differentiated System Description Table (DSDT).* Main table for AML, not changing once loaded and exit boot services is called (or Int 19h).
- *Secondary System Description Table (SSDT).* Modular extensions of the DSDT. These are used for multiple hardware support. Example: depending on the CPU installed, they may have different features that must be defined. They also can be used per OS expectation to allow for new features for newer operating systems and backward compatibility for older ones.
- *Multiple APIC Description Table (MADT).* Describes IOxAPICs and Local CPU APICs. In PIC mode versus APIC mode.
- *Smart Battery Table (SBST).* OEM-specific table depending on the battery mated to the system.
- *Embedded Controller Boot Resources Table (ECDT).* Optionally describes resources used by the embedded controller. The table provides earlier access to the EC than if the system has to wait until the OS loads the EC drivers later in the boot.
- *Boot Graphics Resource Table (BGRT).* Describes location of the board splash screen for OS to load during OS boot to provide a seamless boot experience between the BIOS and OS.
- *Firmware Performance Data Table (FPDT).* Describes pre-OS firmware execution time to the OS or tools without the need for a wall clock or stopwatch.

There are many server and NUMA system tables that provide the operating system with enhanced details of the capabilities of dual and multisocketed systems. These tables include the System Locality Distance Information Table (SLIT) and the System Resource Affinity Table (SRAT).

There are some newer tables defined in the ACPI 5.0 specification that do not deal with Intel architecture (such as GTDT) and can be excluded from the firmware image.

Most of the ACPI tables do not change for the life of the platform and can be considered static. There may be some tables that are ported from board to board (like PCI IRQ routing _PRT). Some tables (such as SSDT) can be dynamically created, loaded, or enabled, depending on the hardware discovered during the system boot and depending on the operating system and/or the usage model requirements. For dynamic SSDTs, "Load" and "Load Table" can be used to update tables during OS load or even runtime before being interpreted by the OS. This allows for hot plugging of docking stations, socketed processors, proprietary daughter cards, and so on, where modular add-in tables make a single firmware image scalable. This SSDT table technique also can be used for dynamically adding instrumentation for debug and performance measurements.

ACPI Namespace

ACPI Namespace is an outline of a system. It is divided into high-level scopes, where nothing exists outside of a scope. A scope is equivalent to a directory, hence the dir tree model in the specification. The base of the tree is the Root Scope. The system bus (SB) scope is for everything physically on the system board. PR is for Processor tree.

ACPI Name space includes both objects (either dynamic or static) and methods (dynamically called by the OS drivers as needed).

Device Objects are defined through ASL-specific language. They are either ACPI enumerated (has an HID for a device) or an _ADR, which is used to supply OSPM with the address of a device on its parent bus. An _ADR object is used when specifying the address of any device on a bus that has a standard enumeration algorithm.

Objects can be a sum of the DSDT and any loaded SSDTs. But what does that mean? And how do we generate it?

You can create DSDT or SSDT from an ASL (ACPI Source Language) source file and generate AML (ACPI Machine Language) using an ASL compiler. Microsoft has a few versions of the compiler and Intel has an ASL compiler called IASL.exe. There are 64- and 32-bit versions of the compiler tools, but even the 32-bit version of the tool will generate a 64-bit version of the ASL code. The ACPICA project (www.acpica.org) also has source to generate a new compiler tool for various operating systems.

On a Windows machine, by looking into a device manager and picking Devices by connection, one can see the results of the ACPI namespace. To actually look at a representation of ASL code on a real machine, the Intel ASL compiler also includes a disassembler and an extractor to pull it from a local machine.

For more information on ACPI:
- For a starting point for ACPI, start with the ACPI specification; it has ample example code at www.apci.info.
- Discover more data at the ACPI Component Architecture website (www.acpica.org). It has the ACPI Component Architecture User Guide and Programmer Reference Manual and the ACPI Source Language Optimizing Compiler and Disassembler User Guide.
- A currently obsolete-but-still-applicable ACPI Implementer's Guide also can be found (still) on the Web. It was produced in the early v1.0 days of the ACPI specification. After the initial industry enabling efforts, it was inactivated. Just make sure that what you find is at least a document from 1998 or later.

Summary

This section covered basic programming for PCI, SATA, USB, and ACPI standards as they apply to the BIOS. Please check on the latest standards through the standards bodies as they are constantly changing. More complete and lower level programming details are available in the respective industry specifications. More complete details about certain characteristics of IO BIOS programming also can be obtained through BIOS specifications, which may be available online.

In the BIOS, standard enumeration algorithms can eliminate much extra work between revisions of boards or systems. These standards can also be tuned, as we will see later per board or per silicon components for best fit and performance.

Chapter 6
System Firmware Debug Techniques

> ... Bloody instructions, which, being taught, return to plague the inventor.
>
> —William Shakespeare, *Macbeth*, Act 1, Scene 7

Shakespeare is often misunderstood, as his writing style is rather unique. So it is with other people's code. Actually, your code can be, as well. Therefore, debugging system firmware can be a daunting task, whether or not the code is yours. Even if no two firmware engineers utilize the exact same set of debugging techniques, they can have many of the same tools at their disposal.

This chapter attempts to provide the reader with the appropriate mindset to debug any kind of firmware on Intel architecture.

Host/Target Debugging Techniques

Most software developers are very familiar with debuggers that operate in application space. Debuggers of this type take a program executable, along with debug information, load the program into memory, and use the processor interrupt infrastructure to allow the user to step through the code with some degree of control in the debugger. This is a host debug methodology.

Debugging firmware is usually done with more than one system: one under test and one under control (or so we hope). This is a host/target debug methodology. While an implementation of firmware may have infrastructure to load/debug firmware components, this is not common.

In order to support a host/target debug methodology, the platform under test must support some kind of hardware capability to control and/or observe what's happening on the target system. In addition, there are software features that can help enhance the debug experience exposed by available hardware capabilities.

Hardware Capabilities

Typical Intel architecture platforms provide a common set of hardware features that may be employed by anybody debugging firmware. Without these hardware features, low-level debug of Intel architecture platforms would be virtually impossible.

No two hardware features are equal, and they all serve a slightly different purpose. The reader should be aware of what to expect from these hardware features.

DOI 10.1515/9781501506819-006

POST Codes

One of the oldest and rudimentary ways of telling a user what's happening on the target platform is to give status visually through on-board components. Many Intel architecture platforms incorporate seven-segment displays that show hexadecimal status codes sent by the firmware. These displays are typically driven by an agent that captures I/O writes to ports 0x80–0x83 and shows the values on the displays.

The amount of information that can be conveyed through hexadecimal number displays is rather limited. The most prevalent use of these codes is to indicate "I got here" to the user. A system crash or hang can sometimes be debugged by using the last POST code as an indication of "this is the last known good point" and understanding what is being done immediately after that point. If you have the capability of run control over a target, it is also possible to capture a sequence of POST codes to illustrate the logic flow of the firmware, which can allow for POST codes to be used for more than one purpose.

BIOS companies typically have a list of standard architectural POST codes common across all platforms. This list is usually documented fairly extensively for customer consumption. If it's not, what good are the POST codes unless you have the entire firmware source code base?

Extending POST Code Usefulness

Consider a platform that only has two seven-segment displays that display the I/O traffic to port 0x80, no serial port, and no ITP port. A fatal error condition may occur. That fatal error could be caused by a number of things. Since the platform has only two seven-segment displays, only 256 static error codes or status codes are possible.

If an error is fatal, there's really nothing for the platform to do once the error is encountered, is there? Instead of simply sending a non-descriptive byte out I/O port 0x80 and halting, consider sending more information. How? Instead of halting, use the system to cycle through more bytes of data that may further help diagnose the problem.

Audio (Beep) Codes

Sometimes used in addition to POST codes, audio beep codes are used to give the user an auditory clue of the state of the target, in applications where visual indicators are not available (such as a motherboard in a closed PC case).

As these are more applicable to consumers of end-products and are not really valuable to firmware engineers, they won't be discussed further.

Serial Port

UARTs are still a prized component of hardware designs. While seven-segment displays allow POST codes to be displayed to the user in a cost-effective manner, UARTs providing text driven output give an infinite number of degrees of freedom in what can be communicated.

Rather than simple hexadecimal data, full strings can be output to textually describe what's going on. Debug information can be displayed, if desired. Steps in complex calibration sequences can be shown to assist in debug of hardware or the firmware algorithms themselves.

Of course, UARTs require that an external cable and host PC be connected in order to run a terminal program to view the serial output. But that's not too much to ask for the flexibility a UART gives you, including in some cases JTAG level access.

Interactive Shells

If you have a UART available, one obvious extension of the console allowed with a UART is the capability of bidirectional traffic (that is, debug shell). This shell can be used for system diagnostics and probing during development. Many commercially available firmware stacks support interactive debug shells.

In-Target Probe (ITP), a Form of JTAG Port

A firmware developer's most prized tool, the ITP is the most useful tool in debugging firmware. An ITP is a piece of hardware connected to both a host and a target system, allowing the host system to have execution control over the target from the beginning of power-on through the life of the target boot.

ITPs allow a host system to perform the following actions:
- Halt the system on a hardware reset.
- Halt the system on processing mode entry/exits.
- Step through atomic assembly instruction execution.
- Change processor registers on the fly.
- Probe/alter system memory.
- Probe/alter system buses and devices (PCI).
- Set breakpoints on code execution.
- Set breakpoints on data access/read/write.
- Set breakpoints on I/O transactions.
- Script several commands into functional groupings.

Basically, just about anything you can do by executing firmware you can also do with an ITP. In fact, ITP hardware and ITP scripts are crucial to bringing new processors and chipsets online in a rapid fashion. You can't find an Intel firmware engineer who doesn't have at least one ITP in his or her possession.

There are several Intel-compatible ITP devices and associated software suites on the market. Other architectures/vendors have In Circuit Emulators (ICE) to do similar/same jobs. Regardless of the vendor, make sure you have one.

Software Debug Methods

In addition to available hardware debug capabilities, several software-based methods may assist in successful debug of Intel architecture firmware.

Console Input/Output

You laugh at your friends who debug with printf, right? That's not so funny in the firmware world. If you don't have access to hardware that allows run control, you need to have as much information as possible at your fingertips. Debug messages can serve as the base of that information.

Abstraction

If some sort of console output is available on a platform, functional abstraction can be a great way to get more meaningful information out of your firmware.

Consider a 32-bit memory-mapped write operation. A quick and dirty way of performing that operation in C would be:

```
*((uint32_t*) mmioAddr) 0x55aa55aa;
```

Now, also consider instead writing an access method to perform that transaction to be used as follows:

```
mmioWrite32  (mmioAddr, 0x55aa55aa);
```

This access method could be easily modified to not only perform the MMIO write, but display debug information on a console:

```
mmioWrite32:  ADDR  (FF0E0FF2)  55AA55AA
```

This is a rather simple example, but it can apply to any kind of hardware access. This instrumentation allows enhanced visibility into the operation of the firmware, as well as the capability to simulate algorithms on other platforms (that is, have the console output in the API, but not the hardware access). Personally, I do this all the time.

Disable Optimization

One of the most forgotten debug techniques is to disable optimization in the compiler. Why is this so important? Whether you are looking at high-level source code in an ITP or straight assembly, what you see in the code window may not be what you expect. Take the following example, for instance.

Where Am I in the Firmware?

So you are running in silicon initialization and the system hangs. How do you know where it is hung?

When using a POST code, it will give you a clue to the last checkpoint called. But then you still have 100 files in which the system may be hung. So you go down and begin the trace code, starting from that checkpoint using an in-target probe (ITP), in-circuit emulator (ICE) or another run-control debug tool.

If you are using the Tiano code with serial debug on, there will be a GUID for the particular code that is executing.

When you get to the point where it stops, there may be absolutely nothing wrong with that line or that file. What do you do? You backtrack and start debugging what the hardware or silicon is doing versus what you think it should be doing, looking at register level details, poring over specifications.

When Hardware Isn't Stable, Where Do I Start?

When your hardware isn't stable, the initialization may inconsistently hang. There are a number of reasons why:
1. Make sure all cards and cables are properly seated. Check your configuration in every way you can; you can spend hours chasing ghosts because someone partially knocked a connection loose or you may not have the right version of the card/cable to support your current debug activity.
2. The previous configuration steps may not be complete or correct (BIOS can fix it).
3. Check the voltage rails on the motherboard and make sure they are stable.

4. The power sequencing or input clocking may not be correct, and the silicon may be in an indeterminate state. If this is the case, there is some other programmable firmware that will likely need to be updated to take this into account.

5. Try the code on a known-good system. If the parts are interchangeable, you can modularly replace parts until you find one that isn't working.

6. Check your schematics and make sure all the parts of the subsystem giving you fits is correct. A "blue wire" may be able to help.

7. If this is a brand new motherboard design, have a hardware person check the Intel design guide and make sure there is nothing obviously wrong. If shortcuts were made, then suspect the motherboard will need to be respun.

8. Check for critical signal integrity with someone who knows what an "eye diagram" is. This would require a motherboard change to fix the routing/layout.

9. If all of the above has failed, it could be silicon issue, as on a brand-new preproduction A0 stepping component; get a silicon design engineer to assist the debug at register level with the specifications open as you trace through the code line by line. Or call your vendor and report a potential issue

Most of the time, the BIOS will be blamed for bad hardware. Even if there is a BIOS workaround that can fix the hardware stability problem, it could still be looked at as a BIOS problem...this comes with the territory.

Debugging Other People's Code

Unless you are writing in a firewalled, green pasture of an environment, this scenario has already happened.

You have to understand the larger picture to understand where to start looking in the code. Study the architecture and understand where it is "safe" to make changes for a patch. Test the patch to make sure it works. You can later go back in and do a more elegant fix.

It is likely that when the person wrote the code, all the new requirements were unknown. Unless you have a lot of time on your hands, and the changed requirements have so overwhelmed the existing code that it is more a rat's nest of patches, you should avoid the common pitfall of jumping into a redesign of the code.

Most of the time, you will have to just "deal with it" until you can and need to do something more formal and longer term.

Debugging PCI Option ROMs or Binary Libraries

For option ROMs, there are a signature and entry/exit points. You don't get much else unless the vendor supplies the code to you under NDA. During the execution, there will be an initialization sequence and an optional runtime component. Various interrupts or services may be called that will access the option ROM.

As with any black box, you have to know what goes into the box and what is expected to come out. Just because the boot halts inside of an option ROM doesn't mean it is the option ROM's problem. There could be a motherboard/hardware reason that it is hanging in the code. The option ROM may be a symptom; it may not be the root cause. As with the unstable hardware section above, there are debug steps you can follow to try to rule out potential external issues first:

1. Make sure all cards and cables are properly seated.
2. The previous configuration steps may not be complete or correct (BIOS can fix it).
3. Check the voltage rails on the motherboard and make sure they are stable.
4. The power sequencing or input clocking may not be correct, and the silicon may be in an indeterminate state. If this is the case, there is some other programmable firmware that will likely need to be updated to take this into account.
5. Try the card/part on a known-good system. If the parts are interchangeable, you can modularly replace parts until you find one that isn't working.
6. Check your schematics and make sure all the parts of the subsystem giving you fits is correct.
7. If this is a brand-new motherboard design, have a hardware person check the Intel design guide and make sure there is nothing obviously wrong. If shortcuts were made, then suspect the motherboard will need to be respun.
8. Check for critical signal integrity with someone who knows what an "eye diagram" is. This would require a motherboard change to fix the routing/layout.
9. If all the above has failed, call your vendor and report a potential issue.

Debugging Library Code (No Source)

Debugging a library function is like the black box option ROM above. The key difference is, with a library, there should be a well-defined API that provides you with more data than an option ROM. With that data, you may be able to create a temporary workaround for that initialization sequence to ensure that the issue is truly in the library. You can then either bring that issue back to the vendor, or you can write your own code and replace the library. It may be the case that the library is in a binary format for production, but that the vendor would be willing to supply a debug version of the source to help you debug the scenario.

It should be noted, however, that for an industry standards library, the code should have been tested sufficiently at the vendor such that any issues being found now are a result of a change from the standard specification or something unique to the hardware that the library is trying to initialize. Before contacting the vendor, it would be a good idea to run through the "unstable hardware" checks to make sure nothing is wrong with the hardware itself.

Debugging Beyond Firmware

You've gotten through firmware execution, loaded the first stage of the OS in memory, and jumped to it. We're all done, right?

No. Not even close.

Except for highly embedded closed box or entirely proprietary systems, most operating systems will rely on some form of runtime support from Intel architecture firmware. There are several types of interactions between the operating system and firmware. This section touches lightly on the types of firmware reliance a boot loader or operating system may have.

Real Mode Interrupts

Legacy operating systems dating from the beginning of the original IBM PC to current day utilize real mode interrupts to request information from the firmware or tell the firmware to do something. These real mode interrupts serve a wide range of functions including:
- Video Services (INT 0x10)
- System Services (INT 0x15)
- I/O Services (various)

As with just about everything in life, there are both good and bad things about real mode interrupts. Let's look at the good things first:
- Once a real mode interrupt is defined, its meaning rarely changes. This means that once firmware supports a real mode interrupt, it rarely has to change.
- The state of the system is well known at the invocation of a real mode interrupt.

Now for the bad things:
- There's a prevalent lack of documentation on many of these real mode interrupts. Since real mode interrupts were an easy way to create interfaces between the operating system and firmware, vendors are free to define any services they desire, as long as it wouldn't trash any expectations set on other real mode interrupt calls existing in the industry. Therefore, many of these are specific to designs and PC types, and the documentation on them cannot be found readily.
- Because any operating system may choose to execute a real mode interrupt in a Virtual x86 task, implementers of real mode interrupts may be tied to keeping the implementation as 16-bit real mode code. Changing into any protected mode in a Virtual x86 task throws an exception.
- Depending on the policies of the operating system, it may also be required that a service (in the case of PCIBIOS32, not really a real mode interrupt) completely reside in one 4-KB page of memory. Failure to do so may result in page faults.

- No two operating systems utilize the exact same set of real mode interrupts (if they even do), and there is no documentation on which services are required for any given operating system.

So, how are you supposed to know what to implement if you were to design your firmware from scratch? Debug.

Debugging Methods

Although the number of real mode interrupt debug methods is vast, this section outlines a few helpful hints that may allow the reader a little help in this complex area.

- IVT Hardware Breakpoints. To determine when a real mode interrupt is called, use hardware breakpoints on the Interrupt Vector Table entries for the real mode interrupts in question. Providing the operating system has not overridden the debug registers, you'll get a hit every time a specific interrupt is called.
- Common Real Mode Interrupt Handler. If you have the flexibility to do so, have all the real mode interrupts utilize one common handler, which takes an interrupt vector. This allows one hardware breakpoint to be used to trace all real mode interrupt calls.
- Console Output. If there's a console available that's accessible in real mode, use it. Your best friend printf may actually come to the rescue a few times.

System Management Mode

System Management Mode (SMM) is a special operating mode of an Intel architecture processor that allows an isolated and secure operating environment for many purposes, including operating system or firmware handshaking, error handling, and hardware abstraction. In many ways, it is very similar to ARM's trust zone implementations in silicon, so heads up realtime programmers. SMM will be encountered in most firmware implementations. A couple of those situations may be:

- ACPI/APM. In both of these power management specifications, SMM is invoked in order to change power states or modes.
- Hardware I/O Traps. Firmware may implement hardware I/O traps to either communicate intentionally with an operating system entity (such as ACPI OSPM), emulate hardware, or perform security-based operations such as preventing GPIO manipulation for unsecured flash programming.

Regardless of the situation, SMM is one of the most difficult parts of firmware code to debug.

Debugging Methods

As the intent of SMM is to be as invisible as possible to the system during runtime, hardware should not have its state modified by SMM code. This means that the concept of a console is probably off limits for debug messages.

The best methods of debugging SMM are:

- POST Codes. The port 0x80–0x83 I/O range is mostly treated as a write-only range and displayed on seven-segment displays. Reads to those I/O ports is not always allowed by Intel architecture chipsets. Therefore, the seven-segment displays may be used to help debug SMM or indicate that SMM or specific SMM handlers are implemented. This is common with the SMM handler for enabling/disabling ACPI.
- Use of ITP. Commercial ITPs usually allow special breakpoints to be placed upon entering and exiting SMM, which allow a user to step through the entire firmware SMM infrastructure or debug code that invoke an SMM handler after the SMM trap.

Industry Specifications

Numerous industry specifications outline communication methods between firmware and higher-level software. No two specifications look entirely the same. The requirements on the locations and styles of the firmware buffers differ between all of them.

Pitfalls

Just because you have a good understanding of a hardware debugger and some knowledge into industry specifications that are supported doesn't mean that debugging the platform after handover to the OS will be a breeze. There are several pitfalls that are very common.

Industry Specification Overlap

Many industry standard specifications document firmware/OS communication methods for the same information in a different manner. The best example of this would be the communication of platform interrupt routing.

Platform interrupt routing may be communicated by the following mechanisms:

- $PIR table per the PCI IRQ Routing Table Specification
- Interrupt entries in the MP table per the MultiProcessor Specification
- _PRT methods per the ACPI Specification

Since there is overlap in the communicated data, you cannot assume that all or any of these are used by the operating system. If you're implementing only one of those methods, your interrupt information may not be consumed by the operating system. If you're implementing all of them, you don't always know which method(s) the operating system is consuming. Therefore, in supporting all these methods, you need to ensure that the information communicated by all of them is consistent. Also, make no assumptions about which method is being used.

Disappearing Breakpoints

Hardware debuggers utilize the debug registers (DR0–DR7) in the processor to control all hardware interrupts. Since these are public processor registers, anybody can modify them. That includes a boot loader or an operating system. It may seem logical that you should be able to set hardware breakpoints on memory accesses to debug boot loader and operating system use of firmware tables. However, if a boot loader or operating system chooses to overwrite the DR0–DR7 register while the target is running, the breakpoints will basically disappear. Therefore, care must be taken when attempting to debug firmware table usage.

Summary

If you understand the hardware capabilities at your disposal, have the appropriate tools, and understand the applicable specifications, you should be able to apply the techniques described in this chapter to make your way through debugging your firmware from the reset vector through the entire boot process.

Chapter 7
Shells and Native Applications

I was like a boy playing on the sea-shore, and diverting myself now and then finding a
smoother pebble or a prettier shell than ordinary, whilst the great ocean of truth lay all undis-
covered before me.

—Sir Isaac Newton

A shell is a very convenient place to run applications, and it allows both developers
and users great access to all the hardware in a platform, and all the shells/applica-
tions they are sitting upon. Many shells have significantly lower overhead to them
than a modern operating system. These two features combine to make them an excellent place to develop and test new hardware and low-level drivers for that hardware,
as well as a place to run diagnostics.

The common features that most shells share are the ability to run external executable images, the ability to be automated, file system access, environment access,
and system configuration.

In Figure 7.1 you can see how a shell command is translated from a human readable string down to a hardware command in the EFI environment.

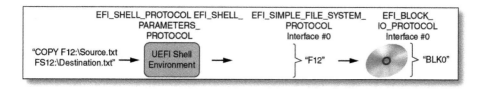

Figure 7.1: A Command Traversing the Driver Stack

The running of external shell applications is critical since that is the method most
used to add a new feature into the shell. This new feature can be anything from the
simple printing of a string to the console for user input all the way up to a complex
program that runs the entire platform. This is the only way to add a completely new
feature to the shell without editing the shell's own code. This is also commonly used
to perform proprietary tasks, such as manufacturing configuration, where the executable is not found on the system afterwards.

Automation is accomplished through script files. These are a set of sequential
commands that can be started automatically upon entering the shell so that they happen whenever the shell is launched. Some shells allow a user to abort the running of
these automatically started scripts.

DOI 10.1515/9781501506819-007

These two sets of extension abilities also can be combined. It is possible for a script file to call some of the extended executables, some commands internal to the shell, and even a different script file.

The features that make the UEFI Shell 2.0 unique have to do with the features that make it especially useful for firmware. This means specifically that the shell can be heavily configured such that the platform can have a shell with a reduced feature set and a similarly reduced footprint size. At least 64 combinations of size and feature set are available in the UEFI Shell, with more available via extensions. This allows for the UEFI Shell to vary in size from ~300 to almost 1000 KB.

The other effect that this reduction in the size of the feature set can have is security. If the end user of the platform is not expected to use the shell, it is possible to restrict the features available to eliminate some risk that they can harm the system, but still leave enough features that the limited shell could be used to initiate a platform debug session. It is even possible to have a limited built-in-shell (with a correspondingly small binary image footprint) launch a large and feature-rich shell from a peripheral storage device, such as USB, DVD, or even over the network.

When in early testing of a new platform, a common use of the shell is as a boot target, normally before the hardware can boot to a full modern operating system. This allows for lots of hardware testing via the internal commands and custom-designed shell applications. Since custom applications have access to the full system, they can easily test memory, run new assembly instructions, test a new peripheral media device, or simply examine the contents of the ACPI table.

Since the EFI and UEFI shells have built-in commands to examine memory, examine drive contents, verify device configuration, use the network, and output logs of what was found, much early testing can be accomplished in this environment. When this is combined with the ability of a shell to run itself with minimal features from the underlying system, it is a clear advantage to use the shell to test and debug new hardware of unknown quality.

The logical continuation of this is that in a system where the hardware is *expected* to be of high quality, but the side effect of the usage model dictates that testing be done still (such as a manufacturing line), it makes a lot of sense to first boot to the shell to do some level of testing and then "continue" the boot onto the operating system. This is easily done from any EFI or UEFI Shell since in both of these cases the operating system loader is just another UEFI application that can be launched from the shell. To do this automatically, you would configure the startup.nsh script file for the UEFI Shell and have that script file do a series of tests and, if they all pass, then launch the operating system loader application. There are features that directly support this type of behavior with the ability to get and set environment variables and use conditional expressions right inside the script files.

Here is an example script file:

```
if exist fs0:\myscript.nsh then
 myscript TEST_INFO1 TEST_INFO1
endif
if %lasterror% == EfiError(8)
 echo  "write  protect  error"
endif
if %lasterror% == 0
 fs0:\OS\OsLoader.EFI
endif
#  note that we  never expect the Loader to return,
#  but we  must  have  the  endif for syntax.
```

Pre-OS Shells

Both the EFI Shell and the UEFI Shell are UEFI applications. This means that they will run on any current UEFI platform (the EFI Shell will run on older implementations of the UEFI and EFI specifications). These applications have very low requirements from the system. They both need memory, SimpleTextInput, SimpleTextOutput, Device-PathToText, and UnicodeCollation, and will use lots more (for example, Simple-FileSystem or BlockIO) if they are present. See the documentation for each UEFI application to verify exactly what protocols are required for that application.

The EFI Shell is a nonstandard shell. That means there is no predefined behavior for a given command and that there is no predefined set of commands that must be present. In practice, there is a de-facto standard for both risk factors due to the prevalence of a single implementation of the EFI Shell dominating in the marketplace. The EFI Shell provides all the standard features already discussed above, but unlike the UEFI Shell there are only two different versions of the EFI Shell to allow for customizing the size requirement. This means that fine-tuning of the binary size cannot occur.

The UEFI Shell 2.0 is the successor to the EFI Shell. This is a standards- based version of a UEFI-compliant shell. It has all the commands the EFI Shell had, but many of these commands have been extended and enhanced and some new commands have also been added to the UEFI Shell. This means that all script files that were written for the EFI Shell will work on the UEFI Shell, but this is not always the case in reverse. It is possible (and recommended) to write the scripts using the new features if the target shell will always be the UEFI Shell, as they greatly simplify and enhance the capabilities of the script files.

Two changes in the UEFI Shell are very significant for script files. The first is the concept of levels and profiles for the shell. These are sets of commands that can be queried for availability before they are called. This is important because if you can't call the shell command GetMtc to get the monotonic tic count or DrvDiag to initiate a driver diagnostic then you may want to verify that it is present in the shell before you call it. With the old EFI Shells you couldn't test for this condition and had to rely on the platform to have the correct version of the shell, but in the newer UEFI Shells, you can query for the presence of the Driver1 profile and thereby know that the DrvDiag command is required to be present. The second change directly affecting script files is the concept of *Standard Format Output* or -sfo. This is a feature, and a parameter, present on some shell commands (like the ls command), which have a lot of columnar output. By specifying -sfo, the output will be output in a specific format defined in the specification so output between different implementations will have no effect. This output is comma delimited and can be redirected to a file and then easily parsed with the parse shell command which did not exist in the EFI Shell. These two changes mean that a script file that works in the UEFI Shell but not in the EFI Shell can have a lot more logic in it and can have multiple methods for getting information such that if one shell command is not present, it could use another, while the same script file, if done in a cross-version method, would have to do a lot more work.

UEFI Shell Application

The UEFI and EFI Shells are themselves UEFI applications. What does this actually mean? Let's start with the word *application*. In the UEFI environment, applications are binary files that are loaded into memory, have their entry-point function called, and are then unloaded from memory. This is different from a driver, which is not unloaded after running the entry-point function. The second part of it means that the application depends on some of the elements of UEFI. There is no defined method to know exactly which part of the interface is defined, but a well-designed application will have some documentation or a clear message about what it requires. The elements of UEFI that can be required are all accessed via the System Table, either through Boot Services or Runtime Services. Note that outside of Operating System Loader applications there are no UEFI applications that operate in the runtime mode of the UEFI environment.

What makes a shell application different? A shell application is one that must run after the shell application (itself a UEFI application) has started. There are a few benefits to this: parameters, file system, environment. We'll go into each of those.

When a UEFI application starts, it gets its parameters as a single long array of CHAR16. This means that the application must carry the logic for parsing this into parameters and then determining associations between the parameters (for example, the use of quotes). When a UEFI Shell application starts, the shell has already performed this parsing and the application is passed Argc and Argv almost as if it were a standard C application. This allows for much smaller applications, much faster application creation, and generally easier to maintain applications.

The file system in the UEFI environment is accessed via DevicePaths. These are not especially easy or fun for a human to read and not especially easy to write. For example:

```
PciRoot(0x0)/Pci(0x1D,0x3)/USB(0x1,0x0)
```

is the DevicePath for a USB hard disk in the system. When the shell runs, it creates a human readable map name for this called FS0: and a consistent map name (stays the same across multiple platforms) called f17b0:. These are much easier to use. For example, echo hello world, fs0:\hi.txt makes a lot of sense and is easily understood by almost any user. However, the UEFI application must interpret the full device path from its command line and try to find the file system represented on that device path and find the required file at the end. This is a compound problem since there are usually multiple file systems and the effort to decode each one will repeat all the work each time the decoding must take place.

The shell environment features things like path, which is a list of places to search for a specified file by default, a series of aliases so that ls and dir are the same command, and environment variables so that %foo% can be automatically replaced by a predetermined (and configurable) value. There are also useful functions for finding files using wild card characters (? and *), finding the names of devices, and getting additional information on files. Configurable elements of these environment features can be changed and configured on the command line of the shell.

A complicating factor is that the method used to access these features from the EFI Shell differs from the method used from the UEFI Shell 2.0. This means you may have to do extra work to support both types of UEFI Shells (or use the UDK 2010 Shell Library)

You have to decide on tradeoffs:
- Is it worth the feature set that the shell provides to require that the application run under it at all? Maybe writing a UEFI application instead of a shell application would be a better solution.
- Is it worth the binary size increase to use the UDK 2010 library and support either of the two (EFI and UEFI) shells? The library will automatically detect the shell version and seamlessly handle the differences.
- Is the target environment a single type of shell such that the library overhead could be minimized by directly using the protocols produced by the shell? Direct access will reduce the binary size, but it also increases the amount of work required for some actions (printing with color is a good example).

The code for a simple Hello World UEFI application follows:

```
EFI_STATUS EFIAPI
UefiMain (
```

```
IN EFI_HANDLEImageHandle, IN EFI_SYSTEM_TABLE *SystemTable
)
{
SystemTable->ConOut->OutputString(SystemTable-
>ConOut, L"Hello World");
return (EFI_SUCCESS);
}
```

The same done as a UEFI Shell application would replace the call to
OutputString with a call to ShellPrintEx(-1,-1,L"Hello World").

As you can see the application in its simplest form is actually quite similar in the
UEFI application and in the UEFI Shell application forms. The difference becomes
more apparent as we look at the code used to open a file.

The UEFI Shell application opening a file named file.txt:

```
gShellProtocol->OpenFileByName(L"File.txt",    &Handle,    EFI_
FILE_MODE_READ);
```

The UEFI application opening a file named file.txt and for simplicity we are not even
trying to search a path for the file (pseudo code):

```
BootServices->LocateHandleBuffer(&Buffer,    &Count,    &Simple-
FileSystemGuid);
for (loop = 0 ; loop < Count ; loop++){ Buffer[loop]->Open-
Root(&RootHandle);
if (RootHandle->OpenFile(L"File.txt") == SUCCESS)
{
//Save the handle... break;
}
CloseHandle(RootHandle);
}
FreePool(Buffer);
If (SavedHandle is valid)...
```

The point here is that the shell does not do anything that any other application (or
driver for that matter) cannot do. It just makes the repeating of these tasks very easy
to do. Don't think that you can't do what the shell does. Think how much you don't
need to do that the shell already is doing for you.

EFI/UEFI Script File

UEFI applications and UEFI Shell applications are pretty well defined up to this point in terms of their capabilities and their restrictions. They are the more powerful of the two types of files that interact with the shell. The other type of file is the shell script file.

Different Features between Script and App

A Script file is always a text file, either UNICODE or ASCII, and because of this can be changed quite easily with no special programs. A small sample shell script is:

```
echo "1 - START"
GOTO label1
echo "1 -  NO"
FOR %a IN a b c echo   "1  - NO"
:label1
echo "1 - NO"
ENDFOR
echo "1 - END"
```

This script is a simple functional test of the goto script-only command. The significant limitation of script files are that they cannot do anything that is not already done in either a shell command or an existing shell application. This means that script files are good for repetitive tasks, but they have their limitations. For example, to output the current memory information to a log file and then compare that with a known good version of the file is an excellent task for completion by a script file. On the other hand, opening a network connection and sending some information to a remote platform is something that is not already encapsulated into a shell command (and assuming there is no special application) means that this would be better done with an application and not a script.

The power behind applications is that they can open and interact with any protocol and any handle that is present in the system. An application has all of the same privileges and rights as a UEFI driver—this means that the application can do pretty much anything. A script, on the other hand, cannot open any protocols; it can interact only with shell commands and applications.

The power behind script files is that they can do large amounts of repetitive work with less overhead than required for an application and that they can fully exercise shell commands and applications with much less development overhead than an application. Script files require no compiler or any development tools at all. They can even be edited via the edit command in the shell and then rerun without using any other software.

For example, the following loop will do some desired action 300 times in a row:

```
echo "2 - START"
FOR %a  RUN  (1 300)
echo "some desired action" ENDFOR
echo "2 - END"
```

This same script could be made more generic by modifying it to use the first parameter to the script itself as the termination condition. This means that the script will run some arbitrary number of times that is controllable at the time the script is launched.

```
echo "2 - START"
FOR  %a  RUN  (1 %1)
echo "some desired action" ENDFOR
echo "2 - END"
```

Customizing the UEFI Shell

The UEFI Shell was both specified and designed with the goal of allowing lots of customization. We already covered the 64 possible combinations of shell levels and shell profiles. For initial silicon bring-up and debugging, it would be best to try to use a level 3 shell with all the profiles installed. This would mean that the binary size would be the biggest of all the combinations, but also that the feature set would be the biggest. There is a defined method for adding additional (custom) profiles into the shell that include any custom shell commands you have developed.

In Figure 7.2 you can see how the UEFI Shell runs on top of the UEFI drivers. You can also see the separation of required and optional components of the shell, which is what allows for the easy customization and modification of the shell.

To add a command set to the UEFI Shell 2.0, located in the UDK2010 available at www.tianocore.org, add a NULL-Named-Library to the shell via your DSC file. This new library must then use the API from UefiShellCommandLib to register its commands with the shell core. The shell core will then call into this new library when the registered commands are invoked from the command line of the shell. This registration will include the name of the command (don't overlap with existing commands in the shell), a function pointer (of a specific prototype) to be called when the command is run, a required level (zero in this case), the name of this profile, and the identifier for the help content in HII. This information is used to populate required shell features:
– The name is used for the required environment variable `profiles`.

- The help content is used if the `help` command is invoked.
- The level would be used to remove the command if the build is set for a lower level.
- The function pointer is for the core to call your library for implementation of the command.

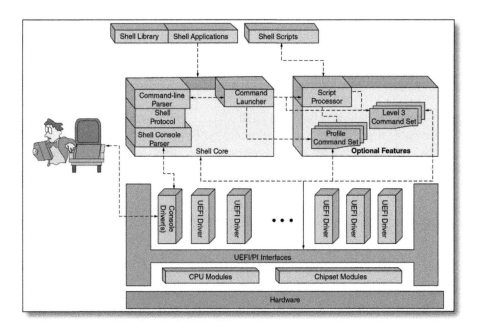

Figure 7.2: UEFI Shell 2.0 Architectural Layout

Note: Per the UEFI Shell 2.0 specification, the distribution is always two files minimum.

Adding a shell application is almost as much overhead in terms of coding work. Although the work to build the library is reduced, more work is required in the distribution of the separate files that are not part of the shell binary itself.

The shell will by default add the root of each drive, as well as the \efi\tools and \efi\boot directories. This means that any tool that wants to appear to be an internal command should reside in one of those three directories.

Note: For automatic help system integration, there should be a help file named the same as the application file and with contents contained in .man file format the same as the shell internal commands (except their information is stored via HII).

Once the internal command (in a profile) or the external application has started, they have the same privileges and almost the same access. A few actions can only be accessed via the UefiShellCommandLib. These actions are centered on internal shell functionality that a few commands need to manipulate:

– Shell script interaction
– Shell alias interaction
– Shell map interaction

Note: Linking a shell application with the library will work, but (per definition)the library functions only when also linked to the shell core so it functions (completely) only for internal shell commands.

The help system built into the UEFI Shell 2.0 core automatically parses a file when someone uses the help command (for example, help <Your_App_ Name>). This file must be in the same location as the application file. The Unicode text file must have file format similar to this:

```
.TH  <AppName>  0  "brief description"\r\n
.SH NAME\r\n
Add  more  detailed  brief description\r\n
.SH SYNOPSIS\r\n
Add  usage  information  including  parameters\r\n
.SH SYNOPSIS\r\n
Add  a list containing each parameter and its  function\r\n
.SH DESCRIPTION\r\n
Add  a  (long)  detailed description\r\n
.SH  EXAMPLES\r\n
Put  some  examples here\r\n
.SH  RETURNVALUES\r\n
SHELL_SUCCESS  The  action  was  completed  as requested.\r\n
Add any  more  return values here.\r\n
```

Once you have this file in place, there is little distinction to a normal user of the shell between your command and an internal command. There are two differences the user can notice:

– Internal commands take precedence over applications with the same name. Specify the file name with the .efi extension to override this behavior. This can also happen with script files; use .nsh to override in this case.
– Internal commands are listed via help command. External applications are not.

Where to Get Shells

Shells are frequently distributed by one of two common methods: binary distribution and code distribution. The benefits of binary distribution are simplicity and convenience without any overhead. The benefit of code distribution is customization, but this brings with it a higher overhead to get the product included in your firmware image.

The binary EFI Shell is distributed in binary form via SVN in the EDK and EDK II standard distributions at http://www.tianocore.org. This binary comes in two sizes, with the larger image having more commands available.

The binary UEFI Shell will be distributed in binary form via SVN in the EDK II and via UDK releases, both located at http://www.tianocore.org.

The source for the EFI Shell is located in an EFI Shell subproject called efi-shell. This is at http://efi-shell.tianocore.org. There are two build files that support the two different versions.

The source for the UEFI Shell is located via SVN in the EDK II and in the UDK distributions at http://edk2.tianocore.org. The customization is controlled by Platform Configuration Database entries and configured in the DSC used for building the shell.

GUIs and the UEFI Shell

There is no inherent support for graphical user interfaces (GUIs) in any of the shells discussed. There are methods in human interface infrastructure (HII) that are possible to use for configuring and performing localized displays. This would be done via the HiiLib (in UDK\EDK II) or directly via the HII protocols (See Chapters 29 and 30 of UEFI specification).

Another possibility is to use libraries to achieve this functionality. You could use the C Library (in UDK\EDK II); it should be possible to compile some standard graphics libraries and use them in the shell.

There are libraries that some companies have developed for application development. Some of these are available for purchase and others are used internally only. One example of a publicly available solution is the AMI Provisioning solution (see ami.com/prov).

Remote Control of the UEFI Shell

Both the EFI and UEFI Shells are remote controllable since all EFI implementations have support for remote control over the serial port of the keyboard and console. This is not a modern over-the-Internet remote desktop style of control, but it is certainly sufficient. This means remote control of a system running a shell requires a second computer to be the host for the testing. A very common technique for remote debugging a platform involves connecting both a hardware debugger and a serial port between a host and the platform-under-development (PUD). Then the engineer doing the debugging remotely (via the modern remote desktop connection of your choice) controls the host computer and then controls the PUD via the hardware debugger and the serial connection. The biggest challenge in this scenario is changing the copy of an application the PUD has access to. I have found that there are KVMs that have a built-in USB switching capability and using that in conjunction with a standard USB drive allows for the UEFI application under debug to be updated without anyone having to physically change anything.

Obviously, if having the PUD physically right next to you is possible, that may be faster and easier, although for some systems the power, sharing, or noise requirements may make that prohibitive to do.

Debugging Drivers and Applications in the EFI and UEFI Shells

Driver and application debugging is an excellent use of shells. Many commands are there explicitly to enable and assist in debugging. In the UEFI Shell these are contained in the "Drivers1" and "Debug1" profiles; in the EFI Shell these are in the Full image.

The basic parts of a driver that can be tested depend on the type of driver. Some drivers are much easier to get higher test coverage than others.

For a driver with a storage medium present, you can verify that the driver installed the correct protocols, verify that the platform built the upper parts of the driver stack, verify writing and reading to/from the storage medium, and verify that the driver frees all the memory it allocated upon unloading. At the same time that you can test all of these things manually, the better method would be to test by running the installation program from a UEFI-aware operating system.

For a driver with no storage medium present, such as a network driver, there may be limited coverage. The "Network1" profile has a ping command that can verify that the network controller can send and receive data, but not much more than that. The best test for this specific case would be a PXE boot test.

If the driver you are testing is for a bus, not for a device, then you need to take into account it needs to create child controllers and usually an intermediate I/O protocol. Then you would use commands like DevTree, Devices, and Drivers to see that the parent-child relationships are correctly established.

Testing an application, even a complex application such as a shell itself, requires a lot of work. The first thing is that an application should, when finished, leave the system with the same amount of memory. The second is that testing an application can utilize StdIn redirection to control the input to the application and use StdOut redirection, combined with script files, to automatically verify the output.

The shell command MemMap can display memory information about the platform. The actual map is, in this case, not the information that is of interest. The interesting information is the other part—about how many bytes of memory are allocated for each type (that is, BootServiceData). The MemMap command is run (recording the data) before and after running an application or loading and unloading a driver and then run again, and the end results are compared with the first run.

The commands Connect, Disconnect, and Map are required for setup and configuration of drivers for devices that are disk drives. Many commands can be used for write, read, and verify on a disk drive. A simple version would be to echo a text file to the new drive and then use the Compare command to verify it.

The End for the Shell

There are many possible end-game scenarios for the shell. They can range from exiting the shell to having it run forever as a background program. They are (vaguely organized from simple to less simple):
- Exit command
- OS Loader
- Shell application as platform
- Runtime application

The simplest example is that a user can run the exit command and return control to the caller (of the shell). This could be done so that the next application in the boot list is called, to un-nest from one instance of the shell to another, or to return control directly to the boot manager or setup screen.

The next simplest of these is when the OS Loader application is run. At some point during the OS Loader application, the ExitBootServices API is called (via the system table), causing the shell to end indirectly. In this case, all memory in the system not marked as Runtime is allowed to be overwritten, including the shell. The goal is that the OS will take over memory management and thus the boot service memory is no longer required.

The next possible method is that a shell application (or UEFI application) is the end-goal of the platform. This means there is no operating system at all and that the platform will forever (until powered off) just run the application. The best example of this scenario is how some Hewlett-Packard printers use an application to do all the work of handling print jobs, controlling the queue, monitoring ink, and so on. This embedded platform has no operating system whatsoever. All it has is an application that runs forever.

The most complex is somewhat of a hybrid of the previous two types. This is an application that handles everything like the preceding example, but uses the Exit-BootServices API as in the second example. This does allow the application to directly access hardware, but it also requires that this new application have drivers to handle this interaction. This distinction between this type of application and a true operating system may be more in the mind of the creator than anything else. It could be easily used for a hardware test where the boot time drivers need to stop interacting with the hardware, but where there is no real replacement of the features provided by an operating system. I do not know of any examples of this type of application.

Summary

A shell is a very convenient place to run applications and provide great access to all of the hardware. New UEFI shell interfaces and scripts provide a convenient, cheap, and flexible solution for simple applications for diagnostics and manufacturing and even simple user applications. The UEFI shell basics are downloadable as open source from www.Tianocore.org and can be quickly implemented on top of a UEFI firmware solution.

For more in depth information, please see the book *Harnessing the UEFI Shell*.

Chapter 8
Loading an Operating System

A fanatic is one who sticks to his guns whether they're loaded or not.

—Franklin P. Jones

When loading the OS, there are many ways to bootstrap the system and jump into the OS. For Intel architecture devices, there are two sets of OS interfaces we need to contend with: EFI and legacy OS. There are a number of second-stage boot loaders for each interface of Microsoft and Linux, the major operating system camps. RTOS and other proprietary operating systems will have either EFI, legacy, or both flavors; or support neither.

There is a third OS interface, the null option: when there is a blind handoff, there is no interface at all and at the end of the BIOS, it just grabs a specific address in a piece of NVRAM, loads it, and jumps to it, and the OS never looks back.

Before we get to the details, let's back up and look into the Boot Device Selection phase theory of operation. In other BIOS implementations, it is known as the *boot services*. How does one get to the disk we want to get to?

The Boot Path

To boot to an OS, you must have the right boot path enabled to get to the target operating system. In a mainstream system, this means you have to hunt and peck to find all the bootable storage devices within the bootable buses and devices, locate a bootable partition somewhere, and then decide whether you want to boot to it or not. But how do you get there?

The Bus

From the CPU and chipset, there is likely a bus or two that must be traversed, such as PCI, AHCI, USB, or SD. We must communicate on that bus in order to know whether the OS is out there on a device somewhere, and that the next-stage boot loader is resident and ready to be loaded and executed. Fortunately, in the EFI case, there is often a bus driver that has been constructed. That bus driver would know the protocols for reads, writes, and so on. This is fundamental regardless of whether you are searching for bootable partitions, locating and identifying the boot target's .efi file, or, in the case of a closed box, just reading a sector and blindly handing off control to it.

DOI 10.1515/9781501506819-008

The Device

Once you can communicate across a particular bus to talk to the device, there may be multiple boot partitions or devices to choose from. For this a boot priority list is a requirement, unless you have only one specific target in mind. While you may be able to hard-code this for a closed box, for recovery cases, it is ideal to have a list of removable media that reflect a higher priority than the default storage. Alternate input methods may be used to drive the boot flow to a particular device (such as the use of jumpers or switches on GPIOs). The boot list can be used for giving priority to recovery, validation, or manufacturing OS over the production boot image.

The Partition Table

This is described in an earlier chapter.

The File System

Which file system is being used? There have been new file systems coming out about every year since 1964. The two we are going to talk about are FAT and EXT.

Microsoft provides a license for FAT to UEFI developers through the UEFI forum. Those using an EFI solution should receive that as part of the EDK. FAT stands for the file allocation table and has been around for many years in different bit-wise fashions. FAT12, FAT16, and FAT32 before NTFS took over. While FAT12 is reserved for floppies, FAT32 handles up to 2 TB of data.

Linux developed an alternative known as EXT, which is gaining favor in open-source communities. There are variations of both FAT and EXT; developers have to look at the requirements to determine which makes sense for them.

Booting via the Legacy OS Interface

There are three basic steps to loading a legacy OS: consuming the MBR, loading the legacy OS loader, and performing the hand off to the operating system itself.

Master Boot Record

Booting a legacy OS (non-EFI) consists of locating the right master boot record (MBR) on one of a potentially large number of bootable media.

On each disk an MBR may be sought by looking at LBA Sector 0 for signature 0xAA55 in the last two of the 512 bytes. In the master boot record, there are four 16-byte partition tables specifying whether there are any partitions and, if so, which are active.

The BIOS can choose any of the active primary partitions in the table for the drive and discover whether any of them are bootable. This bootable partition would then be listed in the boot target list, which can then be prioritized.

Loading the Legacy OS Loader

There are 440 bytes of executable code in the winning MBR that can be loaded into 0x7C00. Depending on the next step, that code can load the volume boot record (VBR) code from that partition into location 0x7C00 again and execute it. At some point down the chain a real OS loader is loaded, jumping to that location while the processor is in 16-bit Real Mode, and starts executing the OS loader.

Legacy BIOS to OS Handoff Requirements

The legacy OS loader relies on legacy BIOS services, including but not limited to:
- Int 13h for disk including RAID option ROMs
- Int 16h for PS/2 keyboard
- Int 10h for video output from video BIOS
- BIOS's SMI handler providing legacy USB keyboard support via port 60/64 emulation.

Depending on the desired features enabled by the boot loader, the OS needs different tables. The following is a list of those tables:
- Memory Map (INT15h / Function E820h)
- Programmable Interrupt Routing ($PIR)
- Multi-Processor Specification (_MP_)
- Minimal Boot Loader for Intel® Architecture
- Advanced Configuration and Power Interface (ACPI)

ACPI tables are needed only if those features are enabled by the boot loader and required by the OS. Most modern operating systems, including RTOS, are ACPI aware.

The _MP_ table is needed if there is more than one Intel processing agent (more than one thread or core) in the system. Details on the _MP_ table may be found in the Multi-Processor Specification.

The $PIR table and interrupt-based memory map are almost always needed. Details on the $PIR table may be found in the $PIR Specification. The memory map is discussed in more detail in the following sections.

The OS loader is often operating-system-specific; however, in most operating systems its main function is to load and execute the operating system kernel, which continues startup, and eventually you load an application. Examples for Linux include U-boot, Grub, and Sys-Linux. Examples for Windows CE are Eboot and ROMboot.

Another term has been used in the past for the OS loader was the *initial program loader* or IPL. While the term predates most of the current mechanisms, it can pop up in certain crowds or segments of industry. The job is the same as a BIOS or a boot loader or an OS loader. The names are just changed to protect the innocent.

Booting via the EFI Interface

Booting a UEFI operating system consists of locating the global partition table record (GPT) on one of the same potentially large number of bootable media.

Default EFI Boot Behavior

By default, UEFI firmware will search the path /EFI/BOOT/ on a FAT GPT partition for an executable second-stage bootloader. Each FAT GPT partition will be checked in its discovered order for an appropriate boot executable. On a 64-bit architecture, the name of the default bootloader will be bootia64.efi; on a 32-bit machine it will be bootia32.efi.

Operating system installation programs will typically rewrite the NvVar that controls the boot process, thus installing a new path to the operating system's standard bootloader. For example: the new path will be /EFI/BOOT/grub.efi for a Linux system or C:\Windows\System32\winload.efi for a Windows system.

A second-stage bootloader, as shown in Figure 8.1, will then hand off control from the second stage to the runtime system by first locating the bootloader configuration file, if any, and then executing commands contained in that configuration file in the following order:

1. Locate a kernel image
2. Locate any ancillary boot data, such as an init RAM disk
3. Optional: convert an EFI memory map to E820h tables, for systems that do not support UEFI Runtime Services
4. Call ExitBootServices()
5. Execute the kernel with parameters given in the boot loader configuration file

Direct Execution of a Linux Kernel

Modern UEFI systems, in conjunction with modern versions of the Linux kernel, can directly execute a Linux kernel without need of a second-stage bootloader such as Grub.

Since the Linux kernel now can get the EFI memory map via a call to UEFI Runtime Services, the necessity of using a second-stage bootloader to convert an EFI memory map to E820h/E801h tables is mitigated.

This extension to the Linux kernel is fully backward compatible, meaning it is possible to add the EFI_STUB kernel configuration option to your kernel configuration and to seamlessly use this to execute the kernel directly from an UEFI firmware, or to execute the kernel as specified above from a standard second-stage boot loader.

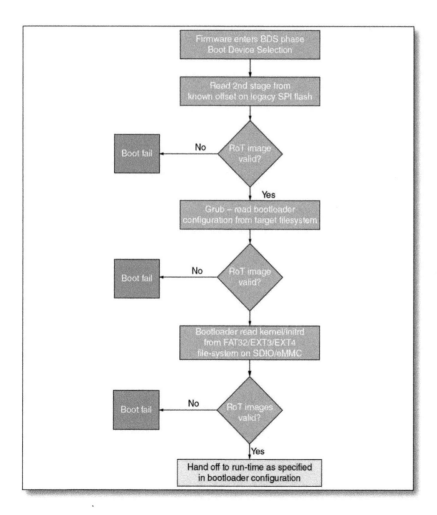

Figure 8.1: Default Second-Stage Boot Loader Flow

UEFI Runtime Services

Operating system kernels such as those used in Windows and Linux systems assume and require the second-stage boot loader to have called ExitBootServices() before handing control over.

In order to support calling UEFI services from a virtual-memory-enabled kernel, however, it is necessary for the kernel and UEFI callback mechanism to agree on a new address structure. Recall UEFI systems operate in protected unpaged mode, whereas Windows and Linux systems are fully fledged paged OS environments. The UEFI runtime subsystem operates in protected unpaged mode, whereas the kernel has switched execution over to paged mode; therefore, when a kernel makes a runtime call to UEFI one of two things must logically happen.

1. Each callback to UEFI could switch the processor back to UEFI's default mode of protected unpaged mode. This is undesirable, however, for a number of reasons:
    –   Slow to switch modes back and forth
    –   Complex to enable/disable paging between the two modes
    –   Considered unsafe security-wise as the UEFI callback has unfettered access to memory.
2. The UEFI callback must now itself operate in paged mode, replacing function and data references/pointers to physical addresses with paged references. Example: data at 0x12345678 physical may now be mapped by Linux to 0xD2345678, and the UEFI system should reference the new address, not the old.

In order to achieve this agreement between a paging kernel and the UEFI Runtime Services, the UEFI standard defines the function SetVirtualAddressMap(). After mapping UEFI runtime data/code to a set of virtual addresses, the OS kernel will make this callback to EFI, before making any further UEFI Runtime Service calls.

Neither Option

This option should be reserved for an RTOS or modified Linux kernel. The OS loader (if there is one) must not rely on any BIOS boot services or legacy BIOS calls. The OS must not rely on any BIOS legacy or runtime services. The system should be a closed box with a single permanent boot path. This is an ideal case if this is an SPI-based (flash-based) operating system, such as a microkernel or free RTOS.

In a UEFI-based solution, a developer may choose to have the OS as a DXE payload where the operating system is loaded and jumped to as part of the initial BIOS driver load.

In a legacy-based solution, it is possible to do something similar with a DMA of the OS kernel in a known memory location and a jump to start the kernel.

While this may prove limiting to the boot solution on the platform, there is an alternative OS-loading model via this solution where the UEFI-based firmware is bifurcated and DXE and later is placed on removable media. A jumper or other physical access is likely required to trigger the alternate boot path, but this is important if the solution is going to go beyond the simple prototype and into high volume manufacturing. The blind handoff to disk means reading the first sector of a target device and jumping to a known (good) address. It is the preference of RTOS vendors who don't call back into system firmware during runtime and have not yet implemented either a legacy OS interface or an EFI interface.

Summary

Loading an operating system after the platform is initialized can be done in a variety of ways. Known and tested standards are the fastest and easiest methods to provide for a flexible solution. More deeply embedded solutions have several other options but must be fully thought through beyond the lab environment if the system is meant for bigger, better, and broader things.

Choose wisely and let the circumstances dictate the development (and boot) path; with UEFI, one doesn't need to be married to a single boot solution.

Chapter 9
The Intel® Architecture Boot Flow

There is no one giant step that does it. It's a lot of little steps.

—Peter A. Cohen

A lot of little steps is exactly the idea of walking the path of the Intel architecture boot flow. The bare minimum firmware requirements for making an Intel architecture platform operational and for booting an OS are presented here in a given order. Design or market segment-based requirements might add, delete, or reorder many of the items presented in this chapter; however, for the vast majority of system designs, these steps in this order are sufficient for a full or cold boot from a state where the power is off to the handoff to the operating system. Depending on the architecture of the BIOS, there may be multiple software phases to jump through with different sets of rules, but the sequence for actually touching the hardware is, at least in the early phases, very much the same.

Hardware Power Sequences (The Pre-Pre-Boot)

When someone pushes the button, the CPU just doesn't jump up and start fetching code from flash.

When external power is first applied to a platform, the hardware platform must carry out a number of tasks before the processor can be brought out of reset. The first task is to allow the power supply to settle down to its nominal state; once the primary power supply settles, there are usually a number of derived voltage levels needed on the platform. For example, on the Intel architecture reference platform, the input supply consists of a 12-volt source, but the platform and processor require a number of different voltage rails, such as 1.5 V, 3.3 V, 5 V, and 12 V. The platform and processor also require that the voltages are provided in a particular sequence. This process, known as *power sequencing*, takes place by controlling analog switches (typically field effect transistors). The sequence is often driven by a complex program logic device (CPLD). The platform clocks are also derived from a small number of input clock and oscillator sources. The devices use phase-locked loop circuitry to generate the derived clocks used for the platform. These clocks also take time to converge. When all these steps have occurred, the power sequencing CPLD de-asserts the reset line to the processor. Figure 9.1 shows an overview of the platform blocks described. Depending on integration of silicon features, some of this logic may be on chip and controlled by microcontroller firmware, which starts prior to the main processor.

DOI 10.1515/9781501506819-009

Nonhost-Based Subsystem Startup

As part of the Intel architecture, a variety of subsystems may begin prior to the main host system starting.

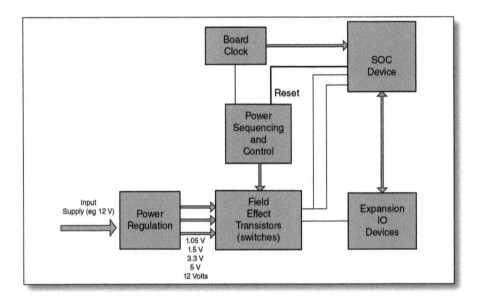

Figure 9.1: Power Sequencing Overview

The Intel Manageability Engine (ME), available on some mainstream, desktop, and server-derived chips, is one such component. While the main system firmware does not initialize these devices, there is likely to be some level of interactions that must be taken into account in the settings of the firmware, or in the descriptors of the flash component for the ME to start up and enable the clocks correctly. The main system firmware also has the potential to make calls and be called from the ME.

Another example is the microengines, which are part of telecommunications segment components in the embedded-market segments. These microengines have their own firmware that starts independently of the system BIOS, but the host system BIOS has to make allowances for this in the ACPI memory map to allow for proper interaction between host drivers and the microengine subsystem.

Starting at the Host Reset Vector

Once the processor reset line has been de-asserted, newer processors may automatically load a microcode update as part of its secure startup sequence. Any correctable errata will be fixed before any executable code kicks off and it ensures security of the system. After the patch is loaded, the processor then begins fetching instructions. The location of these initial processor instructions is known as the *reset vector*. The reset vector may contain instructions or a pointer to the actual starting instruction sequence in the flash memory. The location of the vector is architecture-specific and usually in a fixed location, depending on the processor. The initial address must be a physical address as the MMU (if it exists) has not yet been enabled. For Intel architecture, the first fetching instructions start from 0xFFFF, FFFF0. Only 16 bytes are left to the top of memory, so these 16 bytes must contain a far jump to the remainder of the initialization code.

This code is always written in assembly at this point as (to date) there is no software stack or cache as RAM available.

Because the processor cache is not enabled by default, it is not uncommon to flush cache in this step with a WBINV instruction. The WBINV instruction is not needed on newer processors, but it doesn't hurt anything.

Mode Selection

IA-32 supports three operating modes and one quasi-operating mode:
- *Protected mode is* considered the native operating mode of the processor. It provides a rich set of architectural features, flexibility, high performance and backward compatibility to the existing software base.
- *Real-address mode or* "real mode" is the operating mode that provides the programming environment of the Intel 8086 processor, with a few extensions (such as the ability to switch to protected or system management mode). Whenever a reset or a power-on happens, the system transitions back to real-address mode.
- *System management mode (SMM)* is a standard architectural feature in all IA-32 processors, beginning with the Intel386 SL. This mode provides an operating system or executive with a transparent mechanism for implementing power management and OEM differentiation features. SMM is entered through activation of an external system interrupt pin (SMI#), which generates a system management interrupt (SMI). In SMM, the processor switches to a separate address space while saving the context of the currently running program or task. SMM-specific code may then be executed transparently. Upon returning from SMM, the processor is placed back into its state prior to the SMI.

Normally the system firmware creates an SMI handler, which may periodically take over the system from the host OS. There are normally workarounds that are executed in the SMI handler and handling and logging-off errors that may happen at the system level. As this presents a potential security issue, there is also a lock bit that resists tampering with this mechanism.

Real-time OS vendors often recommend disabling this feature because it has a potential of subverting the nature of the OS environment. If this happens, then the additional work of the SMI handler would either need to be incorporated into the RTOS for that platform or else the potential exists of missing something important in the way of error response or workarounds. If the SMI handler can work with the RTOS development, there are some additional advantages to the feature.

- *Virtual-8086 mode is* a quasi-operating mode supported by the processor in protected mode. This mode allows the processor to execute 8086 software in a protected, multitasking environment.

Intel® 64 architecture supports all operating modes of IA-32 architecture and IA-32e modes.

- *IA-32e mode*—in this mode, the processor supports two submodes: compatibility mode and 64-bit mode. 64-bit mode provides 64-bit linear addressing and support for physical address space larger than 64 GB. Lastly, Compatibility mode allows most legacy protected-mode applications to run unchanged.

Figure 9.2 shows how the processor moves between operating modes.

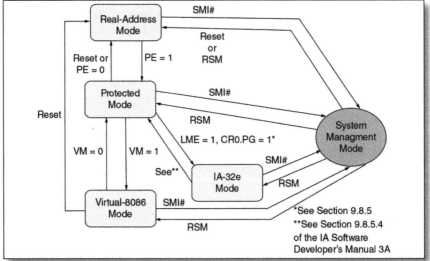

Figure 9.2: Figure 9.2 Mode Switching per Intel® 64 and IA-32 Architectures Software Developer's Manual, Volume 3A

Refer to the Intel® 64 and IA-32 Architectures Software Developer's Manual Volume 3A section titled "Mode Switching" for more details.

When the processor is first powered on, it will be in a special mode similar to real mode, but with the top 12 address lines being asserted high. This aliasing allows the boot code to be accessed directly from NVRAM (physical address 0xFFFxxxxx).

Upon execution of the first long jump, these 12 address lines will be driven according to instructions by firmware. If one of the protected modes is not entered before the first long jump, the processor will enter real mode, with only 1 MB of addressability. In order for real mode to work without memory, the chipset needs to be able to alias a range of memory below 1 MB to an equivalent range just below 4 GB to continue to access NVRAM. Certain chipsets do not have this aliasing and may require a switch into a normal operating mode before performing the first long jump. The processor also invalidates the internal caches and translation lookaside buffers (TLBs).

The processor continues to boot in real mode today, for no particular technical requirement. While some speculate it is to ensure that the platform can boot legacy code (example DOS OS) written many years ago, it is more an issue of introducing and needing to validate the change into a broad ecosystem of players and developers. The backward compatibility issues it would create in test and manufacturing environments and other natural upgrade hurdles will continue to keep the boot mode and Intel reset vector "real" until a high return-on-investment feature requires it to be otherwise.

The first power-on mode is a special subset of the real mode. The top 12 address lines are held high, allowing aliasing, where the processor can execute code from the nonvolatile storage (such as flash) located within the lowest one megabyte as if from the top of memory. Normal operation of the firmware (such as BIOS) is to switch modes to flat-protected mode as early in the boot sequence as is possible. Once the processor is running in protected mode, it usually is not necessary to switch back to real mode unless executing a legacy option ROM, which makes certain legacy software interrupt calls. The flat mode runs 32-bit code and the physical address are mapped on to one with the logical addresses (paging off). The Interrupt Descriptor Table is used for interrupt handling. This is the recommended mode for all BIOS/boot loaders to operate in. The segmented protected mode is not used for the initialization code as part of the BIOS sequence.

Intel produces BIOS specifications or BIOS writer's guides that go into some details about chip-specific and technology-specific initialization sequences. These documents hold fine-grain details of every bit that needs to be set, but not necessarily the high-level sequence in which to set them. The following flows for early initialization and advanced initialization outline that from a hardware architecture point of view.

Early Initialization

The early phase of the BIOS/bootloader will do the minimum to get the memory and processor cores initialized.

In an UEFI-based system BIOS, the Security (SEC) and the pre-EFI initialization (PEI) phases are normally synonymous with "early initialization." It doesn't matter if legacy or UEFI BIOS is used; from a hardware point of view, the early initialization sequence is the same for a given system.

Single-Threaded Operation

In a multicore system, the bootstrap processor is the CPU core/thread that is chosen to boot the normally single-threaded system firmware. At RESET, all of the processors race for a semaphore flag bit in the chipset. The first finds it clear and in the process of reading it sets the flag; the other processors find the flag set and enter a WAIT for SIPI or halt state. The first processor initializes main memory and the application processors (APs) and continues with the rest of boot. A multiprocessor (MP) system does not truly enter MP operation until the OS takes over. While it is possible to do a limited amount of parallel processing during the UEFI boot phase, such as during memory initialization with multiple socket designs, any true multithreading activity would require changes to be made to the DXE phase of the UEFI solutions to allow for this. In order to have broad adoption, some obvious benefits would need to arise.

Simple Device Initialization

The early initialization phase readies the bootstrap processor (BSP) and I/O peripherals' base address registers that are needed to configure the memory controller. The device-specific portion of an Intel architecture memory map is highly configurable. Most devices are seen and accessed via a logical PCI bus hierarchy, although a small number may be memory-mapped devices that have part-specific access mechanisms. Device control registers are mapped to a predefined I/O or MMIO space and can be set up before the memory map is configured. This allows the early initial firmware to configure the memory map of the device needed to set up DRAM. Before DRAM can be configured, the firmware must establish the exact configuring of DRAM that is on the board. The Intel architecture reference platform memory map is described in more detail in Figure 9.3. SOC devices based on other processor architectures typically provide a static address map for all internal peripherals, with external devices connected via a bus interface. The bus-based devices are mapped to a memory range within the SOC address space. These SOC devices usually provide a configurable chip select register, which can be set to specify the base address and size of the memory range enabled by the chip select. SOCs based on Intel architecture primarily use the logical PCI infrastructure for internal and external devices.

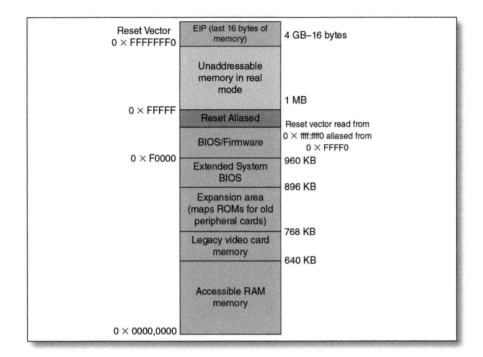

Figure 9.3: Example Intel® Architecture Memory Map at Power On

The location of the device in the host memory address space is defined by the PCI base address register (BAR) for each of the devices. The device initialization typically enables all the BAR registers for the devices required as part of the system boot path. The BIOS will assign all devices in the system a PCI base address by writing the appropriate BAR registers during PCI enumeration. Long before full PCI enumeration, the BIOS must enable PCIe BAR and the PCH RCBA BAR for memory, I/O, and MMIO interactions during the early phase of boot.

Depending on the chipset, there are prefetchers that can be enabled at this point to speed up the data transfer from the flash device. There may also be DMI link settings that must be tuned to optimal performance.

CPU Initialization

This consists of simple configuring of processor and machine registers, loading a microcode update, and enabling the Local APIC.

Microcode Update. Microcode is a hardware layer of instructions involved in the implementation of the machine-defined architecture. It is most prevalent in CISC-based processors. Microcode is developed by the CPU vendor and incorporated into an internal CPU ROM during manufacture. Since the infamous "Pentium flaw," Intel processor architecture allows that microcode to be updated in the field either through a BIOS update or via an OS update of "configuration data."

Today an Intel processor must have the latest microcode update to be considered a warranted CPU. Intel provides microcode updates that are written to the writable microcode store in the CPU. The updates are encrypted and signed by Intel such that only the processor that the microcode update was designed for can authenticate and load that update. On socketed systems, the BIOS may have to carry many flavors of microcode update depending on the number of processor steppings supported. It is important to load the microcode updates early in the boot sequence to limit the exposure of the system to any known errata in the silicon. It is important to note that the microcode update may need to be reapplied to the CPU after certain reset events in the boot sequence.

The BSP microcode update must be loaded before No-Eviction mode is entered.

Local APIC. The Local APIC must be enabled to handle any interrupts that occur early in post, before enabling protected mode. For more information on the Intel APIC Architecture and Local APICs, please see the Intel 64 and IA-32 Intel Architecture Software Developer's Manual, Volume 3A: System Programming Guide, Chapter 8.

Switch to Protected Mode. Before the processor can be switched to protected mode, the software initialization code must load a minimum number of protected mode data structures and code modules into memory to support reliable operation of the processor in protected mode. These data structures include the following:
–   An IDT
–   A GDT
–   A TSS
–   (Optional) An LDT
–   If paging is to be used, at least one page directory and one page table
–   A code segment that contains the code to be executed when the processor switches to protected mode
–   One or more code modules that contain the necessary interrupt and exception handlers

Initialization code must also initialize the following system registers before the processor can be switched to protected mode:
–   The GDTR
–   Optionally the IDTR. This register can also be initialized immediately after switching to protected mode, prior to enabling interrupts.

- Control registers CR1 through CR4
- The memory type range registers (MTRRs)

With these data structures, code modules, and system registers initialized, the processor can be switched to protected mode by loading control register CR0 with a value that sets the PE flag (bit 0).

From this point onward, it is likely that the system will not enter 16b Real mode again, Legacy Option ROMs and Legacy OS/BIOS interface notwithstanding, until the next hardware reset is experienced.

More details about protected mode and real mode switching can be found in the Intel 64 and IA-32 Intel Architecture Software Developer's Manual, Volume 3A: System Programming Guide, Chapter 9.

Cache as RAM and No Eviction Mode. Since no DRAM is available, the code initially operates in a stackless environment. Most modern processors have an internal cache that can be configured as RAM (Cache as RAM, or CAR) to provide a software stack. Developers must write extremely tight code when using CAR because an eviction would be paradoxical to the system at this point in the boot sequence; there is no memory to maintain coherency with at this time. There is a special mode for processors to operate in cache as RAM called "no evict mode" (NEM), where a cache line miss in the processor will not cause an eviction. Developing code with an available software stack is much easier, and initialization code often performs the minimal setup to use a stack even prior to DRAM initialization.

Processor Speed Correction. The processor may boot into a slower mode than it can perform for various reasons. It may be considered less risky to run in a slower mode, or it may be done to save additional power. It will be necessary for the BIOS to initialize the speed step technology of the processor and may need to force the speed to something appropriate for a faster boot. This additional optimization is optional; the OS will likely have the drivers to deal with this parameter when it loads.

Memory Configuration

The initialization of the memory controller varies slightly, depending on the DRAM technology and the capabilities of the memory controller itself. The information on the DRAM controller is proprietary for SOC devices, and in such cases the initialization memory reference code (MRC) is typically supplied by the SOC vendor. Developers should contact Intel to request access to the low-level information required. Without being given the MRC, developers can understand that for a given DRAM technology, they must follow a JEDEC initialization sequence. It is likely a given that the code will be single point of entry and single point of exit code that has multiple boot paths contained within it. It will also likely be 32-bit protected mode code. The settings for various bit fields like buffer strengths and loading for a given number of banks of memory is something that is chipset-specific. The dynamic nature of the memory tests that are run (to ensure proper timings have been applied for a given memory configuration) is an additional complexity that would prove difficult to replicate without a proper code from the memory controller vendor. Workarounds for errata and interactions with other subsystems, such as the Manageability Engine, are not something that can be reinvented, but can be reverse-engineered. The latter is, of course, heavily frowned upon.

There is a very wide range of DRAM configuration parameters, such as number of ranks, 8-bit or 16-bit addresses, overall memory size, and constellation, soldered down or add-in module (DIMM) configurations, page-closing policy, and power management. Given that most embedded systems populate soldered down DRAM on the board, the firmware may not need to discover the configuration at boot time. These configurations are known as *memory-down*. The firmware is specifically built for the target configuration. This is the case for the Intel reference platform from the Embedded Computing Group. At current DRAM speeds, the wires between the memory controllers behave like transmission lines; the SOC may provide automatic calibration and runtime control of resistive compensation (RCOMP) and delay locked look (DLL) capabilities. These capabilities allow the memory controller to change elements such as the drive strength to ensure error- free operation over time and temperature variations.

If the platform supports add-in-modules for memory, there are a number of standardized form factors for such memory. The small outline dual in-line memory module (SODIMM) is one such form factor often found in embedded systems. The DIMMs provide a serial EPROM. The serial EPROM devices contain the DRAM configuration data. The data is known as serial presence detect data (SPD data). The firmware reads the SPD data to identify the device configuration and subsequently configures the device. The serial EPROM is connected via SMBUS, thus the device must be available in this early initialization phase, so the software can establish the memory devices on board. It is possible for memory-down motherboards to also incorporate serial presence detect EEPROMs to allow for multiple and updatable memory configurations to be handled efficiently by a single BIOS algorithm. It is also possible to provide a hard-coded table in one of the MRC files to allow for an EEPROM-less design. In order to derive that table for SPD, please see Appendix A.

Post-Memory

Once the memory controller has been initialized, a number of subsequent cleanup events take place.

Memory Testing

The memory testing is now part of the MRC, but it is possible to add more tests should the design merit it. BIOS vendors typically provide some kind of memory test on a cold boot. Writing custom firmware requires the authors to choose a balance between thoroughness and speed, as highly embedded/ mobile devices require extremely fast boot times and memory testing can take up considerable time.

If testing is warranted for a design, testing the memory directly following initialization is the time to do it. The system is idle, the subsystems are not actively accessing memory, and the OS has not taken over the host side of the platform. Memory errors manifest themselves in random ways, sometimes inconsistently. Several hardware features can assist in this testing both during boot and during runtime. These features have traditionally been thought of as high-end or server features, but over time they have moved into the client and embedded markets.

One of the most common is ECC. Some embedded devices use error correction codes (ECC) memory, which may need extra initialization. After power up, the state of the correction codes may not reflect the contents and all memory must be written to; writing to memory ensures that the ECC bits are valid and sets the ECC bits to the appropriate contents. For security purposes, the memory may need to be zeroed out manually by the BIOS or in some cases a memory controller may incorporate the feature into hardware to save time.

Depending on the source of the reset and security requirements, the system may not execute a memory wipe or ECC initialization. On a warm reset sequence, memory context can be maintained.

If there were any memory timing changes or other configuration changes that require a reset to take effect, this is normally the time to execute a warm reset. That warm reset would start the early initialization phase over again; affected registers would need to be restored.

Shadowing

From the reset vector, execution starts off directly from the nonvolatile flash storage (NVRAM). This operating mode is known as execute in place (XIP). The read performance of nonvolatile storage is much slower than the read performance of DRAM. The performance of the code running from flash is much lower than if it executed from RAM, so most early firmware will copy from the slower nonvolatile storage into RAM. The firmware starts to run the RAM copy of the firmware. This process is sometimes known as *shadowing*. Shadowing involves having the same contents in RAM and flash; with a change in the address decoders the RAM copy is logically in front of the flash copy and the program starts to execute from RAM. On other embedded systems, the chip selects ranges managed to allow the change from flash to RAM execution. Most computing systems run as little as possible in place. However, some constrained (in terms of RAM) embedded platforms execute all the application in place. This is generally an option on very small embedded devices. Larger systems with main memory generally do not execute in place for anything but the very initial boot steps before memory has been configured. The firmware is often compressed instead of a simple copy. This allows reduction of the NVRAM requirements for the firmware. However, the processor cannot execute a compressed image in place.

On Intel architecture platforms, the shadowing of the firmware is usually located below 1 MB.

There is a tradeoff between the size of data to be shadowed and the act of decompression. The decompression algorithm may take much longer to load and execute than it would be for the image to remain uncompressed. Prefetchers in the processor, if enabled, may also speed up execution in place, and some SOCs have internal NVRAM cache buffers to assist in pipelining the data from the flash to the processor.

Figure 9.3 shows the memory map at initialization in real mode. Real mode has an accessibility limit of 1 MB.

Exit from No-Eviction Mode and Transfer to DRAM

Before memory was initialized, the data and code stacks were held in the processor cache. With memory now initialized that special and temporary caching mode must be exited and the cache flushed. The stack will be transferred to a new location in system main memory and cache reconfigured as part of AP initialization.

The stack must be set up before jumping into the shadowed portion of the BIOS that now is in memory. A memory location must be chosen for stack space. The stack will count down so the top of the stack must be entered and enough memory must be allocated for the maximum stack.

If protected mode is used, which is likely following MRC execution, then SS:ESP must be set to the correct memory location.

Transfer to DRAM

This is where the code makes the jump into memory. As mentioned before, if a memory test has not been performed up until this point, the jump could very well be to garbage. System failures indicated by a POST code between "end of memory initialization" and the first following POST code almost always indicates a catastrophic memory initialization problem. If this is a new design, then chances are this is in the hardware and requires step-by-step debug.

Memory Transaction Redirection

For legacy option ROMs and BIOS memory ranges, Intel chipsets usually come with memory aliasing capabilities that allow reads and writes to sections of memory below 1 MB to be either routed to or from DRAM or nonvolatile storage located just under 4 GB. The registers that control this aliasing are typically referred to as programmable attribute maps (PAMs). Manipulation of these registers may be required before, during, and after firmware shadowing. The control over the redirection of memory access varies from chipset to chipset. For example, some chipsets allow control over reads and writes, while others only allow control over reads.

For shadowing, if PAM registers remain at default values (all 0s), all FWH accesses to the E and F segments (E_0000–F_FFFFh) will be directed downstream toward the flash component. This will function to boot the system, but is very slow. Shadowing, as we know, improves boot speed. One method of shadowing the E and F segments (E_0000–F_FFFFh) of the BIOS is to utilize the PAM registers. This can be done by changing the enables (HIENABLE[ ], LOENABLE[ ]) to be 10 (write only). This will direct reads to the flash device and writes to memory. By reading and then writing the same address, the data is shadowed into memory. Once BIOS code has been shadowed into memory, the enables can be changed to 0x01(read only), so memory reads are directed to memory. This also prevents accidental overwriting of the image in memory. See the example in Table 9.1.

Table 9.1: Reading and Writing the Same Address

PAM Registers	Register Address
PAM0	0F0000–0FFFFFh
PAM1	0C0000–0C7FFFh
PAM2	0C8000–0CFFFFh
PAM3	0D0000–0D7FFFh
PAM4	0D8000–0DFFFFh
PAM5	0E0000–0E7FFFh
PAM6	0E8000–0EFFFFh

Consult the chipset datasheet for details on the memory redirection feature controls applicable to the target platform.

Application Processor (AP) Initialization

Even in SOCs, there is the likelihood of having multiple CPU cores, which are considered BSP 1 AP to system initialization. While the BSP starts and initializes the system, the application processors (APs) must also be initialized with identical features enabled to the BSP. Prior to memory, the APs are left uninitialized. After memory is started, the remaining processors are initialized and left in a WAIT for SIPI state. To do this, the system firmware must:

1. Find microcode and then copy it to memory.
2. Find the CPU code in SPI and copy to memory. This is an important step to avoid execution-in-place penalties for the remainder of the boot sequence.
3. Send Startup IPIs to all processors.
4. Disable all NEM settings, if this has not already been done.
5. Load microcode updates on all processors.
6. Enable Cache On for all processors.

Partial details of these sequences are in the Software Developer's Manual; fuller details can be found in the BIOS Writer's Guide for that particular processor or on CPU reference code obtained from Intel.

From a UEFI perspective the AP initialization may either be part of the PEI or the DXE phase of the boot flow or in the early or advanced initialization. At the time of this printing, the location of the AP initialization code may be considered product dependent.

CPUID—Threads and Cores

Since Intel processors are packaged in various configurations, there are different terms that must be understood when considering processor initialization:

- *Thread.* A logical processor that shares resources with another logical processor in the same physical package.
- *Core.* A processor that coexists with another processor in the same physical package that does not share any resources with other processors.
- *Package.* A "chip" that contains any number of cores and threads.

Threads and cores on the same package are detectable by executing the CPUID instruction.

See the Intel® 64 and IA-32 Architectures Software Developer's Manual, Volume 2A for details on the information available with the CPUID instruction on various processor families.

Detection of additional packages must be done "blindly." If a design must accommodate more than one physical package, the BSP needs to wait a certain amount of time for all potential APs in the system to "log in." Once a timeout occurs or the maximum expected number of processors "log in," it can be assumed that there are no more processors in the system.

Startup Inter-Processor Interrupt (SIPI)

In order to wake up secondary threads or cores, the BSP sends a SIPI to each thread and core. This SIPI is sent by using the BSP's LAPIC, indicating the physical address from which the application processor (AP) should start executing. This address must be below 1 MB of memory and must be aligned on a 4-KB boundary.

AP Wakeup State

Upon receipt of the SIPI, the AP starts executing the code pointed to by the SIPI message. As opposed to the BSP, when the AP starts code execution it is in real mode. This requires that the location of the code that the AP starts executing is located below 1 MB.

Wakeup Vector Alignment

The starting execution point of the AP has another important and commonly forgotten architectural restriction. The entry point to the AP initialization code must be aligned on a 4-KB boundary. Refer to the Intel® 64 and IA-32 Architectures Software Developer's Manual, Volume 3A section "MP Initialization Protocol Algorithm for Intel Xeon Processors."

The Intel® 64 and IA-32 Architectures Software Developer's Manual, Volume 3A section "Typical AP Initialization Sequence" illustrates what is typically done in by the APs after receiving the SIPI.

Caching Considerations

Because of the different types of processor combinations and different attributes of shared processing registers between threads, care must be taken to ensure that the caching layout of all processors in the entire system remain consistent such that there are no caching conflicts.

The Intel® 64 and IA-32 Architectures Software Developer's Manual, Volume 3A section "MTRR Considerations in MP Systems" outlines a safe mechanism for changing the cache configuration in all systems that contain more than one processor. It is recommended that this be used for any system with more than one processor present.

AP Idle State

Behavior of APs during firmware initialization depends on the firmware implementation, but is most commonly restricted to short durations of initialization, followed by entering a halt state with a HLT instruction, awaiting direction from the BSP for another operation.

Once the firmware is ready to attempt to boot an OS, all AP processors must be placed back in their power-on state (WAIT for SIPI), which can be accomplished by the BSP sending an INIT ASSERT IPI followed by an INIT DEASSERT IPI to all APs in the system (all except self). See the Intel® 64 and IA-32 Architectures Software Developer's Manual, Volume 3A for details on the INIT IPI, and the MultiProcessor Specification 1.4 for details on BIOS AP requirements.

Advanced Initialization

The advanced device initialization follows the early initialization and basically ensures that the DRAM is initialized. This second stage is focused on device- specific initialization. In a UEFI-based BIOS solution, advanced initialization tasks are also known as Dynamic Execute Environment (DXE) and Boot Device Selection (BDS) phases. The following devices must be initialized in order to enable an embedded system. Not all are applicable to all embedded systems, but the list is prescriptive for most and is particular to an SOC-based- on-Intel architecture.

- General purpose I/O (GPIO)
- Interrupt controller
- Timers
- Cache initialization (could also be done during early initialization)
- Serial ports, console in/out
- Clocking and overclocking
- PCI bus initialization
- Graphics (optional)
- USB
- SATA

General Purpose I/O (GPIO) Configuration

GPIOs are key to the extensibility of the platform. As the name implies, GPIOs can be configured for either input or output, but also can be configured for a native functionality. Depending on weak or strong pull-up or pull-down resistors, some GPIOs also can act like strapping pins, which are sampled at RESET by the chipset and can have a second meaning during boot and runtime. GPIOs also may act like sideband signals to allow for system wakes. GPIO 27 is used for this on most mainstream platforms.

System-on-chip devices are designed to be used in a large number of configurations, the devices often having more capabilities than the device can expose on the

I/O pins concurrently. That is because several functions are multiplexed to a particular I/O pin. The configuration of the pins must be set before use. The pins are configured to either provide a specific function or serve as a general-purpose I/O pin. I/O pins on the device are used to control logic or behavior on the device. General purpose I/O pins can be configured as input or output pins. GPIO control registers provide status and control.

System firmware developers must work through between 64 and 256 GPIOs and their individual options with the board designer (per platform) to ensure that this feature is properly enabled.

Interrupt Controllers

Intel architecture has several different methods of interrupt handling. The following or a combination of the following can be used to handle interrupts:
- Programmable Interrupt Controller (PIC) or 8259
- Local Advanced Programmable Interrupt Controller (APIC)
- Input/Output Advanced Programmable Interrupt Controller (IOxAPIC)
- Messaged Signaled Interrupt (MSI)

Programmable Interrupt Controller (PIC)
When the PIC is the only interrupt device enabled, it is referred to as PIC Mode. This is the simplest mode where the PIC handles all the interrupts. All APIC components are bypassed, and the system operates in single-thread mode using LINT0.

The BIOS must set the IRQs per board configuration for all onboard, integrated, and add-in PCI devices.

The PIC contains two cascaded 8259s with fifteen available IRQs. IRQ2 is not available since it is used to connect the 8259s. On mainstream components, there are eight PIRQ pins supported in PCH, named PIRQ[A# :H#], that route PCI interrupts to IRQs of the 8259 PIC. PIRQ[A#:D#] routing is controlled by PIRQ Routing Registers 60h–63h (D31:F0:Reg 60- 63h). The PIRQ[E# : H#] routing is controlled by PIRQ Routing Registers 68h–6Bh (D31:F0:Reg 68 – 6Bh). See Figure 9.4.

The PCH also connects the 8 PIRQ[A# : H#] to eight individual IOxAPIC input pins, as shown in Table 9.2.

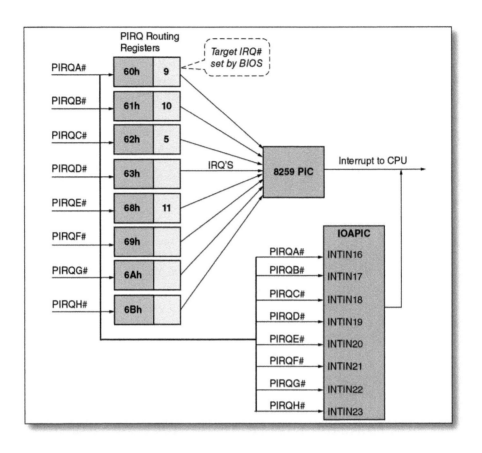

Figure 9.4: Platform Controller Hub (PCH) PIRQ to IRQ Router

Table 9.2: Platform Controller Hub (PCH) PIRQ Routing Table

PIRQ# Pin	Interrupt Router Register for PIC	Connected to IOxAPIC Pin
PIRQA#	D31:F0:Reg 60h	INTIN16
PIRQB#	D31:F0:Reg 61h	INTIN17
PIRQC#	D31:F0:Reg 62h	INTIN18
PIRQD#	D31:F0:Reg 63h	INTIN19
PIRQE#	D31:F0:Reg 68h	INTIN20
PIRQF#	D31:F0:Reg 69h	INTIN21
PIRQG#	D31:F0:Reg 6Ah	INTIN22
PIRQH#	D31:F0:Reg 6Bh	INTIN23

Local Advanced Programmable Interrupt Controller (LAPIC)
The local APIC is contained inside the processor and controls the interrupt delivery to the processor. Each local APIC contains its own set of associated registers, as well as a Local Vector Table (LVT). The LVT specifies the manner in which the interrupts are delivered to each processor core.

Refer to the Intel® 64 and IA-32 Architectures Software Developer's Manual for more information on initializing the local APIC.

I/O Advanced Programmable Interrupt Controller (IOxAPIC)
The IOxAPIC is contained in the ICH/IOH and expands the number of IRQs available to 24. Each IRQ has an associated redirection table entry that can be enabled or disabled and selects the IDT vector for the associated IRQ. This mode is only available when running in protected mode.

Refer to the Chipset BIOS Writer's Guide for more information on initializing the IOxPIC.

Message Signaled Interrupt (MSI)
The boot loader does not typically use MSI for interrupt handling.

Interrupt Vector Table (IVT)

The IVT is the Interrupt Vector Table, located at memory location 0p and containing 256 interrupt vectors. The IVT is used in real mode. Each vector address is 32 bits and consists of the CS:IP for the interrupt vector. Refer to the Intel® 64 and IA-32 Architectures Software Developer's Manual, Volume 3A section titled "Exception and Interrupt Reference" for a list of real-mode interrupts and exceptions.

Interrupt Descriptor Table (IDT)

The IDT is the Interrupt Descriptor Table and contains the exceptions and interrupts in protected mode. There are also 256 interrupt vectors, and the exceptions and interrupts are defined in the same locations as the IVT. Refer to the Intel® 64 and IA-32 Architectures Software Developer's Manual, Volume 3A for a detailed description of the IDT.

Exceptions
Exceptions are routines that run to handle error conditions. Examples include page fault and general protection fault. At a minimum, placeholders (dummy functions)

should be used for each exception handler. Otherwise the system could exhibit unwanted behavior if it encounters an exception that isn't handled.

Real-Mode Interrupt Service Routines (ISRs)

Real-mode ISRs are used to communicate information between the boot loader and the OS. For example, INT10h is used for video services, such as changing video modes and resolution. There are some legacy programs and drivers that assume these real-mode ISRs are available and directly call the INT routine.

Timers

There are a variety of timers that can be employed on today's Intel Architecture system.

Programmable Interrupt Timer (PIT)

The PIT (8254) resides in the IOH/ICH and contains the system timer, also referred to as IRQ0. Refer to the chipset datasheet for more details.

High Precision Event Timer (HPET)

HPET resides in the IOH/ICH and contains three timers. Typically, the boot loader does not need to do any initialization of HPET and the functionality is used only by the OS. Refer to the Chipset BIOS Writer's Guide for more details.

Real Time Clock (RTC)

The RTC resides in the IOH/ICH and contains the system time (seconds/minutes/hours/and so on). These values are contained in CMOS, which is explained later. The RTC also contains a timer that can be utilized by firmware. Refer to the appropriate chipset datasheet for more details.

System Management TCO Timer

The TCO timers reside in the IOH/ICH and contain the Watch Dog Timer (WDT), which can be used to detect system hangs and will reset the system.

Note: It is important to understand that for debugging any type of firmware on Intel architecture chipsets that implement a TCO Watch Dog Timer, it should be disabled by firmware as soon as possible coming out of reset. Halting the system for debug prior to disabling this Watch Dog Timer on chipsets that power on with this timer enabled will result in system resets, which doesn't allow firmware debug. The OS will re-enable the Watch Dog Timer if it so desires. Consult the chipset datasheet for details on the specific implementation of the TCO Watch Dog Timer. Refer to the Chipset BIOS Writer's Guide for more details.

Local APIC (LAPIC) Timer
The Local APIC contains a timer that can be used by firmware. Refer to the Intel® 64 and IA-32 Architectures Software Developer's Manual, Volume 3A for a detailed description of the Local APIC timer.

Memory Caching Control

Memory regions that must have different caching behaviors applied will vary from design to design. In the absence of detailed caching requirements for a platform, the following guidelines provide a "safe" caching environment for typical systems:
1. Default Cache Rule – Uncached.
2. 00000000-0009FFFF – Write Back.
3. 000A0000-000BFFFF – Write Combined / Uncached.
4. 000C0000-000FFFFF – Write Back / Write Protect.
5. 00100000-TopOfMemory – Write Back.
6. TSEG – Cached on newer processors.
7. Graphics Memory – Write Combined or Uncached.
8. Hardware Memory-Mapped I/O – Uncached.

While MTRRs are programmed by the BIOS, Page Attribute Tables (PATs) are used primarily with the OS to control caching down to the page level.

The Intel® 64 and IA-32 Architectures Software Developer's Manual, Volume 3A, Chapter 10, "Memory Cache Control" contains all the details on configuring caching for all memory regions.

See the appropriate CPU BIOS Writer's Guide for caching control guidelines specific to the processor.

Serial Ports

An RS-232 serial port or UART 16550 is initialized for either runtime or debug solutions. Unlike USB ports, which require considerable initialization and a large software stack, serial ports have a minimal register-level interface. A serial port can be enabled very early in POST to provide serial output support.

Console In /Console Out
During the DXE phase, part of the boot services includes console in and console out protocols.

Clock and Overclock Programming

Depending on the clocking solution of the platform, the BIOS may have to enable the clocking of the system. It is possible that a subsystem such as the Manageability Engine or baseboard management controller (BMC) in server platforms have this responsibility.

It is possible that beyond the basic clock programming, there may be expanded configuration options for overclocking such as:

– Enable/disable clock output enable based on enumeration.
– Adjust clock spread settings. Enable/disable and adjust amount. Note: settings are provided as fixed register values determined from expected usages.
– Underclock CPU for adaptive clocking support. If done directly, the BIOS must perform adjustment with ramp algorithm.
– Lock out clock registers prior to transitioning to host OS.

PCI Device Enumeration

Peripheral Connect Interface (PCI) device enumeration is a generic term that refers to detecting and assigning resources to PCI-compliant devices in the system. The discovery process assigns the resources needed by each device, including the following:

– Memory, prefetchable memory, I/O space
– Memory mapped I/O (MMIO) space
– IRQ assignment
– Expansion ROM detection and execution

PCI device discovery applies to all the newer (nonlegacy) interfaces such as PCI Express (PCIe) root ports, USB controllers, SATA controllers, audio controllers, LAN controllers, and various add-in devices. These newer interfaces all comply with the PCI specification.

Refer to the PCI Specification for more details. A list of all the applicable specifications is in the References section.

It is interesting to note that in the UEFI system, the DXE phase does not execute the majority of drivers, but it is the BDS Phase that executes most of the required drives in UEFI to allow the system to boot.

Graphics Initialization

If the platform has a head, then the video BIOS or Graphics Output Protocol UEFI driver is normally the first option ROM to be executed in the string. Once the main console out is up and running, the console in can be configured.

Input Devices

Refer to the board schematics to determine which I/O devices are in the system. Typically, a system will contain one or more of the following devices.

Embedded Controller (EC)

An embedded controller is typically used in mobile or low-power systems. The EC contains separate firmware that controls the power management functions for the system, as well as PS/2 keyboard functionality. Refer to the specific EC datasheet for more details.

Super I/O (SIO)

An SIO typically controls the PS/2, serial, and parallel interfaces. Most systems still support some of the legacy interfaces rather than implementing a legacy- free system. Refer to the specific SIO datasheet for details on programming information.

Legacy-Free Systems

Legacy-free systems use USB as the input device. If pre-OS keyboard support is required, then the legacy keyboard interfaces must be trapped. Refer to the IOH/ICH BIOS Specification for more details on legacy-free systems.

USB Initialization

The USB controller supports both EHCI and now XHCI. To enable the host controller for standard PCI resources is relatively easy. It is possible to not enable USB until the OS drivers take over and have a very well-functioning system. If pre-OS support for EHCI or XHCI is required, then the tasks associated with the USB subsystem become substantially more complex. Legacy USB requires an SMI handler be used to trap port 60/64 accesses to I/O space and convert these to the proper keyboard or mouse commands. This pre-OS USB support is required if booting to USB is preferred.

SATA Initialization

A SATA controller supports the ATA/IDE programming interface, as well as the Advanced Host Controller Interface (AHCI, not available on all SKUs). In the following discussion, the term "ATA-IDE Mode" refers to the ATA/IDE programming interface that uses standard task file I/O registers or PCI IDE Bus Master I/O block registers. The term "AHCI Mode" refers to the AHCI programming interface that uses memory-mapped register/buffer space and a command-list-based model.

A separate document, RS – Intel® I/O Controller Hub 6 (ICH6) Serial ATA Advanced Host Controller Interface (SATA-AHCI) Hardware Programming Specification (HPS), details SATA software configuration and considerations.

SATA Controller Initialization

The general guidelines for initializing the SATA controller during POST and S3 resume are described in the following sections. Upon resuming from S3, System BIOS is responsible for restoring all registers it initialized during POST.

Setting the SATA Controller Mode

The system BIOS must program the SATA controller mode prior to beginning other initialization steps. The SATA controller mode is set by programming the SATA Mode Select (SMS) field of the Port Mapping register (D31:F2:Reg 90h[7:6]). The system BIOS may never change the SATA controller mode during runtime. Please note that the availability of the following modes depends on the SKU of PCH in use.

If system BIOS is enabling AHCI Mode or RAID Mode, system BIOS must disable D31:F5 by setting the SAD2 bit, RCBA 418h[25]. System BIOS must ensure that it has not enabled memory space, I/O space, or interrupts for this device prior to disabling the device.

IDE Mode

IDE mode is selected by programming the SMS field, D31:F2:Reg 90h[7:6] to 00. In this mode, the SATA controller is set up to use the ATA/IDE programming interface. In this mode, the 6/4 SATA ports are controlled by two SATA functions. One function routes up to four SATA ports, D31:F2, and the other routes up to two SATA ports, D31:F5 (Desktop SKUs only). In IDE mode, the Sub Class Code, D31:F2:Reg 0Ah and D31:F5:Reg 0Ah will be set to 01h. This mode may also be referred to as compatibility mode as it does not have any special OS driver requirements.

AHCI Mode

AHCI mode is selected by programming the SMS field, D31:F2:Reg 90h[7:6], to 01b. In this mode, the SATA controller is set up to use the AHCI programming interface. The six SATA ports are controlled by a single SATA function, D31:F2. In AHCI mode the Sub Class Code, D31:F2:Reg 0Ah, will be set to 06h. This mode does require specific OS driver support.

RAID Mode

RAID mode is selected by programming the SMS field, D31:F2:Reg 90h[7:6] to 10b. In this mode, the SATA controller is set up to use the AHCI programming interface. The 6/4 SATA ports are controlled by a single SATA function, D31:F2. In RAID mode, the Sub Class Code, D31:F2:Reg 0Ah, will be set to 04h. This mode does require specific OS driver support.

In order for the RAID option ROM to access all 6/4 SATA ports, the RAID option ROM enables and uses the AHCI programming interface by setting the AE bit, ABAR 04h[31]. One consequence is that all register settings applicable to AHCI mode set by the BIOS must be set in RAID as well. The other consequence is that the BIOS is required to provide AHCI support to ATAPI SATA devices, which the RAID option ROM does not handle.

PCH supports stable image-compatible ID. When the alternative ID enable, D31 :F2 :Reg 9Ch [7], is not set, the PCH SATA controller will report Device ID as 2822h for a desktop SKU.

Enable Ports

It has been observed that some SATA drives will not start spin-up until the SATA port is enabled by the controller. In order to reduce drive detection time, and hence the total boot time, system BIOS should enable the SATA port early during POST (for example, immediately after memory initialization) by setting the Port x Enable (PxE) bits of the Port Control and Status register, D31:F2:Reg 92h and D31:F5:Reg 92h (refer 1 requirement), to initiate spin- up of such drives.

Memory Map

In addition to defining the caching behavior of different regions of memory for consumption by the OS, it is also firmware's responsibility to provide a "map" of the system memory to the OS so that it knows what regions are actually available for its consumption.

The most widely used mechanism for a legacy boot loader or a legacy OS to determine the system memory map is to use real-mode interrupt service 15h, function

E8h, sub-function 20h (INT15/ E820), which firmware must implement (see http://www.uruk.org/orig-grub/mem64mb.html).

Region Types

There are several general types of memory regions described by the legacy interface:
- Memory (1) – General DRAM available for OS consumption.
- Reserved (2) – DRAM address not for OS consumption.
- ACPI Reclaim (3) – Memory that contains all ACPI tables to which firmware does not require runtime access. See the applicable ACPI specification for details.
- ACPI NVS (4) – Memory that contains all ACPI tables to which firmware requires runtime access. See the applicable ACPI specification for details.
- ROM (5) – Memory that decodes to nonvolatile storage (for example, flash).
- IOAPIC (6) – Memory decoded by IOAPICs in the system (must also be uncached).
- LAPIC (7) – Memory decoded by local APICs in the system (must also be un-cached).

Region Locations

The following regions are typically reserved in a system memory map:
- 00000000-0009FFFF – Memory.
- 000A0000-000FFFFF – Reserved for legacy option ROMs and legacy BIOS.
- 00100000-???????? – Memory, where???????? indicates the top of memory changes based on "reserved" items listed below and any other design-based re-served regions.
- TSEG – Reserved.
- Graphics Stolen Memory – Reserved.
- FEC00000-FEC01000* – IOAPIC.
- FEE00000-FEE01000* – LAPIC.

See the applicable component specification for details on chipset-specific memory map requirements. See the appropriate ACPI specification for details on ACPI-related memory map requirements.

For a UEFI system, the UEFI system tables provide the equivalent data.

Loading the OS

Following the memory map configuration, a boot device is selected from a prioritized list of potential bootable partitions. The UEFI "Load Image" command or Int 19h is used to call the OS loader, which in turn loads the OS. The details are covered in the previous chapter.

Summary

The boot sequence outlined in this chapter provides general guidance that will work for most Intel architecture platforms; however, on any given platform there may be a reason to change the sequence, depending on the hardware requirements. Additional secure boot implementations may also be incorporated to check for signatures of binaries prior to execution. Such security additions may be added to future online articles to support Quick Boot.

As always, please refer and defer to the chipset and CPU specifications for your target platform.

Chapter 10
Bootstrapping Embedded

Capitalists are no more capable of self-sacrifice than a man is capable of lifting himself up by his own bootstraps.

—Vladimir Lenin

Bootstrapping to a computing device is the act of bringing the system up without any manual entry. It may be an antiquated term, but most operating systems are not native software on Intel® architecture (which start at 0xFFFFFFF0h) and cannot bootstrap themselves. BIOS and boot loaders have one main task to do—the bare minimum required to initialize enough hardware, and then get out of the way for the more robust operating system to take over. In some cases, the BIOS or bootloader should query the user or system for preferences, perform scans for bootable partitions, enumerate expansion buses, or run diagnostics in the case of a unit failure. These are usages where the OS seems unreachable or something seems incorrect with the hardware, but people typically just want to get to the OS to run their application or answer their email or phone or play the latest YouTube† video from the Internet; they do not want to wait for a BIOS to boot.

As a system designer, you can look at the Apple iPad† for the latest industry benchmark in bootstrapping. As with most embedded computing devices, it doesn't boot, *it turns on*. While the comparison may not be fair in that the iPad isn't actually booting most of the time, it is just coming out of a lower power state; the end user doesn't care. Consumers will be expecting that level of responsiveness going forward. One could easily argue that mobile phones really boot once, then have a short turn on/off time similar to that of a PC's standby sleep mode. But until the likes of Windows† and Linux decide to bootstrap themselves natively from a true OFF without the need for a BIOS or bootloader, we as system developers will have to adapt tried and true BIST and POST to a new world order, in innovative ways, or have our products stay on the shelf at the store and then get moved directly to a museum, still in the original packaging. We need to understand how to optimize the boot times for performance; this is especially true for the embedded-market space, where the system needs to effectively turn on, not boot.

But first, we need to put things in perspective.

Optimization Using BIOS and Bootloaders

Some of the typical optimizations that can be applied include:
- Platform policy rethink
- Turn off debugging
- Decrease flash size

DOI 10.1515/9781501506819-010

- Reordering flash image
- Cache as RAM pre-memory during PEI phase
- Intel SpeedStep® technology enabled early
- BDS optimization (boot devices)
- Platform memory speed
- Remove PS/2 keyboard/mouse
- Remove BIOS setup
- Remove video option ROM
- Remove BIOS USB functional support
- Eliminate unnecessary data table creation
- Booting to UEFI operating systems
- Using UEFI drivers instead of option ROMS
- Using UEFI services
- Removed setup menu
- Using a solid-state drive versus hard-disk drive to eliminate spin-up time and accelerate OS loading

This is not an all-inclusive list. Let's look at each of them individually that can be applied per design and then look at a better architectural method.

Platform Policy (What Is It and Why Is It Here?)

One of the first considerations when looking at a system BIOS and the corresponding requirements is whether you can limit the number of variables associated with what the user can do with or to the system.

> You're pirates. Hang the code, and hang the rules. They're more like guidelines anyway.
> —Elizabeth to crew of the Black Pearl
> in Pirates of the Caribbean

For instance, it might be reasonable to presume that in a platform with no add-in slots, a user will not be able to boot from a RAID controller, since there is no integrated component for RAID in the chipset or down on the board. The user cannot expect it to be initialized.

This is where a designer enters the "platform policy zone." These policies are dynamic; when you truly understand the "what" and the "why," you can institute changes. You can question everything and not stand on tradition. Even though a platform may not expose an add-in slot, the platform might expose a USB connection. A conscious decision needs to be made for how and when these components are used. We need to make informed decisions in these cases.

In some cases, it is determining what you don't need to do in the BIOS space versus the operating system space. This can be more important for boot time reductions than what you need to do during the boot flow. Example: If the OS kernel or drivers are going to repeat the bus/device enumeration of the entire PCI subsystem, for SATA, or for USB hubs/devices, then you only need to do what you must to get the OS loaded and executing and skip the rest. Too often, the standard PC BIOS handles many inane corner cases that can be found in one or two devices on the market for the sake of ultimate backward compatibility, all the way back to DOS. A standard PC BIOS fills out every line of every legacy data table in memory regardless of whether the OS or application needs the data. It has been considered a real added value that someone in the universe who buys this motherboard may install some legacy application, and we may want to make sure it is a very robust solution. Some devices will need to comprehend all the baggage because there will continue to be that part of the market. In all cases for fast boot, however, developers are encouraged to reduce, reduce, reduce.

For instance, since a user can connect anything from a record player to a RAID chassis via USB, users might think they can boot from a USB-connected device. Though this is physically possible, it is within the purview of the platform design to enable or disable this feature.

A good general performance optimization statement would be: *If you can put off doing something in BIOS that the OS can do, then put it off!* Look at the whole boot chain between bootloader, potential second-stage agents, the OS, and shutdown. You need to be examining the concept of moving the finish line closer to the ball, understanding there are tradeoffs between firmware and OS initialization. This is advanced because you need to have control and insight into each of the phases of the boot flows for a platform.

Ask the second part of the question: why is it here? If it is for a keyboard or mouse input during runtime, or to a USB stick to copy files locally to and from the system during runtime, then we probably will not need to fully enumerate the bus during boot time or incorporate a full USB firmware stack.

In Example 1 below, the decision was made to not support booting from USB media and to not support the user interrupting the boot process via keyboard/mouse. This means that during the DXE/BDS phase, the BIOS can avoid initializing the USB infrastructure to get keystrokes and save 0.5 seconds of boot time.

It should be noted that PCI resources were assigned to the USB controllers on the platform, but by eliminating BIOS USB enumeration we saved 0.5 seconds. Upon launching the platform OS, the OS still could interact with plugged- in USB devices without a problem because the OS drivers will normally reset the USB controllers and re-enumerate the USB bus/devices to suit its own needs. No wonder the OS takes so long to boot ... what else may the OS reinitialize and re-enumerate during a cold or warm boot?

Platform policy ultimately affects how an engineer responds to the remaining questions.

Case Study Summaries

We have experimented with boot times and presented case studies in the Intel Developer's Forum (IDF) in the past. Here are two examples.

Example 1

The overall performance numbers used in this example are measured in microseconds and the total boot time is described in seconds. Total boot time is measured as the time between the CPU coming out of reset and the handoff to the next boot agent.

The hardware used was:
- 1.8 Ghz Intel® Atom™–based netbook design
- 1 GB DDR2 memory
- 2 MB flash
- Western Digital 80GB Scorpio Blue 5400 RPM drive
- Intel® Solid State Drive X25-E

It should also be noted that this proof of concept was intended to emulate real-world expectations of a system BIOS, meaning nothing was done to achieve results that could not reasonably be expected in a mass-market product design. The steps that were taken for this effort should be easily portable to other designs and should largely be codebase-independent.

Table 10.1 lists the performance numbers achieved while maintaining broad market requirements.

Table 10.1: Performance Measurement Results – Before/After

Boot Phase	Normal Boot Time	Optimized Boot Time	Delta	Percentage Reduction in Boot Times
SEC (μs)	26342	25419	923	3.503
PEI (μs)	1230905	763315	467590	37.98
DXE (μs)	998234	443021	555213	55.61
BDS (μs)	7396050	766778	6629272	89.63
Total (s)	9.651531	1.999533	7.651998	79.28%

Example 1 Details —— **139**

Example 2

Measurements were taken starting from a configuration based on the original Intel Atom processor. The performance numbers achieved are listed in Table 10.2.
- Intel Atom Processor Z530/Z10 (C0 stepping)
- Intel® SCH US15W chipset (D1 stepping)
- 512 MB DDR2 memory at 400 MHz
- 2 MB flash

Table 10.2: Performance Measurements for Example 2

Boot Phase	Normal Boot Time	Optimized Boot Time	Delta	Percentage Reduction in Boot Times
Total (s)	11.66	1.65	10.01	85.85%

While a different combination of techniques was used between these two teams in these examples, it should be noted that the second trial was more focused on the embedded market scenarios and striving to simply reduce boot times as much as possible without regard to the broad market. The difference, while noticeable, would not be that great.

Example 1 Details

Some of the details are listed in Table 10.3.

Table 10.3: Example 1 Details

Change	Boot Time (in seconds)	Incremental boot time improvement (in seconds)
Initial configuration	9.65	—
Eliminate SMBIOS tables	9.25	0.4
Booting to UEFI target	8.75	0.5
Using UEFI drivers instead of option ROMs	5.75	3.0
Using an SSD versus HDD to eliminate spin-up time	3.65	2.1
Using UEFI services	3.40	0.25
Removed setup menu	1.99	1.41

Admittedly, broad marketing requirements are not the first thing that comes to mind when a developer sits down to optimize a firmware for performance; however, the reality is that marketing requirements form the practical limits for how the technical solution can be adjusted.

Answering some basic questions can help you make decisions that will set outer bounds and define the performance characteristics of the system. Since this section details the engineering responses to marketing requirements, it does not provide a vast array of code optimization tricks. Unless the code has a serious set of implementation bugs, the majority of boot speed improvements can be achieved from the following guidelines. There are codebase-independent tricks spelled out.

What Are the Design Goals?

How does the user need to use the platform? Is it a closed-box system? Is it more of a traditional desktop PC? Is it a server-based system with some unique add-ons? How the platform is thought of will ultimately affect what users expect. Making conscious design choices to either enable or limit some of these expectations is where the platform policies can greatly affect the resulting performance characteristics.

What Are the Supported Target Operating Systems?

Understanding the requirements of a particular platform-supported OS will greatly affect what optimization paths can be taken in the BIOS. Since many "open" platforms have a wide variety of operating systems that they support, this limits some of the choices available. In the case of the proof-of-concept platform, there were only two main operating systems that were required to be supported. This enabled the author to make a few choices that allowed the codebase to save roughly 400 ms of boot time by avoiding the reading of some of the DIMM SPD data for creating certain SMBIOS records since they weren't used by the target operating systems.

Changes in the BIOS codebase that avoided the unnecessary creation of certain tables saved roughly 400 ms in the boot time.

Do We Have to Support Legacy Operating Systems?

Are the target operating systems UEFI-compliant or not? If all the OS targets are UEFI-compliant, then the platform can save roughly 0.5 second in initialization of the video option ROM. In this case, there were two operating systems that needed to be booted

Example 1 Details —— **141**

on the same motherboard. We had conflicting requirements where one was UEFI-compliant and one was not. There are a variety of tricks that could have been achieved by the platform BIOS when booting the UEFI- compliant OS but for purposes of keeping fair measurement numbers, the overall boot speed numbers reflect the overhead of supporting legacy operating systems as well (the compatibility segment module [CSM] was executed).

Do We Have to Support Legacy Option ROMs?

Whether or not to launch a legacy option ROM depends on several possible variables:
- Does the motherboard have any devices built-in that have a legacy option ROM?
- Does the platform support adding a device that requires the launch of a legacy option ROM?
- If any of the first two are true, does the platform need to initialize the device associated with that option ROM?

Trick: To save an additional 0.5 second or more of boot time when booting a UEFI-compliant OS, the BDS could analyze the target BOOT#### variable to determine if the target was associated with an OS loader—thus it is a UEFI target. The platform in this case at least has the option to avoid some of the overhead associated with the legacy compatibility support infrastructure.

One reason why launching legacy option ROMs is fraught with peril for boot performance is that there are no rules associated with what a legacy option
ROM will do while it has control of the system. In some cases, the option ROM may be rather innocuous regarding boot performance, but in other instances that is not the case. For example, the legacy option ROM could attempt to interact with the user during launch. This normally involves advertising a hot key or two for the user to press, which would delay the BIOS in finishing its job for however long the option ROM pauses waiting for a keystroke.

Trick: For this particular situation, we avoided launching all the drivers in a particular BIOS and instead opted to launch only the drivers necessary for reaching the boot target itself. Since the device we were booting from was a SATA device for which the BIOS had a native UEFI driver, there was no need to launch an option ROM. This action alone saved approximately three seconds on the platform. More details associated with this trick and others are in the Additional Details section.

Are We Required to Display an OEM Splash Screen?

This is a crucial element for many platforms, especially from a marketing point of view. The display of the splash screen itself typically does not take that much time. Usually, initializing the video device to enable such a display takes a sizable amount of time. On the proof-of-concept platform, it would typically take 300 ms. An important question is how long does marketing want the logo to be displayed? The answer to this question will focus on what is most important for the OEM delivering the platform. Sometimes speed is paramount (as it was with this proof of concept), and the splash screen can be eliminated completely. Other times, the display of the logo is deemed much more important and all things stop while the logo is displayed. An engineer's hands are usually tied by the decisions of the marketing infrastructure.

One could leverage the UEFI event services to take advantage of the marketing-driven delay to accomplish other things, which effectively makes some of the initialization parallel.

What Type of Boot Media Is Supported?

In the proof-of-concept platform description, one element was a bit unusual. There was a performance and a standard configuration associated with the drive attached to the system. Though it may not be obvious, the choice of boot media can be a significant element in the boot time when you consider that some drives require 1 to 5 seconds (or much more) to spin up. The characteristics of the boot media are very important since, regardless of whatever else you might do to optimize the boot process, the platform still has to read from the boot media, and there are some inherent tasks associated with doing that. Spin-up delays are among those tasks that are unavoidable in today's rotating magnetic media.

For the proof of concept, the boot media of choice was one that incurs no spin-up penalty; thus, a solid-state drive (SSD) was chosen. This saved about two seconds from the boot time.

What Is the BIOS Recovery/Update Strategy?

How a platform handles a BIOS update or recovery can affect the performance of a platform. Since this task can be accomplished in many ways, this may inevitably be one of those mechanisms with lots of platform variability. There are a few very common cases on how a BIOS update is achieved from a user's perspective:
1. A user executes an OS application, which he or she likely downloaded from the OEM's Web site. This will eventually cause the machine to reboot.

Example 1 Details ——— **143**

2. A user downloads a special file from an OEM's website and puts it on a USB dongle and reboots the platform with the USB dongle connected.
3. A user receives or creates a CD or flash drive with a special file and reboots the platform to launch the BIOS update utility contained within that special file.

These user scenarios usually resolve into the BIOS, during the initialization caused by the reboot, reading the update/recovery file from a particular location. Where that update/recovery file is stored and when it is processed is really what affects performance.

When Processing Things Early

Frequently during recovery, one cannot presume that the target OS is working. For a reasonable platform design, someone would need to design a means by which to update or recover the BIOS without the assistance of the OS. This would lead to user scenarios 2 or 3 listed above.

The question engineers should ask themselves is, how do you notify the BIOS that the platform is in recovery mode? Depending on what the platform policy prescribes, this method can vary greatly. One option is to always probe a given set of possible data repositories (such as USB media, a CD, or maybe even the network) for recovery content. The act of always probing is typically a time-consuming effort and not conducive to quick boot times.

There is definitely the option of having a platform-specific action that is easy and quick to probe that "turns on" the recovery mode. How to turn on the recovery mode (if such a concept exists for the platform) is very specific to the platform. Examples of this are holding down a particular key (maybe associated with a GPIO), flipping a switch (equivalent of moving a jumper) that can be probed, and so on. These methods are highly preferable since they allow a platform to run without much burden (no extensive probing for update/recovery.)

Is There a Need for Pre-OS User Interaction?

Normally the overall goal is to boot the target OS as quickly as possible and the only expected user interaction is with the OS. That being said, the main reason people today interact with the BIOS is to launch the BIOS setup. Admittedly, some settings within this environment are unique and cannot be properly configured outside of the BIOS. However, at least one major OEM (if not more) has chosen to ship millions of UEFI-based units without exposing what is considered a BIOS setup. It might be reasonable to presume for some platforms that the established factory default settings are sufficient and require no user adjustments. Most OEMs do not go this route. However, it is certainly possible for an OEM to expose applets within the OS to provide some of the configurability that would have otherwise been exposed in the pre-OS phase.

With the advent of UEFI 2.1 (and more specifically the Human Interface Infrastructure [HII] content in that specification), it became possible for configuration data in the BIOS to be exposed to the OS. In this way, many of the BIOS settings can have methods exposed and configured in what are not traditional (pre-OS) ways.

If it is deemed unnecessary to interact with the BIOS, there is very little reason (except as noted in prior sections) for the BIOS to probe for a hot key. This only takes time from a platform boot without being a useful feature of the platform.

A Note of Caution

When trying to optimize the settings for hardware and OS interaction features, such as power management flows, which are enabled and controlled via a combination of hardware and software, it is important not to oversimplify the firmware setting. Often, the tradeoffs and ramifications are going to be beyond the simple boot flow to get to the OS. For these settings, extreme care should be taken to understand the downstream usage model and workloads that are going to be exercising these features. Experiment with these settings, but do not be surprised if the resulting data does not support your original hypothesis.

Additional Details

When it comes time to address some codebase issues, the marketing requirements clearly define the problem space an engineer has to design around. With that information, there are several methods that can help that are fairly typical of a UEFI-based platform. This is not intended to indicate these are the only methods, but they are the ones most any UEFI codebase can exercise.

Adjusting the BIOS to Avoid Unnecessary Drivers

It is useful to go into and understand the details of how we avoided executing some of the extra drivers in our platform. It is also useful to reference the appropriate sections in the UEFI specification to better understand some of the underlying parts that, for conciseness, cannot be covered in this book.

The BDS phase of operations is where various decisions are made regarding what gets launched and what platform policy is enacted. That being said, this is the code (regardless of which UEFI codebase you use) that will frequently get the most attention

Example 1 Details —— **145**

in the optimizations. If we refer again to the boot times for our proof of concept, it should be noted that the BDS phase was where the majority of time was reduced. Most of the reduction had to do with optimizations as well as some of the design choices that were made and the phase of initialization where that activity often takes place.

At its simplest, the BDS phase is the means by which the BIOS completes any required hardware initialization so that it can launch the boot target. At its most complex, you can add a series of platform-specific, extensive, value-added hardware initialization not required for launching the boot target.

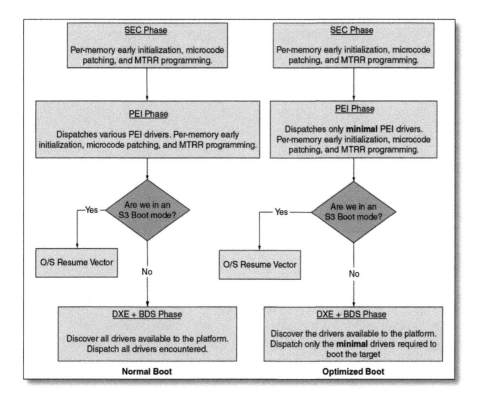

Figure 10.1: Architecture Overview of Boot Process

What Is a Boot Target?
The boot target is defined by something known as an EFI device path (see the UEFI specification). This device path is a binary description of where the required boot target is physically located. This gives the BIOS sufficient information to understand what components of the platform need to be initialized to launch the boot target.

Below is an example of just such a boot target:

```
Acpi(PNP0A03,0)/Pci(1F|1)/Ata(Primary,Master)/
HD(Part3,Sig00110011)/"\EFI\Boot"/"OSLoader.efi"
```

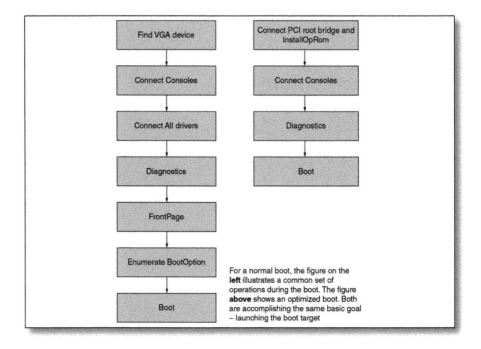

Figure 10.2: Functional Boot Flow

Steps Taken in a Normal and Optimized Boot

Figure 10.1 indicates that between the normal boot and an optimized boot, there are no design differences from a high level (UEFI) architecture point of view. So optimizing a platform's boot performance does *not* mean that one has to violate any of the EFI platform initialization design specifications.

It does mean that you have to go through each module and ask the big questions: Can I eliminate it entirely? Can I reduce the corner cases? Are there going to be variables in this equation or bit field? (See Figure 10.2.)

Loading a Boot Target

The logic associated with the BDS optimization focuses solely on what is the minimal behavior associated with initializing the platform and launching the OS loader. When customizing the platform BDS, you can avoid calling routines that attempt to connect all drivers to all devices recursively, such as BdsConnectAll(), and instead connect

Example 1 Details ━━ **147**

only the devices directly associated with the boot target. Figure 10.3 shows an example of that logic.

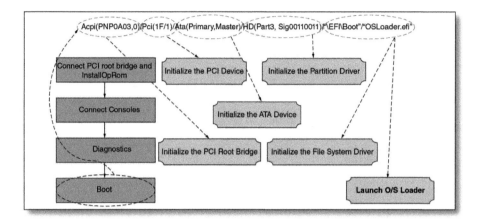

Figure 10.3: Deconstructing the BDS Launch of the Boot Target

Organize the Flash Effectively

In a BIOS that complies with the PI specification, there is a flash component concept known as a firmware volume (FV). This is typically an accumulation of BIOS drivers. It would be reasonably expected that these FVs are organized into several logical collections that may or may not be associated with their phase of operations or functions. There are two major actions the core initiates that are associated with drivers. The first is when a driver is dispatched (loaded into memory from flash), and the second one is when a driver is connected to a device. Platform policy could dictate that the DXE core avoids finding unnecessary drivers. For instance, if the USB device boot is not needed, the USB-related drivers could be segregated to a specific FV, and material associated with that FV would not be dispatched.

Minimize the Files Needed

Since one of the slowest I/O resources in a platform is normally the flash part on which the BIOS is stored, it is prudent to minimize the amount of space a BIOS occupies. The less space it occupies, the shorter the time for routines within the BIOS to read content into faster areas of the platform (such as memory). This can be done by minimizing the drivers required by the platform, and pruning can typically be accomplished by a proper study of the marketing requirements.

Example 2 Details

Table 10.4 depicts the results of the boot time investigation, followed by in- depth discussion of each change.

Table 10.4: Boot Time Results

Change	Boot time (in seconds)	Incremental boot time improvement (in seconds)
Initial configuration	11.66	-
Turn off debugging	8.39	3.27
Decrease flash size	8.18	0.21
Caching of PEI phase	7.91	0.27
Intel SpeedStep® technology enabled early	7.82	0.09
BDS optimization (boot devices)	7.53	0.29
Platform memory speed	7.43	0.10
Remove PS/2 keyboard/mouse	7.36	0.07
Remove BIOS setup	5.43	1.93
Remove video option ROM	3.33	2.10
Remove BIOS USB support	1.65	1.68

Turn Off Debugging

Turning off debugging removes the serial debugging information and turns on C Compiler optimizations. Because framework BIOS is almost entirely written in C (unlike earlier BIOS versions, which were written in assembly language), enabling compiler optimizations is particularly useful.

EFI BIOS makes extensive use of spewing debugging information over a serial port to aid development and debug of the BIOS. While this debugging information is valuable in a development environment, it can be eliminated in a production environment. In addition to the boot time improvements realized, there are also IP considerations to shipping a BIOS developed in a higher-level language that has debugging information enabled.

Likewise, compiler optimizations must be disabled when it is desired to perform source level debug of the C language BIOS code. However, in production this can be eliminated.

Example 2 Details — **149**

Decrease Flash Size

This step represents modifying the BIOS build process to use a 1 MB flash part instead of the original 2 MB flash part. This includes decreasing the number of flash blocks used in the board process. The framework BIOS uses a flash file system to store PEI and DXE modules as well as other entities. Decreasing the number of blocks in this file system improves the access time each time a module is accessed.

Caching of PEI Phase

Many of the PEI modules in framework BIOS must be executed prior to platform memory being initialized. Once memory is initialized, the remaining portions of the BIOS are copied to system memory and executed out of memory. Because the framework BIOS uses cache-as-RAM (CAR) for pre-memory storage and stack, it runs all the PEI modules in place directly from the flash part without caching. It is possible, however, on the Intel® Atom™ processor to simultaneously enable CAR plus one 64 KB region of normally cached address space. The BIOS must be arranged in such a way to take full advantage of this one prememory cacheable region. This means having a separate flash file system used exclusively by the PEI modules that are run prior to memory initialization and placing that file system in the region that will be cached. By employing this technique to cache the portion of the flash part that includes the PEI modules executing prior to initialization of memory, performance is increased. For this effort, the 64 KB region was unable to cover all the PEI modules. Through further reduction in size of PEI, more improvement is possible.

Intel SpeedStep® Technology Enabled Early

Intel SpeedStep® technology is a power savings technology used to limit the processor speed based on current software demand on the system. When the system is in heavy use, the processor is run at full speed. At idle and near idle, the system is run at slower speed "steps."

The BIOS role in initialization of Intel SpeedStep technology includes detection of Intel SpeedStep technology capabilities, initialization of the processor speed for all processor threads, and advertisement of Intel SpeedStep capabilities for the operating system. The above "initialization of all processor threads" is typically to the "power on" speed, which is normally equal to the lowest supported speed. This is to ensure increased stability during the boot process. The operating system will then enable the faster steps.

To increase boot speed, the BIOS, instead of enabling the "power on" feature of Intel SpeedStep® technology, can enable the highest speed setting. This not only increases the speed of the processor during a BIOS post, but also increases the speed of loading the operating system.

BDS Phase Optimization

The framework BIOS BDS phase normally looks for potential boot devices from hard drives, CD-ROM drives, floppy drives, and network. On the investigation platform, the requirements were for boot from hard disk. This optimization removes the BDS checks for boot devices on CD-ROM, floppy, and network since they are not supported on this platform. If the operating system is being loaded from flash instead of hard disk, the hard disk would be replaced with an optimized flash boot.

Platform Memory Speed

Noticeable boot time improvement was realized by using the highest memory speed supported on the platform. On platforms featuring the Intel Atom processor, this is determined by a set of jumpers on the board. On other platforms, this may be a setting in BIOS setup.

Remove PS/2 Keyboard/Mouse

Initialization of the PS/2 keyboard and mouse in the BIOS takes a considerable amount of time due to the specification of these devices. This eliminates the possibility of interacting with the BIOS during the BIOS post and operating system loader. If BIOS setup has been removed as discussed below, user input is not needed during the BIOS. On a fielded embedded device, keyboard and mouse are typically not needed and therefore do not need to be initialized. During device development and debug this feature might be better left on until the device is operational.

Remove BIOS Setup

During the boot process, the BIOS provides an opportunity for the user to hit a hot key that terminates the boot process and instead displays a menu used to modify various platform settings. This includes settings such as boot order, disabling various processor or chipset features, and modifying media parameters. On an embedded device, BIOS setup (and any similar settings provided by an operating system loader) is more

Example 2 Details —— **151**

of a liability since it gives the end user access to BIOS features that are potentially untested on the device. It is better to have a set of setup options that may be chosen at BIOS build time. Removal of the BIOS setup also saves significant BIOS post time.

Remove Video Option ROM

The video option ROM on platforms featuring the Intel Atom processor and many other newer platforms is quite slow due to the many different video interfaces that must be supported and the display detection algorithms that must be employed. Replacement of a highly optimized DXE video driver in place of the video option ROM saves significant boot time. The speed of this optimized DXE video driver is highly dependent on the exact display chosen and video features required by the platform prior to installation of the operating system graphics driver. On the investigation platform, a fixed splash screen was displayed. It was unchanged during the boot process until the operating system graphics driver initialized the display. To achieve this, the capability to display text was removed from the DXE graphics driver. As a result, none of the normal BIOS or operating system initialization messages is displayed. This yields additional performance and a cleaner boot appearance.

Remove BIOS USB Support

Since USB-boot and a USB input device like a keyboard/mouse were not requirements on the investigation platform, initialization of USB was completely removed from boot flow. USB is still available from the operating system once the driver is loaded but not during the BIOS or OS loader.

Divide Long Lead Pieces into Functional Blocks and Distribute Across the Boot Flow

While BIOS today is not multithreaded, there are some things that can still be done in parallel. Not waiting around for long timeouts or scans and breaking up the activities between multiple functions across the boot flow are two good ways to eliminate idle delay times. Example: command the hard drives to spin up early in the boot flow. It should be noted that even solid-state drives have a firmware readiness time minimum before data can be retrieved. This can be mitigated by warming up the drives. Similarly, newer LCD displays may have a minimum time required to turn on the backlight, or perform a costly 900 ms reset on each power cycle.

Keeping the CPU fully occupied as well as any DMA engine during OS loading or BIOS shadow is another method of running some of the longer lead activity in parallel. One can start to load the data from the storage to memory at the same time you are executing other items. Bottom line: don't stand around whistling while you wait for hardware or timeouts when you can be doing real work.

Summary

This chapter covers several potential optimizations that can be implemented on a broad array of embedded platforms, depending on the policy decisions and requirements of the platform.

It is important to note that some latent firmware bugs were found that only became apparent when optimizations were enabled. For this reason, rigorous validation is recommended after enabling these and optimizations.

In creating new paths for optimizations, it is important to get as much data as you can from experts on a particular component or subsystem. Often the details will not be written down in specifications.

> None of us got where we are solely by pulling ourselves up by our bootstraps. We got here because somebody—a parent, a teacher, an Ivy League crony or a few nuns—bent down and helped us pick up our boots.
>
> —Thurgood Marshall

Chapter 11
Intel's Fast Boot Technology

A little simplification would be the first step toward rational living, I think.

—Eleanor Roosevelt

One of the key objectives of computing platforms is responsiveness. BIOS boot time is a key factor in responsiveness that OEM manufacturers, end users, and OS vendors ask firmware developers to deliver. Here the focus is on system startup time and resume times.

Traditional Intel architecture BIOS has labored through the years to design itself to boot on any configuration that the platform can discover, each time it boots it works to rediscover anything it can about a change to the machine configuration that may have happened when it was off. This provides the most robust, flexible experience possible for dynamic open boxes with a single binary. However, this has also resulted in a bloated boot time upwards of 30 seconds for the BIOS alone. As we have covered in other chapters, when properly tuned and equipped, a closed box consumer electronics or embedded computing device powering on can easily boot in under two seconds. This normally requires a customized hard-coded solution or policy-based decisions, which can cost several months of optimizations to an embedded design. By following the methods contained in this chapter, even open-box PCs can be as fast as embedded devices and consumer electronics, less than two seconds. And the benefit to embedded designs is that they need not spend weeks and months of analysis per design to get the desired effect on boot speed.

The Human Factor

Assuming the device being created will interact with people, it is important to understand how the human brain reacts to stimulus, or what it expects in response with regards to timing.

DOI 10.1515/9781501506819-011

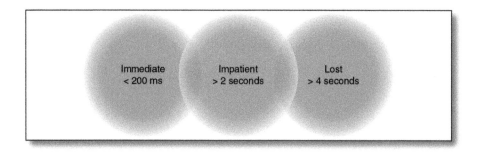

Figure 11.1: Response Time in Man-Computer Conversational Transactions

Back in 1968, a psychologist named Robert B. Miller, working at IBM in Poughkeepsie, New York, conducted experiments between people and computers using the latest input devices at the time. While the devices have changed over the last few decades, the human brain has not (Miller, 1968).

In Miller's experiments, he showed that a person would believe that, in terms of response time, less than 200 milliseconds (ms) is considered to be immediate, greater than two seconds makes people start to get impatient, and after four seconds, communication between human and machine is broken (see Figure 11.1).

Four decades later, another psychologist, Steven Seow, authored a book with a similar set of experimental results in his responsiveness chapter.[1] While Seow's experiments were geared toward a software UI instead of simple input device responses, the results are strikingly similar to Miller's, as illustrated in Figure 11.2.

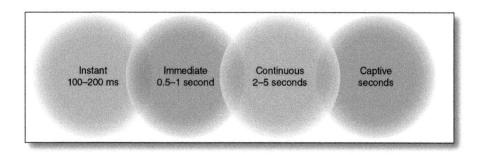

Figure 11.2: Seow's Responsiveness Time Definitions

---

1 S.C. Seow, *Designing and Engineering Time: The Psychology of Time Perception in Software*, Addison-Wesley Professional, 2008, Chapter 4.

Seow broke up responsiveness into four categories:
- *Instantaneous* was measured in the range 100–200 ms, where the maximum was 100 ms for a key press and a maximum of 200 ms for a menu draw.
- *Immediate implied* 500–1000 ms, where the end user perceives information is available and being displayed.
- *Continuous* was coined for the range of 2000–5000 ms, where the machine is reacting, but the user expects feedback on progress at longer durations.
- *Captive* lasted from 7000 through 10000 ms, the maximum time a user will maintain focus before switching to some other task (abandon as background).

The next set of similarities was determining, without a stopwatch, a delta between times. Variations may not be noticeable to the untimed eye.

Seow suggested a basic "20 percent rule" for perceptible differences. Miller's data was a bit more refined (as Figure 11.3 shows):
- 75%of people cannot detect change of ±8 percent between 2 and 4 seconds
- From 0.6 to 0.8 seconds, there was 10 percent variation
- From 6 to 30 seconds, a 20–30 percent variation

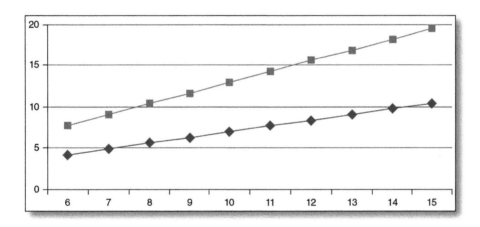

Figure 11.3: Miller's Results

For typical system boot times where the BIOS executes in 6 seconds to 15 seconds, the times would have to be improved between 1.2 and 4.5 seconds for someone to take notice and appreciate the work of a developer trying to make improvements at the millisecond level.

It should be noted that many little changes can add up to a lot. Even in the subsecond range, where Miller's results imply a need for approximately 80 milliseconds to see results, a series of small changes of 5 to 10 ms can easily reach a noticeable timing result.

Responsiveness

Looking across the system, in order to achieve what your brain thinks is the right timing, many things must be aligned for speed and performance, not just during runtime, but during startup and resume operations, as well as during sleep and shutdown. Every millisecond wasted burns milliwatts, costing time and energy.

We need responsiveness across all levels of the platform, as shown in Figure 11.4:

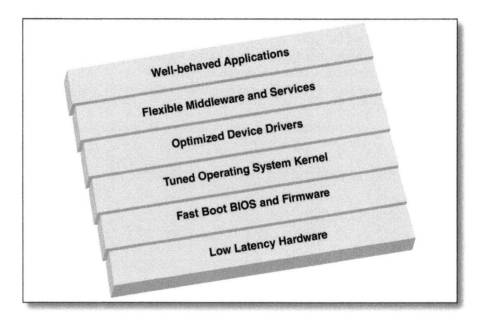

Figure 11.4: The Platform Level Stack Responsiveness

- *Low latency hardware.* Today's silicon and hardware provide much greater speed than they are normally tuned for. While people think of a PC as booting in 45 seconds or more, the same hardware, properly tuned, can execute a viable boot path in less than 1 second.
- Along these lines, power sequencing of the various power rails on the platform is an area that needs to be examined. Between 300 and 700 ms can be absorbed by just the power sequencing. This is before the CPU comes out of reset and the system firmware starts operating.

- *Fast boot BIOS and firmware*. System BIOS and embedded microcontroller firmware components are moving forward in ways that they didn't in years past, or didn't need to. Silicon vendors often provide sample boot code that works to enable the platform through initialization. What is needed is more responsive silicon reference code.
- *Operating system*. Intel has been working with OS vendors to optimize the user experience. For developers, it is easy to see where a very modular and diverse mix of components can work if architected correctly, but many solutions are not fully optimized. Linux teams in the Intel Open Source Technology Center (OTC) are engaged to speed up the experience from kernel load and driver startup times. And other operating systems are not being ignored.
- *Driver optimizations*. Intel OS drivers are measured using various tools, depending on the OS. Intel is reducing the load and execution times for all of our drivers. We are continually investigating any optimizations possible to improve the responsiveness of our ingredients, including the graphics and wireless device drivers.
- *Middleware*. This is a topic that you will have to consider: the applications that use it and how it can be altered to take advantage of offload engines on the system.
- *Applications*. Like other companies, Intel is investing in its application store, as well as working with others in the industry to streamline their applications with various tools from the Intel tools suites. There are a variety of applications we provide which assist in the debug and monitoring of the system that we provide to all of our customers.

Depending on the use of solid-state drives, there are fundamental things that can be done differently at the OS and application levels that can have a profound impact on application responsiveness. This is an area we need to work on, this is where our customers work, and this is where it will count the most. The user experience is here, if we did the rest of our jobs correctly.

And let's not forget that responsiveness doesn't end at the platform level; it extends into the local network and into the ubiquitous cloud.

The (Green) Machine Factor

Assuming the device being created will interact with other machines, it is important to understand how the delays in the system will affect the overall effectiveness. Timing requirements between machines can be much tighter or much looser than when dealing with people.

Mission-critical systems may have single-digit millisecond responsiveness requirements in certain responses where the system cannot be put into a lower power idle state without significant risk or limitations to the overall network. Other systems require only low data amounts and infrequent access, and can stand to wait several seconds or minutes or hours for a system to resume from slumber and complete a task.

Real-time systems allow for setting priority on devices as well as execution threads so they can predetermine if there is any millisecond wait at all for anything in the system. The more responsive the system is, the more flexibility the real time system designer may have.

The faster the response times can be, the deeper the sleep state can be and the less power is required to keep the system active over time. Example: If the system can be made to boot in less than two seconds from an OFF (S4) state, where power is normally 2 mW, then why put the system into S3, where the resume time is about 1 second and the power is several hundred mW? Obviously, it depends on the resume times, power requirements, and usage model tradeoffs. But the faster response times from lower power states can prove extremely beneficial. Another example is Enhanced Intel SpeedStep® Technology, where the CPU can dynamically enter a lower power state and run at a lower frequency until the performance is required. Average power is a key factor when working on more ecologically sensitive, green infrastructures, from servers to sensors. Responsiveness capabilities provide an ability to lower power overall and create more easily sustainable technology.

Boot Time Analysis

In order to properly measure the responsiveness of a system, a stopwatch doesn't work. Counting aloud "one Mississippi, two Mississippi, three Mississippi...," doesn't work either. For the right level of granularity, there are timers on both the Intel processors (Time Stamp Counter, TSC, with millisecond timing) and in the chipsets (High Performance Event Timers, HPET, microsecond timing) that can be implemented as part of a logging mechanism in the firmware. While firmware or hardware architecture limit the straight usage of either, it is possible to incorporate a mechanism with reasonable accuracy for the need of boot time analysis. Logging of the various milestones in the boot flow can be added by outputting to a serial port as an example. A temporary storage location in local memory reserved from the OS known location is preferred, though, for two reasons: no port requirements and no additive delay creating an observer effect. This data can also be dropped into an ACPI table for the log to be retrieved and reviewed later.

If using Tiano implementations, EFI PERF Monitor functions can be added quickly to various EFI code modules in all phases of the Tiano boot flow.
- In the PEI phase, we use PEI_PERF_START(), PEI_PERF_END(), PEI_SER_PERF_START(), and PEI_SER_PERF_END().
- In the DXE, BDS, and Shell phases, we use PERF_ENABLE(), PERF_ START(), PERF_END(), and finally PERF_UPDATE().

These logging routines will dump data into a reserved memory location from a cold boot for retrieval later.

You also need to know how to get around a few limitations:

1. The first limitation is that when you are doing CPU or memory initialization, a reset is required to either the CPU or the platform. When this happens, the timers may also get reset. Finding a scratchpad region that is "sticky," which means it maintains its data across a warm reset or cold boot, is required such that you can save/restore the TSC for accurate measurement/logging across the entire boot path, instead of from just the last reset executed by the firmware.

2. Some basic framework processing overhead can happen outside of the instrumented routines that will not be counted. Between main PEI or DXE cores operating, the processes in between may not be fully instrumented in a particular code base. While this should not be the case, a few milliseconds here or there could slip through the cracks.

3. Over the course of a system S3 sleep/resume cycle, all the timers are reset and you must reserve a memory region from the OS that you can access when memory is "active." As S3 has been on the order of several hundred milliseconds versus tens of seconds, some people choose to use this state as their low-power fast boot option.

4. The TSC or HPET timers may not be set up by default at power on. The firmware will have to initialize them and some tens of milliseconds may be lost in the setup before the first logging can occur.

One way to overcome the software logging issue is to have the hardware instrumented with a logic analyzer. Depending on the motherboard layout and test points available, you should be able to probe the motherboard for different signals that will respond to the initialization as it happens. If no known good test point exists, a GPIO can be set up as the start and end point. Sending the I/O commands takes some time, so it is not ideal.

Using hardware measuring techniques brings further complications. It is likely that the hardware power sequencing takes upwards of 100 ms alone to execute before the processor is taken out of reset and the BIOS or bootloader code can begin to execute. From a user's perspective, it should be considered as they "pushed the button" and their eyes are expecting a response in less than a few seconds. So from a BIOS point of view, this hardware power sequencing is a required handicap.

With the addition of any large number of experimental test points, it is possible to incur an observer effect or to change the boot environment, slowing it down with the extra cycles being added. Example: if you turn on debug mode, or if you do an excessive number of I/Os, the performance can be heavily affected by up to 30 percent in some cases. Be aware of this effect and don't chase ghosts. This concept is outlined in Mytkowicz et al. (2008).

Once we have the data, then the fun truly begins. A quick Pareto chart, where summarizing the timing data per block may quickly help developers focus on the top 20 percent of the longer latency, which may total up to 80 percent of the boot time. These items can be reduced first; then dig into the shorter portions. When looking at attacking this problem, it is a good idea to step back and look at the bigger picture before charging ahead and tackling the problem feature by feature.

First Boot versus Next Boot Concept

In ACPI system state description, the system starts up from G3, G2/S5, or G1/S4, and ends in a G0/S0 working system state. Orthogonal to Global and Sleep states of the ACPI, Intel has defined Fast Boot states that can be thought of as:

– *B0.* First boot, in order to robustly boot on any configuration, firmware dynamically scans all enumerable buses and configures all applicable peripherals required to boot the OS.
– *B1.* Full boot, similar to first boot, whenever a configuration change is noted.
– *BN.* Typical subsequent boot, which reuses data from previous scans to initialize the platform. This results in a sub-two-second user experience.

Figure 11.5 is a diagram of the Fast Boot State.

After a full boot and with no configuration changes, a fast path is taken in the subsequent BIOS boot, resulting in faster boot time. Fast Boot can be implemented without missing any platform features, assuming that the idea is to hand off to the OS loader. This fast path is a "normal" or "typical" boot path.

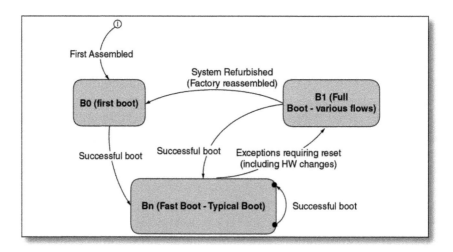

Figure 11.5: Boot State Diagram

Some environments may not be suitable for such a Fast Boot scenario: IT activity, development activity, or a lab environment may not provide enough flexibility. For those cases, the atypical full boot path or first boot paths continue to be supported. Decisions can be made automatically or triggered by user or other external trigger.

Boot Mode UEFI Configuration Setting

In general, the B-states can be aligned to the UEFI-defined boot modes listed in Table 11.1.

Table 11.1: UEFI-Defined Boot Modes

Full Boot Configuration		Fast Boot
B0	B1	B(n)
BOOT_WITH_DEFAULT_SETTINGS	BOOT_WITH_FULL_CONFIGURATION	BOOT_WITH_MINIMAL_CONFIGURATION

The following list shows a high-level breakdown of the two-second budget. It does not assume the scripted boot method, which may be faster in certain scenarios:

1. SEC/PEI phase budget – 500 ms, where:
   - Memory is configured, initialized, and scrubbed (if needed).
   - BIOS has been shadowed to memory and is currently executing from memory.
   - ME-BIOS DID handshake is done and no exception or fall back request was raised.
   - Long latency hardware (such as HDD, eDP panel) has been powered up.
   - CPU is completely patch-updated, including the second CPU patch microcode update.

2. DXE phase budget – 500 ms:
   - Greater than 5 ms each for about 100 existing modules (most are in 1-ms range).
   - Each DXE module has a time budget of 10 ms, unless explicitly waived otherwise.
   - DXE module that issues proper delay to allow other module to run will not have the delay time counts against it.
   - CPU DXE, PCH DXE each has extended time budget – 100 ms.
   - ME DXE budget – 10 ms (no MEBx during Bn).
   - Option ROM – 0 ms, no legacy option ROMs are allowed.
   - Raid Storage Technology ROM - 0 ms as AHCI mode does not need RST option ROM.

3. BDS phase budget – 500 ms – only one boot target:
   - GOP does not display dynamic text – 100 ms.
4. TSL (transient layer), – 500 ms:
   - OS bootloader time is after the BIOS boot ended. However, it does affect the overall end-to-end boot time.

Fallback Mechanisms

There are several events that could cause a full boot to transpire following the next system reset, including hardware, BIOS, or software level changes.
- Certain hardware changes that are relatively easily detected by BIOS include CPU, memory, display, input, boot target, and RTC battery errors.
- BIOS setting changes that will cause an event may include changes to the boot target and console input/output changes.
- Software changes include UEFI updates.

Not every exception event is likely to trigger a full boot on the next boot sequence or involve interrupting the current boot with a system reset. Table 11.2 depicts the different types of exceptions that could occur.

Table 11.2: Types of Exceptions

Exception Type	Current Boot Flow	Requires RESET	Next Boot Flow
Type 1	Fast Boot	No	Fast Boot
Type 2	Fast Boot up until Exception, remainder of boot sequence is Full Boot	No	Fast Boot
Type 3	N/A	Yes	Full Boot with Fast MRC
Type 4	N/A	Yes	Full Boot with Full MRC training

A Type 1 Exception can be completely handled within an EFI module and the remainder of the BIOS boot flow will continue with the *BOOT_WITH_ MINIMAL_CONFIGURATION* flag. Optionally, the exception can be logged for diagnostic purposes.

A Type 2 Exception occurs if a BIOS module encounters an issue that will prevent the rest of the BIOS from continuing the Fast Boot framework. The remainder of the boot sequence may execute slower than anticipated but no reset is needed. The boot will continue and it is recommended that a logging of the vent occurs.

A Type 3 Exception requires an interruption of the current boot flow with a system reset. The next boot will be a full boot (without *BOOT_WITH_ MINIMAL_CONFIGURA-TION* flag) to handle the exception. It is unlikely, unless the error was generated during memory initialization, that a full MRC training would be required on top of the full boot.

A Type 4 Exception is similar to Type 3, except that after the system reset, the BIOS is in Full Boot mode, and Memory Initialization needs to perform full training.

Table 11.3 lists a series of exceptions and the probable type casting. Several of these can be different, depending on the policy decisions of the designer.

Table 11.3: Exceptions and Probable Type Casting

Type	Exception	Example
3	BIOS Setup	Fast boot setting override, setup option changes
4	Boot Failure	No successful first/full boot, watch dog timeout
4	Hardware Change	ConOut changed, RTC power loss, CMOS clear, 4-second power button override is pressed
4	Hardware Override	Recovery jumper, MFG jumper, critical CPU error
2	Software Override	UEFI capsule
4	User/Setup	User interrupt, separate from dock
4	Memory Changed	DIMM change, no DIMM ID, CPU changed?

Baseline Assumptions for Enabling Intel Fast Boot

The following assumptions are made in the Fast Boot feature:
1. A stable platform configuration is reachable. Following the initial provisioning boot, small modifications to platforms are allowed, but the majority of systems boot continuously with the same configuration, from the same drive for the life of the system to the same operating system for the life of the system, in a very limited number of environments (example: at home, at work, or in a single industrial application).
   - There are no reconfigurations allowed after the first boot. This means that after the platform is provisioned out of the box, the configuration is not changing.
   - Boot device list does not change, the BIOS setup menu does not change, and the non-PCI devices on external buses/ports do not require BIOS discovery and initialization. Finally, device initialization needs do not change.
   - Minimum configuration boot when boot target is a nonstandard or user-defined OS. Provide only a static splash screen display only, as opposed to dynamic video prior to OS.

2. No UEFI shell or Serial Redirecting debug console as any user interaction or configuration change will negate Fast Boot times.
3. UEFI only boot. A legacy boot may be necessary for older OS loader and operating systems, but this will inevitably delay the boot times as well as open the system to potential root kit attacks.
4. Setup Menu or other user entry (hot keys) during boot is not required. If it is to be entered, then, when entered, boot speed is not a key requirement.
5. When referring to sub-two-second timing the start and finish lines are described in the following manner:
   - The Start Line is when the processor comes out of reset and starts to fetch code from the SPI. While the starting line can be from the power button, depending on the scope of the parameters, the BIOS is not responsible for the approximately +300ms of power sequence time between the button until the CPU comes out of reset.
   - The Finish Line is when the UEFI BIOS calls LoadImage() for the OS loader image. On loading of the image, the system enters a handoff phase where the OS loader is responsible much more so than the BIOS.

Intel Fast Boot Timing Results

How effective is it? Based on experiments with a variety of systems from 2010 through 2012, system boot times were decreased from:
- seconds (full boot)
- As low as 1 second (Fast Boot) in some cases
- Typically, 2 seconds for a Fast Boot is achievable for PCs, imagine what a true embedded system can do?

Summary

This chapter introduced a very powerful Fast Boot mechanism that can be applied to UEFI solutions. While this mechanism provides dynamic and reliable time savings over a monotonic long, slow boot, other optimizations must still be performed for optimum results. As we have seen in other chapters, hardware selection, OS loader optimizations, and OS interface come into play. Due diligence of the development and design teams is vital to a successful Fast Boot user experience.

Developers should read Chapter 12, and then reread Chapters 10, 11, and 12. Then ask yourself and others the right questions, including: "What will it take to do this?"

Chapter 12
Collaborative Roles in Quick Boot

Every sin is the result of a collaboration.

—Lucius Annaeus Seneca

Collaboration between hardware, firmware, and software is vital to achieve a fast boot experience on the system. If the hardware chosen is incapable of achieving a sub-second initialization time, or if the software is not optimized to take advantage of a Fast Boot time, then the investment spent in firmware optimization with either custom activity or implementing a systematic Fast Boot architecture is wasted. Below are several examples of ways and techniques that can improve the boot times through picking the right device, optimizing the way that device is initialized, or doing the minimum for a future driver to take full advantage of a particular subsystem through loading it's driver.

Power Hardware Role

Before the first instruction set, hundreds of milliseconds have elapsed.

Power Sequencing

If measuring time from the power button, then the motherboard hardware power sequencing can provide a source of delay. If simplified power plans merge the Manageability Engine's power plane with other devices, then an additional 70 ms may be required.

Power Supply Specification

If you're using PCI or PCIe add-in cards on a desktop system, then the PC AT power supply (silver box) will have an additional 100 ms delay for the PCI add-in card onboard firmware to execute. If you're using a system with an embedded controller (mobile client or an all-in-one desktop), then there can be an additional power button debounce in embedded controller firmware that can be as much as 100 ms.

Flash Subsystem

The system should use the highest speed SPI flash components supported by the chipset.

DOI 10.1515/9781501506819-012

High Speed SPI Bus for Flash

When selecting an SPI component, a slower 33 MHz clock for a SPI chip can slow the system boot time by 50 percent as compared with a 50 MHz SPI component. Single-byte reads versus multiple-byte reads can also affect performance. Designers should select at least a 50 MHz component. Intel series 6 and 7 chipsets support 50 MHz DOFR (Dual Output Fast Read). There are also components that will support Quad Fast Read. As the SPI interface is normally a bottleneck on boot speed, this small change can mean a lot to overall performance, and it is a relatively small difference on the bill of material.

Flash Component Accesses

Besides configuring for faster read access and prefetch enabling, further optimizations can be done to reduce its accesses. For example: BIOS option setup data could be a few kilobytes in size and, each time a setup option is referenced, it could cost about 1 ms for 33 MHz SPI, and there could be several references. Optimization can also be done by reinstalling the read-only variable PPI with a new version, which has a copy of the setup data in CAR/ memory and thus the setup data is read only once from the SPI. It could also be cached in memory for S3 needs to prevent unnecessary SPI access during S3 resume.

SPI Prefetch and Buffer

It is possible to enable the buffers on the components to prefetch data from the flash device. If the chipset is capable, set up the SPI Prefetch as early as the SEC phase. It is recommended to do performance profiling to compare prefetch-enabled boot time of each of the individual UEFI modules to determine potential impact. The time when firmware volumes are shadowed can be particularly interesting to examine.

SPI Flash Reads and Writes

BIOS can minimize the number for flash writes by combining several writes into one. Any content in SPI flash should be read at most once during each boot and then stored in memory/variable for future reference. Refer to PCH BIOS Writer's Guide for the optimal SPI prefetch setting. The PCH prefetching algorithm is optimized for serial access in the hardware; however, if the firmware is not laid out in a sequential nature, the prefetch feature may need to be turned off if the read addresses are random (see also "EDK II Performance Optimization Guide – Section 8.3").

SPI flash access latency can be greatly improved with hardware and firmware co-design. Table 12.1 presents some guidelines that, when followed, can provide improvements of several seconds off a boot.

Table 12.1: Improving SPI Flash Access Latency with Hardware and Firmware Co-Design

Chipset Hardware (SPI)	Board Hardware	Chipset Firmware	System Firmware (BIOS)
Fast read mode (multiple data cycles per control cycle)		Soft-strap setting of SPI mode	Maximize SPI read in sequential block
Quad data pin support (4 bit per clock) for read	4 data lanes routing and signal integrity		Minimize single lane write (write combine)
Maximum clock rate at 50 MHz (from default of 25 MHz)	50 MHz signal integrity	SPI usage collision avoidance with BIOS	SPI usage collision avoidance with BIOS
Software-controllable prefetch mode			Dynamic mode setting depending on usage

Slow Interface and Device Access

Interface and device accesses can be time consuming, either due to the nature of the interfaces and/or devices, or the necessity of issuing multiple accesses to the particular controller, bus, and device.

DMI Optimizations

If the PCH and CPU are both capable of flexible interface timings, then faster DMI settings minimize I/O latency to PCH and onboard devices. The BIOS should be using the highest DMI link speed, as the DMI default link speed may not be optimal. The BIOS should enable Gen2 (or highest) DMI link speed as early as possible (in the SEC phase), if this does not conflict with hardware design constraints. The reason for this quirk is predictable survivability: the default value for DMI link speed is 2.5 GT/s (Gen 1). A faster DMI link helps in I/O configuration speed by 6 to 14 percent. Thus, it should be trained to 5 GT/s (Gen 2 speed), at an early SEC phase. There may be reasons why the link should not run at top speeds all the time. If the BIOS option controls the DMI link speed, when the option may only be read later in the boot, and down speed training.

Processor Optimizations

The following section describes processor optimizations.

CPU Turbo Enabling

Starting on Sandy Bridge CPUs, which launched in 2010, the CPU frequency at reset is limited to the lowest frequency supported by the processor. To enable CPU performance state (P-state) transitioning, a list of registers must be configured in the correct order. For the Intel Fast Boot, the following is expected:
1. Every Full Boot shall save the necessary register setting in UEFI Variables protocol, as nonvolatile content.
2. On Fast Boot, the necessary registers needed for enabling P-state will be restored as soon as possible. By the time that DXE phase is entered, the boot processor shall be in P0 with turbo enabled (if applicable).

Streamline CPU Reset and Initial CPU Microcode Update

Precise time budgeting has been done for the following sequence of events— from platform reset to initial BIOS code fetch at the reset vector (memory address). The key steps within this sequence are:
1. CPU timestamp counter zeroed and counting started at maximum nonturbo frequency.
2. DMI initialization completed.
3. Soft strap and dynamic fusing of CPU completed.
4. CPU patch microcode update read from SPI flash (only once).
5. All logical processors (APs) within the CPU package patch-updated (using the cached copy of the CPU patchMU).
6. BSP (bootstrap processor) starts fetching the BIOS at reset vector for execution.

Efficient APs Initialization

In addition to patch-updating, the BIOS needs to replicate memory range and other CPU settings for all APs (application processors) in a multicore, multithreaded CPU. The best optimized algorithm may be CPU specific but, in general, the following guidelines apply:
1. Parallelize microcode updating, MTRR, and other operations in logical core.
2. Minimize synchronization overhead using the best method for the particular CPU microarchitecture.

3. Execution from memory and not XIP from SPI.

Caching Code and Data

All BIOS code must be executed in cache-enabled state. The data (stack) must be in cache. These apply to all phases of the BIOS, regardless of memory availability. Unless an intentional cache flush operation is done (for security or other reasons), second access to the same SPI address should be hitting the CPU cache (see also "EDK II Performance Optimization Guide – Section 8.2," but included here for completeness).

Main Memory Subsystem

The following section describes the main memory subsystem.

Memory Configuration Complexity

When looking at memory configuration, the higher frequency memory will provide faster boots. Like the processor, the simpler the physical makeup of the memory, the faster the boot will be. Fewer banks of memory will boot faster than greater numbers of memory. If the memory's overall size is smaller, then the runtime performance will be limited. Balance the smaller number of banks with high bit technology memory to allow for a small but agile memory footprint.

Fast and Safe Memory Initialization

Since 2010, with the Intel® Core™ series CPU, fast memory initialization flow has been available for typical boot. To accomplish this, for the first boot with a new memory stick and/or a new processor, there is an involved and intensive (time-consuming) training algorithm executed to tune the DDR3 parameters. If the same CPU and DIMM combination are booted subsequently, major portions of the memory training can be bypassed.

In fast memory initialization, the MRC is expected to support three primary flows:
1. *Full (slow) Memory Initialization.* Create memory timing point when CPU and memory are new and never seen before.
2. *Fast Memory Initialization.* If CPU and DIMM have not changed since previous the boot, this flow is used to restore previous settings.
3. *Warm Reset.* Power was not removed from DIMM. This flow is used during platform reset and S3 resume.

The three flows can be used in conjunction with the Fast Boot states; however, they may operate independently of the main Fast Boot UEFI flag setting.

Hardware-Based Memory Clearing

On some SKUs of memory controllers offered by Intel, the hardware can be set to zero memory for security or ECC requirements. This is not part of the two-second BIOS boot time budgeting. Traditionally, a complete software- based memory overwrite is a very time-consuming process, adding seconds to every boot.

Efficient Memory Operations Instruction Usage

Starting on the Sandy Bridge generation CPU, new CPU instructions have been added to the speed up string operation. For memory operations, such as clearing large buffers, using optimized instructions helps. For more information, please see EDK II Performance Optimization Guide – Section 8.5.

SMBus Optimizations (Which Applies to Memory Init)

The PCH SMBus controller has one data/address lane and clock at 100 KHz. There are three ways to read data:
- SMBus Byte Read: A single SMBUS byte read makeup is 39 bits long, and thus at minimum one SMBUS byte read would take 0.39 ms.
- SMBus Word Read: A SMBus word read is 48 bits, hence 0.48/2 bytes or 0.24 ms/byte. Word reads are 40 percent more efficient than byte reads, but the bytes we need to read are not always sequential in nature on full boots.
- I2C Read: Where I2C is an alternate mode of operation supported by the PCH SMBus controller.

With the MRC code today on fast boots, we do not read all the SPD bytes all the time; we read only the serial number of the DIMMs, unless the DIMMs change. The serial number can be performed with sequential reads. Experiments prove that using the I2C read saves a few milliseconds, which count overall.

Minimize BIOS Shadowing Size, Dual DXE Paths for Fast Path versus Full Boot

UEFI BIOS is packaged into multiple firmware volumes. The Fast Boot is enhanced when there are several DXE firmware volumes instead of one monolithic one. That means the DXE phase of the BIOS should be split into two or more DXE firmware volumes; for example, a fast one and a slow one (a full one). The fast-boot-capable DXE firmware volume contains the minimum subset of module needed for IFB typical boot, and the other DXE firmware volume contains the rest of the module needed for full boot.

This requirement affects only the firmware volumes that have to be decompressed from SPI flash into memory before execution. To optimize decompression speed, the BIOS needs to avoid decompressing unnecessary modules that will not be executed.

This may be done at the DXE driver boundary; however, there is no restriction preventing module owners from creating a smaller fast boot module and a separate full boot module for the two different volumes.

PCIe Port Disable Algorithm

There are Mini PCIe enumeration needs for detections that ultimately lead to function-disable of the particular PCIe port. These include PCIe port without card detected, and NAND over PCIe initialization flow. All these must be combined and get done in a single Mini PCie enumeration.

Manageability Engine

The Manageability Engine (ME) is a security processor subsystem and offload engine inside the PCH. There are two SKUs of the firmware that runs on the device: 1.5 MB and 5.0 MB SKUs. The 5.0 MB SKU is associated with advanced security features, such as Intel® Active Management Technology. The 5.0 MB firmware requires a setup option ROM called the Manageability Engine BIOS Extension (MEBx), which up until 2011 ran on every boot, which took time. There are also ME/BIOS interactions during boot, regardless of the firmware SKUs.

Eliminating MEBx

Starting with 2012 platform controller hubs, the Intel PCH 5.0 MB eliminates the need to execute MEBx on Fast Boots. Instead of running MEBx on every boot, MEBx is run only as needed within the framework on a typical boot per the UEFI flag.

Reducing Manageability Engine and BIOS Interactions

In addition to the 2012 MEBx optimization, starting in 2012 platforms, during normal boot there are only two architecturally defined sync-points between ME and BIOS remaining:

1. *Device Initialization Done (DID)*. This happens as soon as memory is available for ME use following MRC initialization. The time is estimated to be between 50 ms and 120 ms after TSC starts, depending on the MRC and CPU requirements.
2. *End of POST (EOP)*. This happens before a BIOS process boot list (at the end of DXE phase). It is estimated to be 700 ms after TSC starts.

All other ME-BIOS communication will happen asynchronously outside of these two sync-points (that is, no waiting for the other execution engine). The MEBx (ME BIOS extension) module is not expected to be called in a typical BIOS boot. If it is needed, it can be called via the exception handling methodology defined in Intel Fast Boot framework.

Hardware Asset Reporting for Intel® Active Management Technology (Intel AMT)

Within the Fast Boot framework, SMBIOS, PCI Asset, and ASF tables are always updated and passed to the ME Intel AMT firmware (5MB in size) regardless of boot mode.

For the media table, the BIOS will enumerate all storage controllers and attached devices during full boot and upon request by the Intel AMT firmware. Upon detecting an Intel AMT firmware request, BIOS will enumerate all media (except USB) devices to generate and pass the media table. The heuristic on how frequent Intel AMT will request this is the responsibility of the Intel AMT design.

USB Flash Drive Provisioning for Intel® AMT

Instead of supporting USB provisioning for Intel AMT in a typical fast boot, a BIOS following the Fast Boot framework will support USB flash drive provisioning only in full boot mode. By definition, any type 2 or type 3 exceptions will cause the BIOS to fall back into full boot mode. For example, one mechanism is when a user interrupts the boot processing by a hot key, stalling the boot; an exception will be triggered. If BDS phase is in full boot mode, a USB stick provisioning of Intel AMT will need to function as expected.

Graphics Subsystem

The following section describes the graphics subsystem.

Graphics Device Selection

When looking at video and graphics devices, the panel timings were mentioned above. The controller timing and speed are also important to boot speeds—the faster the better. The timing numbers can be modified if required to help to achieve this in a BMP utility on the UEFI GOP driver. A UEFI Graphics Output Protocol driver will provide faster boot speeds than a legacy video BIOS. Finally, a single graphics solution will be faster to boot than a multiple display/controller configuration.

Graphics Output Protocol (GOP) Support for CSM-Free Operating Systems

For operating systems that support a CSM-free boot, the GOP driver will be loaded by BIOS instead of CSM legacy video option ROM. This eliminates the time spent on creating legacy VGA mode display services (INT 10). Benefits can be seen in Figure 12.1 in microseconds based on different ports/monitor selection.

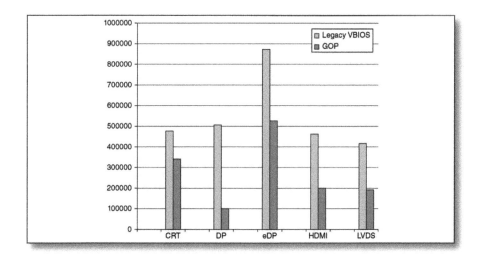

Figure 12.1: Benefits of Graphics Output Protocol Support

Panel Specification

If you are using an Embedded DisplayPort† (eDP) panel, using the panel startup time per the industry specification, then 250 ms is required during the boot to just reset power on the panel. This is a ridiculously long time to wait for hardware, as an entire PC motherboard takes about that time to come up through power sequencing. If the timing is adjusted to what the hardware actually requires to cycle power, then eDP may prove adequate.

Start Panel Power Early

Like the disk drives, the panel now must be started early to parallelize the delays in the hardware during boot. A PEI module to power up the eDP panel is needed if the target display panel has a noticeable delay in the power-up sequence. For example, if a panel requires 300 ms to power up, a PEI module to enable (power up) the eDP port needs to be executed at least 300 ms before the video module is reached in BDS phase of BIOS.

Storage Subsystems

The following section describes storage subsystems.

Spinning Media

For spinning media storage devices, the spin-up time for a hard drive is 2seconds minimum. Even if the BIOS starts the initialization a short time after it gets control of the system, the drive may not be ready to provide an OS.

Utilizing Nonblocking Storage I/O

The Intel PCH integrated SATA controller supports Nonblocking Command Queuing (NCQ) in native AHCI mode operation. Unless required by the target operating system, the BIOS should access the storage subsystem in the most efficient way possible. For example: in all Windows operating systems since Windows XP, AHCI mode should be the default SATA storage mode.

Early SATA COMRESETs: Drive Spin-Up

Generally, in client platforms, the disk feature of *power up in standby* (PUIS) is disabled. The hard disk would automatically spin up once it receives a COMRESET, which is sent when the BIOS enables the related SATA port. Spinning up the hard drive as early as possible at the PEI phase is required by enabling ports right after setting the SATA DFT.

While SATA SSD NAND drives do not literally spin up, the wear-leveling algorithms and databases required to track the bits take hundreds of milliseconds before data is ready to be fetched (including identifying drive data). While this can be mitigated with SSD firmware enhancements or controller augmentation to store such data, numbers in the range of 800 ms are probable with the latest SATA3 SSDs at the time of this writing.

CSM-Free Intel® Raid Storage Technology (Intel RST) UEFI Driver

The Intel RST UEFI driver is required to allow for SSD caching of a slower hard drive. The SSD performance far outweighs the HDD in both read/write and spin-up readiness. This newly optimized UEFI driver is needed to support the CSM-free Class Two and Class Three UEFI boot mechanism. Elimination of CSM is the primary time saving; however, the optimizations made to the new UEFI driver over the legacy Intel RST option ROM are dramatic. As with the MEBx UEFI driver, the Intel RST driver will follow the recommendation of the UEFI flag for Fast Boot. One of the fallback conditions for Fast Boot must also be that for any drive configuration change, the BIOS must inform the UEFI option ROMs via the UEFI boot mode flag.

In SDR0 (Single Disk RAID 0) Intel RST caching mode, the Intel RST driver does not wait for HDD to spin up. It needs to allow data access (read) to OS boot loader as soon as cached data in SSD are available.

The fastest HDD (at the writing of this chapter) takes about 1.4 to 3 seconds from power-up to data availability. That is far slower than the 800 ms power- up to data availability on Intel SSD (X25M).

Minimizing USB Latency

Intel integrated USB host controller and integrated hubs have much smaller latencies than the generic host controller and hub settings spelled out in the USB specifications. The BIOS can be optimized for the integrated components (as they are always present in the platform), by replacing the default USB specification timing with Intel PCH USB timing, as published in the PCH USB BIOS writer's guide.

For example, the minimum time needed to enumerate all the USB ports on PCH (as if they are empty) is approximately 450 ms. Using Intel PCH silicon-specific timing guideline can cut that down by more than half.

Power Management

The following section describes power management.

Minimizing Active State Power Management Impact

On several buses in the platform, there is a recommendation for active state power management (ASPM). The ASPM setting is important in extending battery life during runtime; however, there is nonzero latency in ASPM state transition. The impact can be seen in Table 12.2 for both boot and resume times.

Intel DMI bus supports a PCI ASPM lower link power scheme. To eliminate potential side effects, enabling of DMI ASPM should be done at the last possible moment in the BIOS initialization flow. Actually, it can be made *after* the POST is completed.

To delay the setting of the DMI ASPM link states (L0s/L1) to the last possible moment in the boot, there are three possible options:
1. At ExitBootServices()
2. In ACPI
3. One-shot SMI timer, heuristically determined by experiment, say 8 seconds after ExitBootServices(), to cover the OS booting period

Option 1 is to be selected if we are interested only in BIOS boot time improvement. Option 2 and 3 could be explored for OS boot time improvement. If we aim to improve the OS load time as well, we could use the SMI timer for the S4/S5 path, and use the ACPI method _BFS to set the DMI ASPM for the S3 path, assuming an ACPI compliant OS.

Table 12.2: Active State Power Management Impact

Responsiveness Phase from Microsoft's VTS tool on an Intel Sandy Bridge CRB Board/BIOS	Baseline ASPM - ON	ASPM - OFF
BIOS Post (seconds)	8.89	8.87
Boot to Desktop (seconds)	5.39	5.14
Boot Complete (seconds)	7.31	6.97
Resume (seconds)	0.6	0.57

Security

Security at a high level is often a tradeoff versus boot speeds and responsiveness. Trusted Platform Modules and measured boots will add noticeable time to a boot flow. Single-threaded Boot ROMs, HW Root of Trust and subsequent daisy chaining of authentication takes a very long time if not architected for speed (and security). You need to look at the platform requirements carefully and balance security and responsiveness. There are some things we can do to mitigate security impact to platform boot times.

Intel® Trusted Execution Technology (Intel TXT)

Intel Trusted Execution Technology included additional BIOS binary modules that execute to assist in authentication of subsequent code execution and provide a secure environment for that activity. It takes time to execute these modules, and it takes a small amount of time to do authentication prior to executing code in these environments. Other authentication schemes have similar setup and execution penalties.

TPM Present Detect and Early Start

Trusted platform modules hash and save results as variables during a secure or measured boot. The delay associated with a TPM can be between 300 ms to upwards of 1 second, depending on the TPM vendor, the TPM firmware revision, and the size of the BIOS firmware volumes being hashed. There are several techniques that can save time when using a TPM:
1. Use the fastest SPI flash part available.
2. Use the fastest TPM within the budget.
3. Where possible, execute longer latency TPM commands in parallel with other BIOS code. TPM_Startup and TPM_ContSelfTest commands are usually the slowest commands. This will allow for continued BIOS execution and access to the TPM while the diagnostics are completed. Specifically:
   – Finish measurement of last FV in SEC/PEI before executing TPM_ContSelfTest in PEI.
   – Delay checking for TPM_ContSelfTest until the next TPM command in DXE, and delay the next TPM command if possible. Interrupting SelfTest in some cases causes additional delay.
4. Measure only what is needed. Do not measure free space or boot block if it cannot be modified.
5. If TPM supports legacy, turn off I/O port 0x4E/0x4F.

6. Depending on the BIOS settings and configuration algorithm optimization, there could be several access attempts to 0xfed40000 to detect whether TPM existed on the platform, and each access could cost about 7 ms. Adding an HOB, a UEFI hand off block, to save the data after the very first access to the 0xfed40000 could be used to indicate whether TPM is present on the board or not. The rest of the components should then reference to this HOB instead of checking for the presence of the TPM on system. Read the same information across IO just one time...

7. Copying data into memory before hashing will save time over hashing-in-place.

Operating System Interactions

The following section describes operating system interactions.

Compatibility Segment Module and Legacy Option ROMs

In a UEFI BIOS, a Class 3 UEFI solution will normally be more than 100 ms faster than a legacy OS-supported solution; that is, the CSM time to execute (without additional delay due to legacy option ROMs). Again, this is a tradeoff between OS compatibility support with older operating systems and boot speeds. Setup menu options can disable the CSM if it is not required.

OS Loader

If the OS is being examined, then the OS loader times also can be improved by looking at the OS image size. Limiting the OS requirements for pre-OS keyboard can speed up boot by tens to hundreds of milliseconds. Loading the user interface sooner in the boot flow of the kernel will make a noticeable difference to the end user. Device driver load and start times and usage of services can be streamlined to positively affect boot performance.

During runtime, the UEFI capabilities are very limited and not all the UEFI drivers that were used to boot the platform are available for the OS to call. Once Exit-BootServices() is called by the OS loader and it assumes control of the platform, much information is lost.

The OS loader can collect quite a bit of data about the platform above and beyond the typical ACPI table standard set of information accessing the BIOS through UEFI function calls. Before exiting boot services, the OS loader can both get and give data directly to the BIOS.

An example of the OS level of interactions is setting up for the graphics resolution of the splash screen such that it will match the OS via a hint during OS loading.

Legacy OS Interface

Windows 7 and other legacy operating systems that require a CSM in the BIOS to provide Int 10h (and other legacy software interrupts) execute hundreds of milliseconds to several seconds slower due to the nature of their boot flow. Initialization of each and every legacy option ROM serially is just one reason why it may be many seconds slower than UEFI boot flows. If the OS was not optimized for boot during the kernel and driver loading, then any reasonable amount of BIOS improvement is going to be lost anyway (even a zero-second boot is too long if the OS takes more than ten seconds to boot).

Reducing Replication of Enumeration Between Firmware and OS

The OS often repeats enumeration of buses in the post-boot space that the BIOS firmware has performed in the pre-boot. Ideally this would be a source of timing savings. However, upon further inspection, there are multiple reasons for this replication, including but not limited to the following:
1. Firmware may not have done a complete job of enumerating the entire enumerable subsystem, expecting software to repeat the enumeration when the OS level drivers load. This may be due to the BIOS not requiring use of that portion of the system in the pre-boot space.
2. Virtualization: the firmware can perform a full enumeration of a bus, then expose a different set or a subset of hardware to the operating system through virtualization technology.
3. The firmware may not have done an accurate job.
4. The initial enumeration may not work well with the kernel or device driver stack designed by the operating system developers.

At the end of the day, the BIOS must enumerate the portions of the design only just enough to boot the operating system. Assuming the operating system has the proper enumeration support for the system hardware, the enumeration will be repeated and in a more complete manner than in the BIOS. Standard enumerable bus architecture allows for this replication and the system may require it. Examples include PCI and USB enumeration. The whole USB network under a port may not need to be enumerated five-plus hubs deep. The BIOS really needs to initialize all the hardware that cannot be enumerated through industry standards (such as i2C). The coordination can be made tighter in an embedded design where an RTOS and a custom firmware have minimum overlap in enumeration.

Other Factors Affecting Boot Speed

Certain devices or configurations are known to extend the boot times, including but not limited to the following items.

No Duplication in Hardware Enumeration within UEFI

While replication of enumeration maybe required between BIOS and OS, it is not required within the UEFI domain itself. If necessary, the BIOS can pass information between modules via UEFI variables or HOBs. For example, we can use an HOB to pass CPUI BIST information from SEC to PEI, and memory information from MRC to the SMBIOS module. It is recommended that we not access the same hardware I/O twice unless the data is expected to change.

Minimize Occurrences of Hardware Resets

Most hardware have a long power reset sequence. Question whether a hardware reset is necessary, or if it can be handled in software without reinitializing hardware. It is possible that CPU initialization, memory initialization, or ME initialization may all require an extra system or CPU reset, which will add time, as the boot is partly replicated for that given boot. Fast Boot eliminates most possibilities of system resets.

Intel Architecture Coding Efficiency

Intel architecture performance can be sensitive to coding arrangement (just like any other computer architecture). Follow coding optimization guide at the Intel Software portal is the best-known method. At a minimum, code and data structure alignments should be optimized as described in the optimization guide. (See also EDK II Performance Optimization Guide – Section 8.10.)

Network Boot Feature

A network boot (booting to an OS image over LAN) takes several seconds to negotiate with the DHCP server for an IP address. Fast Boot is not really an option.

Value-Add, But Complex Features

Complexity and robust feature sets will likely result in a flexible, but slower boot performance than a simple configuration. RAID is a feature that adds a lot of value, but
can decrease the speed of the boot due to an option ROM execution requirement. Here
UEFI drivers can help with some of the boot speeds, but cannot completely compensate for the tradeoffs.

Tools and the User Effect

Tools being used to measure speed can produce an observer effect if not properly implemented. Using file I/O, or serial output, or post codes, or other slow recording
mechanisms can add to a boot flow. And the more precise the data collection is, the
greater the effect. Methods can vary broadly per tool, but the best tools will use
memory to store the data during the boot flow and then read it off the platform afterwards. For a complete picture of the boot flow (into the OS level), the best tools are
from the OS vendor that has incorporated the Firmware Performance Data Table
(FPDT), where the BIOS reports the data into a memory location inside the ACPI tables. Runtime tools can read the data after the fact.

Human Developer's Resistance to Change

As Confucius said, "Only the wisest and stupidest of men never change." The developer's attitudes toward the challenge of boot speeds can have a huge impact on the
results. "It's only a few milliseconds" can add up quickly. "S3 is fast enough" will
leave many milliwatts and milliseconds on the table. "It's a systemic problem, what
can I do?" will leave others to solve the problem if they choose to. "Even if the BIOS
disappeared entirely, the OS is still too slow," but that cannot be said any more.

Intel architecture platforms have not all been optimized with this technology to
date. Customers need to work with their independent BIOS vendors to see if the capability has been included with their BIOS release to achieve Fast Boot optimization.

Motherboards can be developed to encompass the right sequencing with the right
parts. Tradeoffs can be worked through for the right reasons. Tools can be obtained
and code modules instrumented properly. And with the right approach, developers
can streamline the entire boot path into something truly responsive.

Summary

When combined with a systematic Fast Boot framework and policy decision around major subsystems, hardware selection and initialization nuances complete the picture of a quick boot solution.

The list discussed is far from complete, focusing on today's Intel® Core™ based platforms. Similar activities are feasible on any platform with due diligence and time.

Chapter 13
Legal Decisions

I go to jail one time for no driver license.

—Bob Marley

When creating new works of firmware, it is important to consider both the incoming license terms (if not starting from scratch), and the distribution license terms and conditions. Examples include proprietary BSD and GPL. If creating a derivative work, it is important to consider all of this before starting the work so that time isn't wasted developing something that someone else may claim later to be his or her private intellectual property (IP) or public IP based on association with the original license of the code used. As the work progresses, there cannot be ambiguity on the path or strategy used; code hygiene and discipline is key.

Often it is difficult for new software to be considered an island, and when it is not original, it is important to consider how and if the new software is statically or dynamically linked to older code in the final design. Beyond the technical challenge of combining old and new code, legally it can be very confusing. Developers are highly encouraged to get professional legal assistance from a quality source that has experience in software and patents.

Of course, if someone is in the business for a long time and the organization or team is steeped in either proprietary or general public license (GPL) ideology, then it is likely that team members will already know the rules; or at least what the rules were. New team members should be walked through the company norms. DO NOT ASSUME that the new smart people (and not so new smart people) who you hired will just know.

Also, as the law is somewhat fluid in nature, even if you are an old hand, it is very important to get *fresh* advice from a professional, because the terms can be nuanced. The nuances change from year to year without a great deal of advertisement to the broader community. The company may change their policies, etc. The following is an example of some of the basics, at the writing of this book. This is not a ruling by a judge, and this was not written by a lawyer.

Proprietary License

Under a proprietary license, the distribution and reusability rules are defined by the originators, but developers have to be very careful in how they define things. Terms can vary broadly. The people you license from will also be potentially interested in your licensing terms, and it may take each party's lawyers many months to walk

DOI 10.1515/9781501506819-013

through everything and agree, should the need arise. This puts any development performed during the negotiation timeframe at risk of being unusable.

Many name-brand software packages come with forms of a proprietary license. While brand-name companies make money directly or indirectly with proprietary licenses, some forms of the proprietary license are in fact freeware (no-cost).

Berkeley Software Distribution (BSD) License

Under a BSD License, there are three versions to consider with varying degrees of compatibility between proprietary and GPL and other BSD licensed software. There have been multiple versions of the BSD license: four-clause, three-clause, and two-clause. The full license texts can be found online, but below are some key difference.

Key Four Clauses to the Original License

The following are the four key clauses of the original license:
1. Redistributions of source code must retain the above copyright notice, this list of conditions and the following disclaimer.
2. Redistributions in binary form must reproduce the above copyright notice, this list of conditions and the following disclaimer in the documentation and/or other materials provided with the distribution.
3. All advertising materials mentioning features or use of this software must display the following acknowledgement: This product includes software developed by the <organization>.
4. Neither the name of the <organization> nor the names of its contributors may be used to endorse or promote products derived from this software without specific prior written permission.

The four-clause BSD license was not GPL-compatible, and the mandatory product message advertising the BSD developers was not wanted by product developers downstream.

Three-Clause BSD

The newer BSD License (three clauses) is compatible with GPL. The third clause appears below for comparison to the fourth clause above.

* Neither the name of the <organization> nor the names of its contributors may be used to endorse or promote products derived from this software without specific prior written permission.

In addition to the three-clause version, there is also a simplified BSD license (two clauses) that is similar in that it is compatible with GPL where the third clause above was considered optional. The two clauses are as follows:
1. Redistributions of source code must retain the above copyright notice, this list of conditions and the following disclaimer.
2. Redistributions in binary form must reproduce the above copyright notice, this list of conditions and the following disclaimer in the documentation and/or other materials provided with the distribution.

One key benefit of the BSD license is that companies that create their own proprietary software can take BSD-licensed code to start with, create derivative works, or augment their existing code. Companies that create their own firmware or software regularly take the BSD drivers that are created by silicon vendors and weave their goodness into these "free" offerings. Intel® BLDK also uses a form of this license for the reused Tiano-based source code that it releases.

General Public License (GPL)

With GPL, software is considered free speech. It is free to use ... but it has hooks in that you have to pass on that freedom of any derivative work or changes. The different versions of GPL spell out how free and how evasive that freedom level is on the rest of the system. For details, please see: http://www.gnu.org/licenses/gpl.html.

One of the chief complaints about the GPL third version is the "viral" like nature of the code base. If someone takes GPLv3 code and reuses it, the code base that it was used on may be considered to be GPLv3 as well, depending on one's interpretation. For that reason, some prefer GPLv2.

Lesser GPL (LGPL)

The main difference between lesser GPL and GPLv3 is the ability to link to LGPL libraries by proprietary code bases without the "spider plant" effect of GPLv3 code. In nature, a spider plant is very easy to propagate from one place to another with just a small piece being transplanted. There are multiple versions of LPGL, which for the sake of time, I leave to the reader to research online.

Separating and Segregating Code

Mixing code covered by different legal agreements presents a challenge.

For example, linking between the GPL code and non-GPL code has been hotly contested. The concepts of *dynamically linked* versus *statically linked* versus *not linked* and the licensing hooks that then tie linked code to GPL are not clear at times, and this is a matter for the courts. Be extremely careful if you are shipping products based on GPL code, thinking through what you can/should/will do with that code and its availability to others after that ship date. Of course, it may be possible to never ship the software derived from GPL and to only use that code internally; then you would not have to reissue the code changes or make it available afterwards. Various manufacturers and their legal representatives have a varied view of GPL needs. Consult your lawyer.

It can be legally questionable to link GPL code to proprietary code, depending on the version of GPL and the terms of the proprietary code. This is exacerbated by terms in GPL v3, which has been referred to as "viral." While that may or may not be friendly, GPL v3 does present challenges in that the attachment of GPL v3 code to a proprietary source code base puts the proprietary nature of the other agreement in question.

If the code is not linked dynamically or statically at build time, but executed through standalone interfaces as part of an operating system or shell or other industry standard, then clearly defined partitions between code entities can be maintained. One could have a proprietary first-stage boot loader, a GPL OS loader, and a BSD OS; and combinations of these.

Unlike the GPL-to-proprietary-code combination, it is much more plausible to link BSD code to proprietary code in that the BSD license allows for derivative works free of entanglements, and proprietary license would tend to govern the end solution.

While BSD seems like it would be a neutral option, linking BSD code to GPL code will bind the developer to hand back the GPL code if it ships. And if it is GPL v3, then the BSD code could be forced to act as if it were governed by the GPL.

Conclusion

Avoid cross-contamination of your products. From a legal point of view, it is important not to link BSD code (like that in Intel BLDK or Tiano), or any proprietary code (like a commercial BIOS) to GPL code (like Linux). It may help to keep GPL code firewalled and separated as much as possible, either physically or logically, from other code whose license types are such that one entity does not cross-pollinate with the other. Execution during one phase should know nothing about the next phase except where to jump to once that black box code is loaded. In this manner, there is no linking performed. It should be noted that some legal experts believe that linking is irrelevant and it is the actual intent that matters.

- Any non-GPL code would frown upon being linked at this point to any GPL v3 code.
- LGPL libraries, from reading through several references, appear to not have this linking problem that GPL code has.
- There are open-source tools to allow creation of a firmware image that concatenates the blocks into an FWH or SPI image such that it can be flashed or upgraded.

When looking at the debate between proprietary, BSD, and GPL licenses, it can be equated roughly to an in-depth political, ideological discussion. The rules can be drastically different. The viewpoints are as diverse as they would be between passionate and insightful people debating the merits and demerits of capitalism, socialism, and communism (respectively). And comparing the three, the analogy can play out along these lines. But when going from the theoretical to the implementation, the differences can make or break your solution.

Appendix A
Generating Serial Presence Detection Data for Down Memory Configurations

I have no data yet. It is a capital mistake to theorize before one has data. Insensibly one begins to twist facts to suit theories, instead of theories to suit facts.

—Sherlock Holmes in "A Scandal in Bohemia"

This appendix provides guidance on how to create the SPD data required for motherboard designs that have the DDR3 SDRAM chips soldered directly onto the motherboard. Modular DIMMs normally have an SPD EERPOM that contains this information, which is used by the BIOS to correctly configure the system during Memory Reference Code. Without this data, the system will not boot; or at best it will try to boot with slow settings.

Since memory-down designs do not include DIMMs, they do not have ready-made SPD data on an EEPROM for the BIOS to read, and the board designer must assist BIOS or firmware developers to create the data. The data can then be put into an onboard EEPROM off the SMBus (as a physical DIMM would have), or the data can be hard-coded into the BIOS or placed into a table (or tables) where the BIOS can access the data during memory initialization. There are tradeoffs between these methods:

Method	Pros	Cons
SPD EEPROM on motherboard	Single BIOS for any memory configuration	1. Cost of the EEPROM, 2. Need to program the SPD data during manufacturing 3. Minor delay during initialization to fetch data across slower SMBus (several ms)
Hard-coding inline in the memory code	1. No EEPROM cost. 2. No programming of SPD on the line 3. No added delay during initialization	1. BIOS has to change for every memory configuration 2. Complexity during manufacturing ensuring correct BIOS per memory configuration
Tables with optional hardware strap, point memory init. code to read from data file instead	1. No EEPROM 2. No programming on line. 3. No SMBus Read delays 4. BIOS can read strap to know which memory configuration exists 5. Possible to upgrade with binary modification with a rebuild	1. Takes up hardware strap 2. BIOS will change when new configurations are designed

DOI 10.1515/9781501506819-014

Hardcoding is not recommended for any solutions. Developers and designs should agree to include tables in the BIOS for various memory configuration (mimicking SPD data), or populate an actual SPD EEPROM on the board.

The following table shows the full list of the DDR3 SPD data that needs to be calculated for a memory-down solution. It assumes no SPD onboard. Each field can be calculated by analyzing the board's topology and/or by using the datasheet for the SDRAM components used on the board. A "Typical Value" with its associated definition is also provided.

Byte (Dec)	Byte (Hex)	Field Name	Typ. Value	Typical Value Definition
0	0×00	Number of Bytes	0×11	256 Bytes Total 128 Bytes Used
1	0×01	SPD Rev	0×10	Rev 1.0
2	0×02	Device Type	0×0B	DDR3 SDRAM
3	0×03	Module Type	0×03	SO-DIMM
4	0×04	SDRAM Density & Banks	0×03	8 Banks 2 Gb
5	0×05	SDRAM Rows & Columns	0×19	15 Rows 10 Columns
6	0×06	Nominal Voltage, V_{DD}	0×00	1.5V
7	0×07	Ranks & Device DQ Count	0×01	Rank = 1 Width = x8
8	0×08	Module Bus Width	0×0B	72 bits (ECC)
9	0×09	Fine Timebase Dividend/Divisor	0×52	2.5ps
10	0×0A	Medium Timebase Dividend	0×01	0.125ns
11	0×0B	Medium Timebase Divisor	0x08	0.125ns
12	0×0C	Cycle Time (T_{CK}-min)	0×0F	1.875ns
13	0×0D	Reserved	0×00	---
14	0×0E	CAS Latencies Supported (CL4-CL11)	0×1E	CL=5, 6, 7, 8
15	0×0F	CAS Latencies Supported (CL12-CL18)	0×00	CL=5, 6, 7, 8
16	0×10	CAS Latency Time (T_{AA}-min or T_{CL})	0×69	13.125ns
17	0×11	Write Recovery Time (T_{WR}-min)	0×78	15ns
18	0×12	RAS# to CAS# Delay (T_{RCD}-min)	0×69	13.125ns
19	0×13	Min. Row Active to Row Active Delay (T_{RRD}-min)	0×3C	7.5ns
20	0×14	Min. Row Precharge Delay (t_{RP}-min)	0×69	13.125ns
21	0×15	Upper Nibble of T_{RAS} & T_{RC}	0×11	---
22	0×16	Min. Active to Precharge Delay (T_{RAS}-min) LSB	0×2C	37.5ns
23	0×17	Min. Active to Active Refresh Delay (T_{RC}-min) LSB	0×95	50.625

Byte (Dec)	Byte (Hex)	Field Name	Typ. Value	Typical Value Definition
24	0×18	Min. Refresh Recovery Delay (T_{RFC}-min) LSB	0×00	---
25	0×19	Min. Refresh Recovery Delay (T_{RFC}-min) MSB	0×05	160ns
26	0×1A	Min. Write to Read Cmd Delay (T_{WTR}-min)	0×3C	7.5ns
27	0×1B	Min. Read to Precharge Cmd Delay (T_{RTP}-min)	0×3C	7.5ns
28	0×1C	T_{FAW} Upper Nibble	0×01	---
29	0×1D	Min. Four Activate Window Delay(T_{FAW}-min)	0×2C	37.5ns
30	0×1E	SDRAM Optional Features	0×83	RZQ/7, RZQ/6, and DLL-Off Mode Support
31	0×1F	SDRAM Thermal and Refresh Options	0×07	Extended Temp. Ranges & Auto Self Refresh (ASR)
32	0×20	Module Thermal Sensor	0×00	None
33	0×21	SDRAM Device Type	0×00	Normal DRAM
34 59	0×22- 0×3B	Reserved	0×00	---
60	0×3C	Unbuffered Module Nominal Height **	0×00	Height<15mm
61	0×3D	Unbuffered Module Max. Thickness **	0×00	Thickness<1mm
62	0×3E	Unbuffered Reference Raw Card Used **	0×00	RAW Card A, x64
63	0×3F	Unbuffered Address Mapping from Edge Connector to DRAM **	0×00	Standard
64 116	0×40- 0×74	Unbuffered RESERVED **	0×00	---
117	0×75	Module Manufacturer ID Code, LSB	0×80	Micron Technology
118	0×76	Module Manufacturer ID Code, LSB	0×2C	---

** Grayed out fields are different for Unbuffered and Registered DDR3 DRAM

Analyzing the Design's Memory Architecture

The first step in creating the SPD data is to carefully analyze the design's schematics to determine the overall memory architecture.

Calculating DIMM Equivalents

The used memory channels must be identified, and the number of "DIMM Equivalents" must be calculated by carefully noting which chip select pins on the DRAM controller are routed to the SDRAM chips.

Each "DIMM Equivalent" will require its own block of SPD data. The specific chip select pins, CS#[7:0] (the actual number of chip select pins can vary depending on the specific memory controller being used), have to be carefully analyzed to see which are being used by the SDRAM chips. It's possible for designs to support single-rank, dual-rank, and quad-rank DIMM equivalents.

As an example, Figure A.1 shows an abstract view of DIMMs located on a single memory channel. Since each DIMM has only two CS# pins routed to the connector, this design supports two dual-rank DIMMs. If all four chip select pins were routed to a single DIMM, then the design would support a single, quad-rank DIMM.

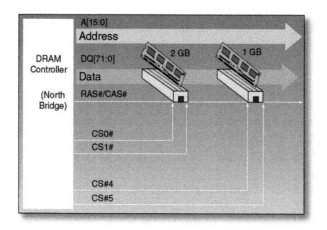

Figure A.1: Chip Select Pins for a Single Memory Channel

Memory-down designs don't use DIMMs; the SDRAM chips are soldered directly onto the motherboard. The chip select signals will be routed to the SDRAM chips in the same manner, however. In Figure A.2 below, on channel 0, only CS#[0] is connected to all eight SDRAM chips. Channel 0 is supporting only one single-rank DIMM equivalent. Channel 1 is also supporting a single- rank DIMM equivalent.

ECC Calculation

The data signals on the schematics must be analyzed to determine whether the down-on-board memory is implementing ECC or not. If the ECC data signals DDR_CB[7:0] (DDR "check bits," although different chipsets might use different nomenclature) are being used as data signals on one of the SDRAM chips, then the memory subsystem on the board is implementing ECC Support. Some of the SPD fields must be set to indicate that the DIMM supports ECC.

SDRAM Width Determination

The DRAM width can be determined by carefully analyzing the number of data signals, DDR_DQ[63:0], that are routed into each SDRAM chip. It will either be four, eight, sixteen, or thirty-two. This will indicate the DRAM width for the DRAM chip in this DIMM equivalent.

The DRAM width is part of SPD field 7, and often there are slight timing differences in the datasheet depending on the width of the specific DRAM being used.

SDRAM Chip Datasheet

The vendor and exact part number of the SDRAM chips used in the design is extracted from the schematics. The full datasheet must be obtained in order to calculate all of the needed SPD fields.

SDRAM Architecture Analysis Example

Figure A.2 shows a typical memory-down implementation. Sixteen SDRAM chips are split evenly across two of three available channels. All the SDRAM chips on a given channel are connected to a single chip select signal. Since each SDRAM chip is connected to eight data signals, this design consists of two single-rank DIMM equivalents using ×8 width MT41J256M8HX-187-EITF SDRAM devices. Since the ECC data lines are not being used (not shown, but they would have required the use of an additional ×8 SDRAM chip per channel), both DIMM equivalents are non-ECC.

Analyzing the schematics provides the SDRAM width and rank information (SPD field #7). All the other information required in the SPD data block will have to be extracted from the MT41J256M8HX-187-EITF datasheet. This process is described in the next section.

Calculating Specific SPD Data Based on SDRAM Datasheet

This section will go through each SPD field and explain how to extract the data for the field out of the SDRAM datasheet. This section will use the SDRAM configuration shown in Figure A.2, using the MT41J256M8HX-187-EITF datasheet. Note that each section number will correspond to the SPD field offset.

Each field will contain:
− The exact definition out of the JEDEC DDR3 specification.
− The appropriate section out of the MT41J256M8HX-187-EITF datasheet

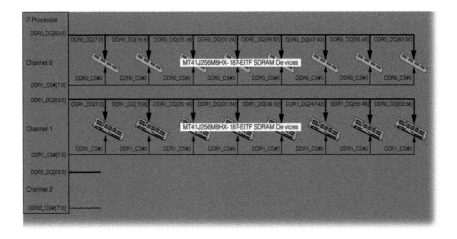

Figure A.2: Schematic Analysis Example

See the "References" section at the end of this appendix for links to the exact documents used.

SPD Field 0x00: Number of Bytes

SPD EEPROMs typically contain 256 bytes. Down-on-board memory designs should use 0x11 for this field.

Byte (Dec)	Byte (Hex)	Field Name	Typ. Value	Definition
0	0×00	Number of Bytes	0×11	256 Bytes Total 128 Bytes Used

Byte 0: Number of Bytes Used/Number of Bytes in SPD Device/CRC Coverage

The least significant nibble of this byte describes the total number of bytes used by the module manufacturer for the SPD data and any (optional) specific supplier information. The byte count includes the fields for all required and optional data. Bits 6–4 describe the total size of the serial memory used to hold the Serial Presence Detect data. Bit 7 indicates whether the unique module identifier (found in bytes 117–125) is covered by the CRC encoded on bytes 126 and 127.

Bit 7	Bits 6:4	Bits 3:0
CRC Coverage	SPD Bytes Total	SPD Bytes Used
0 = CRC covers bytes 0–125 1 = CRC covers bytes 0–116	Bit [6, 5, 4]: 000 = Undefined 001 = 256 All others reserved	Bit [3, 2, 1, 0]: 0000 = Undefined 0001 = 128 0010 = 176 0011 = 256 All others reserved

SPD Field 0×01: SPD Revision

Down-on-board memory designs should use 0×10 for this field.

Byte (Dec)	Byte (Hex)	Field Name	Typ.Value	Definition
1	0×01	SPD Rev	0×10	Rev 1.0

Byte 1: SPD Revision

This byte describes the compatibility level of the encoding of the bytes contained in the SPD EEPROM, and the current collection of valid defined bytes. Software should examine the upper nibble (Encoding Level) to determine if it can correctly interpret the contents of the module SPD. The lower nibble (Additions Level) can optionally be used to determine which additional bytes or attribute bits have been defined; however, since any undefined additional byte must be encoded as 0×00 or undefined attribute bit must be defined as 0, software can safely detect additional bytes and use safe defaults if a zero encoding is read for these bytes.

Production	SPD	Encoding Level					Additions Level			Hex
Status	Revision	Bit 7	Bit 6	Bit 5	Bit 4	Bit 3	Bit 2	Bit 1	Bit 0	
Pre- production	Revision 0.0	0	0	0	0	0	0	0	0	00

Production	SPD	Encoding Level				Additions Level				Hex
Status	Revision	Bit 7	Bit 6	Bit 5	Bit 4	Bit 3	Bit 2	Bit 1	Bit 0	
	Revision 0.1	0	0	0	0	0	0	0	1	01
	...	.	.	.	.	.	.	.	.	.
	Revision 0.9	0	0	0	0	1	0	0	1	09
Production	Revision 1.0	0	0	0	1	0	0	0	0	10
	Revision 1.1	0	0	0	1	0	0	0	1	11
	...	.	.	.	.	.	.	.	.	.
Undefined	Undefined	1	1	1	1	1	1	1	1	FF

The Additions Level is never reduced even after an increment of the Encoding Level. For example, if the current SPD revision level were 1.2 and a change in Encoding Level were approved, the next revision level would be 2.2. If additions to revision 2.2 were approved, the next revision would be 2.3. Changes in the Encoding Level are extremely rare, however, since they can create incompatibilities with older systems.

The exceptions to the above rule are the SPD revision levels used during development prior to the Revision 1.0 release. Revisions 0.0 through 0.9 are used to indicate sequential pre-production SPD revision levels; however, the first production release will be Revision 1.0.

SPD Field 0×02: Device Type

DDR3 DIMMs are programmed with the value 0×0B.

Byte (Dec)	Byte (Hex)	Field Name	Typ. Value	Definition
2	0×02	Device Type	0×0B	DDR3 SDRAM

Per JEDEC Specification, Byte 2: Key Byte/DRAM Device Type
This byte is the key byte used by the system BIOS to determine how to interpret all other bytes in the SPD EEPROM. The BIOS must check this byte first to ensure that the EEPROM data is interpreted correctly. Any DRAM or module type that requires significant changes to the SPD format (beyond defining previously undefined bytes or bits) also requires a new entry in the key byte table below.

Line #	SDRAM/Module Type Corresponding to Key Byte	Bit 7	Bit 6	Bit 5	Bit 4	Bit 3	Bit 2	Bit 1	Bit 0	Hex
0	Reserved	0	0	0	0	0	0	0	0	00
1	Standard FPM DRAM	0	0	0	0	0	0	0	1	01
2	EDO	0	0	0	0	0	0	1	0	02
3	Pipelined Nibble	0	0	0	0	0	0	1	1	03
4	SDRAM	0	0	0	0	0	1	0	0	04
5	ROM	0	0	0	0	0	1	0	1	05
6	DDR SGRAM	0	0	0	0	0	1	1	0	06
7	DDR SDRAM	0	0	0	0	0	1	1	1	07
8	DDR2 SDRAM	0	0	0	0	1	0	0	0	08
9	DDR2 SDRAM FB-DIMM	0	0	0	0	1	0	0	1	09
10	DDR2 SDRAM FB-DIMM PROBE	0	0	0	0	1	0	1	0	0A
11	DDR3 SDRAM	0	0	0	0	1	0	1	1	0B
.	.	.	.	.	.	.	.	.	.	.
253	Reserved	1	1	1	1	1	1	0	1	FD
254	Reserved	1	1	1	1	1	1	1	0	FE
255	Reserved	1	1	1	1	1	1	1	1	FF

SPD Field 0×03: Module Type

This field is typically set to 0×02 for Unbuffered DIMMs or 0×03 when using SO-DIMMs. If the specific chipset/CPU ONLY supports SO-DIMMs, use 0×03 so as not to confuse the BIOS.

Byte (Dec)	Byte (Hex)	Field Name	Typ. Value	Definition
3	0×03	Module Type	0×03	SO-DIMM

Per JEDEC Specification, Byte 3: Key Byte/Module Type
This byte is a Key Byte used to index the module specific section of the SPD from bytes 60–116. Byte 3 identifies the SDRAM memory module type, which implies the width (D dimension) of the module. Other module physical characteristics, such as height (A dimension) or thickness (E dimension) are documented in the module-specific section of the SPD. Refer to the relevant JEDEC JC-11 module outline (MO) documents for dimension definitions.

Bits 7:4	Bits 3:0
Reserved	Module Type
X	0000 = Undefined
	0001 = RDIMM (width = 133.35 mm nom)
	0010 = UDIMM (width = 133.35 mm nom)
	0011 = SO-DIMM (width = 67.6 mm nom)
	0100 = Micro-DIMM (width = TBD mm nom)
	0101 = Mini-RDIMM (width = 82.0 mm nom)
	0110 = Mini-UDIMM (width = 82.0 mm nom)
	0111 = Mini-CDIMM (width = 67.6 mm nom)
	1000 = 72b-SO-UDIMM (width = 67.6 mm nom)
	1001 = 72b-SO-RDIMM (width = 67.6 mm nom)
	1010 = 72b-SO-CDIMM (width = 67.6 mm nom)
	1011 = LRDIMM (width = 133.35 mm nom)
	1100 = 16b-SO-DIMM (width = 67.6 mm nom)
	1101 = 32b-SO-DIMM (width = 67.6 mm nom)
	All others reserved

Definitions:
RDIMM: Registered Dual In-Line Memory Module
LRDIMM: Load Reduction Dual In-Line Memory Module
UDIMM: Unbuffered Dual In-Line Memory Module
SO-DIMM: Unbuffered 64-bit Small Outline Dual In-Line Memory Module
Micro-DIMM: Micro Dual In-Line Memory Module
Mini-RDIMM: Mini Registered Dual In-Line Memory Module
Mini-UDIMM: Mini Unbuffered Dual In-Line Memory Module
Mini-CDIMM: Clocked 72-bit Mini Dual In-Line Memory Module
72b-SO-UDIMM: Unbuffered 72-bit Small Outline Dual In-Line Memory Module
72b-SO-RDIMM: Registered 72-bit Small Outline Dual In-Line Memory Module
72b-SO-CDIMM: Clocked 72-bit Small Outline Dual In-Line Memory Module
16b-SO-DIMM: Unbuffered 16-bit Small Outline Dual In-Line Memory Module
32b-SO-DIMM: Unbuffered 32-bit Small Outline Dual In-Line Memory Module

SPD Field 0×04: SDRAM Density and Banks

Byte (Dec)	Byte (Hex)	Field Name	Typ. Value	Definition
4	0×04	SDRAM Density and Banks	0×03	8 Banks 2 Gb

Byte 4: SDRAM Density and Banks

This byte defines the total density of the DDR3 SDRAM, in bits, and the number of internal banks into which the memory array is divided. These values come from the DDR3 SDRAM datasheet.

Bit 7	Bits 6:4	Bits 3:0
Reserved	Bank Address Bits	Total SDRAM Capacity in Megabits (Mb)
	000 = 3 (8 banks)	0000 = 256 Mb
	001 = 4 (16 banks)	0001 = 512 Mb
	010 = 5 (32 banks)	0010 = 1 Gb
	011 = 6 (64 banks)	0011 = 2 Gb
	All others reserved	0100 = 4 Gb
		0101 = 8 Gb
		0110 = 16 Gb
		All others reserved

2Gb: ×4, ×8 ×16 DDR3 SDRAM
Features

DDR3 SDRAM

MT41J512M4 – 64 Meg × 4 × 8 Banks
MT41J256M8 – 32 Meg × 8 × 8 Banks
MT41J128M16 – 16 Meg × 16 × 8 Banks

SPD Field #4: "SDRAM Density and Banks" Example from Micron T41J256M8 Datasheet

This field is typically extracted directly from the SDRAM datasheet. Often the bank bits are specified instead of the number of banks (that is, three bank bits would provide eight banks, total). Likewise, in the odd situation where the DRAM density (or capacity) is not obviously spelled out in the datasheet, it can be calculated by multiplying the full address range by the DRAM width:

Density (Capacity) $= 2^{(Rows + Columns + Bank Bits)} \times$ DRAM Width

SPD Field 0×05: SDRAM Rows and Columns

Byte (Dec)	Byte (Hex)	Field Name	Typ. Value	Definition
5	0×05	SDRAM Rows and Columns	0×19	15 Rows 10 Columns

From JEDEC Specification, Byte 5: SDRAM Addressing

This byte describes the row addressing and the column addressing in the SDRAM device. Bits 2–0 encode the number of column address bits, and bits 5–3 encode the number of row address bits. These values come from the DDR3 SDRAM datasheet.

Bit 7:6	Bits 5:3	Bits 2:0
Reserved	Row Address Bits	Column Address Bits
	000 = 12	000 = 9
	001 = 13	001 = 10
	010 = 14	010 = 11
	011 = 15	011 = 12
	100 = 16	All others reserved
	All others reserved	

Table 2 Addressing

Parameter	512 Meg × 4	256 Meg × 8	128 Meg × 16
Configuration	64 Meg × 4 × 8 banks	32 Meg × 8 × 8 banks	16 Meg × 16 × 8 banks
Refresh count	8K	8K	8K
Row addressing	32K (A[14:0])	32K (A[14:0])	16K (A[13:0])
Bank addressing	8 (BA[2:0])	8 (BA[2:0])	8 (BA[2:0])
Column addressing	2K (A[11,9:0])	1K(A[9:0])	1K(A[9:0])

SPD Field #5: "SDRAM Rows & Columns" Example from Micron MT41J256M8 Datasheet

Rows and columns are the number of address signals that are active when the RAS# and CAS# signals strobe respectively. The row and column values required by the SPD data are extracted directly from the SDRAM datasheet as shown above. Here, A[9:0] consists of ten individual address lines, not nine. Both column and row fields required in the SPD data are not nibble aligned. This is a common mistake with this field.

SPD Field 0×06: Nominal Voltage, VDD

Below is an example of a 1.5V part; this will be modified per the components used in the design.

Byte (Dec)	Byte (Hex)	Field Name	Typ. Value	Definition
6	0x06	Nominal Voltage, V$_{DD}$	0×00	1.5V only

Byte 6: Module Nominal Voltage, VDD
This byte describes the Voltage Level for DRAM and other components on the module such as the register if applicable. Note that SPDs or thermal sensor components are on the VDDSPD supply and are not affected by this byte. "Operable" is defined as the VDD voltage at which module operation is allowed using the performance values programmed in the SPD. "Endurant" is defined as the VDD voltage at which the module may be powered without adversely affecting the life expectancy or reliability. Further specifications will exist to define the amount of time that the "Endurant" voltage can be applied to the module. Operation is not supported at this voltage.

Bit 7:3	Bit 2	Bit 1	Bit 0
Reserved	Module Minimum Nominal Voltage V$_{DD}$		
	0 = **NOT** 1.25 V operable	0 = **NOT** 1.35 V operable	1 = 1.35 V operable
	1 = 1.25 V operable	0 = 1.5 V operable	1 = **NOT** 1.5 V operable
	1.35 V LV DDR3 devices are required to be 1.5 V operable. All DDR3 devices are required to be 1.5 V endurant.		
	The value on Bit 0 uses a different polarity as compared with Bits 1 and 2 for backward compatibility with previous DDR3 SPD definitions.		
	000 = 1.5 V only 001 = N/A 010 = 1.35 V or 1.5 V 011 = 1.35 V and1.5 V endurant 100 = 1.25 V or 1.5 V 101 = 1.25 V and 1.5 V endurant 110 = 1.25 V, 1.35 V, or 1.5 V 111 = 1.25 V or 1.35 V. 1.5 V-endurant		

The nominal Voltage parameter is extracted directly from the SDRAM datasheet, usually on the front page.

SPD Field 0×07: Ranks & Device DQ Count

Byte (Dec)	Byte (Hex)	Field Name	Typ. Value	Definition
7	0×07	Ranks & Device DQ Count	0×01	Rank = 1
				Width = x8

From the JEDEC Specification, Byte 7: Module Organization
This byte describes the organization of the SDRAM module. Bits 2–0 encode the device width of the SDRAM devices. Bits 5–3 encode the number of physical ranks on the module. For example, for a double-rank module with ×8 DRAMs, this byte is encoded 00 001 001, or 0×09.

Bit 7:6	Bits 5:3	Bits 2:0
Reserved	Number of Ranks	SDRAM Device Width
	0 00 = 1 Rank	000 = 4 bits
	001 = 2 Ranks	001 = 8 bits
	010 = 3 Ranks	010 = 16 bits
	011 = 4 Ranks	011 = 32 bits
	All others reserved	All others reserved

2Gb: ×4, ×8, ×16 DDR3 SDRAM
Features

DDR3 SDRAM

MT41J512M4 – 64 Meg × 4 × 8 Banks
MT41J256M8 – 32 Meg × 8 × 8 Banks
MT41J128M16 – 16 Meg × 16 × 8 Banks

SPD Field #7: "Ranks & Device DQ Count" Example from Micron MT41J256M8 Datasheet

The SDRAM device width also can be easily discerned by looking at the schematics and noting the number of data lines used by each SDRAM device. SDRAM devices use four, eight, sixteen, or thirty-two data signals. The Number of Ranks is trickier to calculate. This parameter is not associated with the SDRAM chips, but is a parameter relating to the DIMM itself. It is the number or rank signals or chip selects used in the DIMM equivalent. The proper value to use must be extracted from the schematics. Note the specific chip select pins being used on a given channel. If only CS0 is routed to the SDRAM chips, then the down-on-board memory solution is single rank (1 rank). If both CS0 and CS1 are routed to all of the SDRAM chips, the down-on-board memory solution is dual rank (two ranks). Some server chipsets also support quad-rank DIMMs.

In extreme cases, it might be necessary to analyze the chipset's datasheet and design guide to discern *exactly* which DIMM equivalent(s) are being used in the down-on-board memory design.

As an example, let's assume that an Intel® 5100 chipset based design has SDRAM chips connected using all four rank signals (CS[3:0]#). This implementation could either be a single quad-rank DIMM equivalent, or two dual-rank DIMM equivalent. As shown in the two figures below, taken from this document: *Intel® Xeon® Processor 5000 Sequence with Intel® 5100 Memory Controller Hub Chipset for Communications, Embedded, and Storage Applications Platform Design Guide* (PDG) April 2009 Revision 2.3 Document Number: 352108–2.3.

All other memory interface signals have to be analyzed. For example, if the design is routing a SINGLE clock to all of the SDRAM chips (DCLKP/N [0]), then the implementation is similar to that in Figure 37; it's a single quad-rank DIMM implementation. However, if half of the SDRAM chips are connected to DCLKP/N[0], and the other half are connected to DCLKP/N[1], then the design is implementing two DIMM equivalents of dual-rank DIMMs.

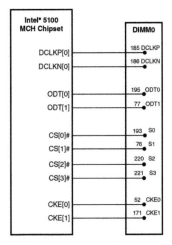

Figure 37 Configuration 1.1 - Clock and Control Signal DIMM Pin Mapping (One DIMM per Channel - 32 GB Mode, Quad-rank with S3 Support)
Figure 37 from *Intel® 5100 Platform Design Guide*–Single QuAD- Rank DIMM equi1valent

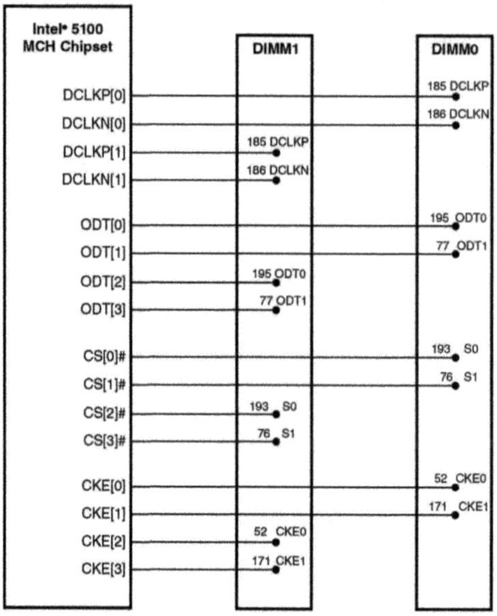

Notes: 1. DIMM pin numbers and name definitions come from the JEDEC specified DDR2 240-pin Registered DIMM Pinouts.

Figure 38 Configuration 2.1 - Clock and Control Signal DIMM Pin Mapping (Two DIMMs Per Channel - 32 GB Mode)
Figure 38 from *Intel*® 5100 Platform Design Guide–Single QuAD-Rank DIMM equivalent

SPD Field 0×08: Module Bus Width

This field is set t0 0×0Bh (72 bits) if the design is implementing ECC. Otherwise, set this field to 0×03h.

Byte (Dec)	Byte (Hex)	Field Name	Typ. Value	Definition
8	0×08	Module Bus Width	0×0B	72 bits (ECC)

Byte 8: Module Memory Bus Width
This byte describes the width of the SDRAM memory bus on the module. Bits 2–0 encode the primary bus width. Bits 4–3 encode the bus extensions such as parity or ECC.

Bit 7:5	Bits 4:3	Bits 2:0
Reserved	Bus width extension, in bits	Primary bus width, in bits
	000 = 0 bits (no extension)	000 = 8 bits

001 = 8 bits	001 = 16 bits
All others reserved	010 = 32 bits
	011 = 64 bits
	All others reserved

Examples:

- 64-bit primary bus, no parity or ECC (64 bits total width): xxx 000 011
- 64-bit primary bus, with 8 bit ECC (72 bits total width): xxx 001 011

SPD Field 0×09: Fine Timebase Dividend/Divisor

Setting this value to 0×52 (2.5ps) works well for implementing the other timing fields based on this value. Most DDR3 DIMMs use 0×52 for this field.

Byte (Dec)	Byte (Hex)	Field Name	Typ. Value	Definition
9	0×09	Fine Timebase Dividend/Divisor	0×52	2.5ps

Per JEDEC Specification, Byte 9: Fine Timebase (FTB) Dividend/Divisor
This byte defines a value in picoseconds that represents the fundamental timebase for fine grain timing calculations. This value is used as a multiplier for formulating subsequent timing parameters. The fine timebase (FTB) is defined as the fine timebase dividend, bits 7–4, divided by the fine timebase divisor, bits 3–0.

Bits 7:4	Bits 2:0
Fine Timebase (FTB) Dividend	**Fine Timebase (FTB) Divisor**
Values defined from 1 to 15	Values defined from 1 to 15

Examples:

Dividend	Divisor	Timebase (pS)	Use
5	1	5	5ps
5	2	2.5	2.5ps
1	1	1	1ps

SPD Field 0×0A and 0×0B: Medium Timebase Dividend/Divisor

Most DDR3 DIMM's SPD data use 0×01h (0.125 ns) for this value.

Byte (Dec)	Byte(Hex)	Field Name	Typ.Value	Definition
10	0×0A	Medium Timebase Dividend	0×01	0.125ns
11	0×0B	Medium Timebase Divisor	0×08	0.125ns

Byte 10: Medium Timebase (MTB) Dividend
Byte 11: Medium Timebase (MTB) Divisor
These bytes define a value in nanoseconds that represents the fundamental timebase for medium grain timing calculations. This value is typically the greatest common divisor for the range of clock frequencies (clock periods) supported by a particular SDRAM. This value is used as a multiplier for formulating subsequent timing parameters. The Medium Timebase (MTB) is defined as the Medium Timebase Dividend (byte 10) divided by the medium timebase divisor (byte 11).

Byte 10, Bits 7:0	Byte 11, Bits 7:0
Medium Timebase (MTB) Dividend	Medium Timebase (MTB) Divisor
Values defined from 1 to 255	Values defined from 1 to 255

Examples:

Dividend	Divisor	Timebase (nS)	Use
1	8	0.125	For clock frequencies 400–1066 MHz

To simplify BIOS implementation, DIMMs associated with a given key byte value may differ in MTB value only by a factor of two. For DDR3 modules, the defined MTB values are:

Dividend	Divisor	Timebase (nS)	Use
1	8	0.125	For clock frequencies 400–1066 MHz
1	16	0.0625	Reserved for future use

SPD Field 0x0C: Cycle Time (t$_{CK}$min)

This field can be tricky to calculate.
1. Find the lowest tCK number in the SDRAM datasheet for CAS Latencies supported by that SDRAM chip (see SPD field 14 below). The example above from the Micron MT41J256M8 gives 1.875 ns.
2. This number must be divided by the Medium Timebase Divisor, the value in 0×0B. In our example this is 0.125 ns.
3. 1.875 ns / 0.125 ns = 15 = 0×0F.

Byte (Dec)	Byte (Hex)	Field Name	Typ. Value	Definition
12	0×0C	Cycle Time (t$_{CK}$min)	0×0F	1.875ns

Per JEDEC Specification, Byte 12: SDRAM Minimum Cycle Time (tCKmin)
This byte defines the minimum cycle time for the SDRAM module, in Medium Timebase (MTB) units. This number applies to all applicable components on the module. This byte applies to SDRAM and support components as well as the overall capability of the DIMM. This value comes from the DDR3 SDRAM and support component datasheets.

Bits 7:0
Minimum SDRAM Cycle Time (tCKmin) MTB Units
Values defined from 1 to 255

If tCKmin cannot be divided evenly by the MTB, this byte must be rounded up to the next larger integer and the Fine Offset for tCKmin (SPD byte 34) used for correction to get the actual value.

tCKmin (MTB units)	MTB(ns)	tCKmin Offset (FTB units)1	FTB(ns)	tCKmin Result(ns)	Use
20	0x14	0.125	0	0	0.001	2.5	DDR3-800 (400 MHz clock)
15	0x0F	0.125	0	0	0.001	1.875	DDR3-1066 (533 MHz clock)
12	0x0C	0.125	0	0	0.001	1.5	DDR3-1333 (667 MHz clock)
10	0x0A	0.125	0	0	0.001	1.25	DDR3-1600 (800 MHz clock)
9	0x09	0.125	-54	0xCA	0.001	1.071	DDR3-1866 (933 MHz clock)
8	0x08	0.125	-62	0xC2	0.001	0.938	DDR3-2133 (1067 MHz clock)

Notes: 1. See SPD byte 34

Table 53 DDR3-1066 Speed Bins

DDR3-1066 Speed Bin		-187E		-187			
CL-^{t}RCD-^{t}RP		7-7-7		8-8-8			
Parameter	Symbol	Min	Max	Min	Max	Units	Notes
ACTIVATE to internal READ or WRITE delay time	^{t}RCD	13.125	-	15	-	ns	
PRECHARGE command period	^{t}RP	13.125	-	15	-	ns	
ACTIVATE-to-ACTIVATE or Refresh command period	^{t}RC	50.625	-	52.5	-	ns	
ACTIVATE-to-PRECHARGE command period	^{t}RAS	37.5	9 × tREFI	37.5	9 × tREFI	ns	1
CL = 5	CWL = 5	^{t}CK (AVG)	3.0	3.3	3.0	3.3	ns	2, 3
	CWL = 6	^{t}CK (AVG)	Reserved		Reserved		ns	3
CL = 6	CWL = 5	^{t}CK (AVG)	2.5	3.3	2.5	3.3	ns	2
	CWL = 6	^{t}CK (AVG)	Reserved		Reserved		ns	2, 3
CL = 7	CWL = 5	^{t}CK (AVG)	Reserved		Reserved		ns	3
	CWL = 6	^{t}CK (AVG)	1.875	< 2.5	Reserved		ns	2, 3
CL = 8	CWL = 5	^{t}CK (AVG)	Reserved		Reserved		ns	3
	CWL = 6	^{t}CK (AVG)	1.875	<2.5	1.875	< 2.5	ns	2
Supported CL settings		5, 6, 7, 8		5, 6, 8		CK	

DDR3-1066 Speed Bin		-187E		-187			
CI-^{t}RCD-^{t}RP		7-7-7		8-8-8			
Parameter	Symbol	Min	Max	Min	Max	Units	Notes
Supported CWL settings		5, 6		5, 6		CK	

Notes:
1. ^{t}REFI depends on T_{OPER}.
2. The CL and CWL settings result in ^{t}CK requirements. When selecting ^{t}CK, both CL and CWL requirement settings need to be fulfilled.
3. Reserved settings are not allowed.

SPD Field #12: "Cycle Time (t_{CK}min)" Example from Micron MT41J256M8 Datasheet

SPD Field 0×0E and 0×0F: CAS Latencies Supported

The supported CAS latencies can be found in the SDRAM datasheet as shown above. Each supported CAS latency must have its bit set in fields 14 and 15.

Byte (Dec)	Byte (Hex)	Field Name	Typ. Value	Definition
14	0×0E	CAS Latencies Supported (CL4-CL11)	0×1E	CL=5, 6, 7,8
15	0×0F	CAS Latencies Supported (CL12-CL18)	0×00	CL=5, 6, 7, 8

From the JEDEC Specification:
Byte 14: CAS Latencies Supported, Least Significant Byte
Byte 15: CAS Latencies Supported, Most Significant Byte
These bytes define which CAS Latency (CL) values are supported. The range is from CL = 4 through CL = 18 with one bit per possible CAS Latency. A 1 in a bit position means that CL is supported, a 0 in that bit position means it is not supported. Since CL = 6 is required for all DDR3 speed bins, bit 2 of SPD byte 14 is always 1. These values come from the DDR3 SDRAM datasheet.

Byte 14: CAS Latencies Supported Low Byte							
Bit 7	Bit 6	Bit 5	Bit 4	Bit 3	Bit 2	Bit 1	Bit 0
CL = 11	CL = 10	CL = 9	CL = 8	CL = 7	CL = 6	CL = 5	CL = 4
0 or 1	0 or 1	0 or 1	0 or 1	0 or 1	1	0 or 1	0 or 1
Byte 15: CAS Latencies Supported High Byte							
Bit 7	Bit 6	Bit 5	Bit 4	Bit 3	Bit 2	Bit 1	Bit 0
Reserved	CL = 18	CL = 17	CL = 16	CL = 15	CL = 14	CL = 13	CL = 12
0	0 or 1	0 or 1	0 or 1	0 or 1	0 or 1	0 or 1	0 or 1

For each bit position
0 means this CAS Latency is not supported
1 means this CAS Latency is supported.

SPD Field #14 and #15: "CAS Latencies Supported" Definition from JEDEC DDR3 SPD Specification

Table 53 DDR3-1066 Speed Bins

DDR3-1066 Speed Bin		-187E		-187			
CI-^{t}RCD-^{t}RP		7-7-7		8-8-8			
Parameter	Symbol	Min	Max	Min	Max	Units	Notes
ACTIVATE to internal READ or WRITE delay time	^{t}RCD	13.125	-	15	-	ns	
PRECHARGE command period	^{t}RP	13.125	-	15	-	ns	
ACTIVATE-to-ACTIVATE or Refresh command period	^{t}RC	50.625	-	52.5	-	ns	
ACTIVATE-to-PRECHARGE command period	^{t}RAS	37.5	9 × tREFI	37.5	9 × tREFI	ns	1
CL = 5 CWL = 5	^{t}CK (AVG)	3.0	3.3	3.0	3.3	ns	2, 3
CWL = 6	^{t}CK (AVG)	Reserved		Reserved		ns	3
CL = 6 CWL = 5	^{t}CK (AVG)	2.5	3.3	2.5	3.3	ns	2
CWL = 6	^{t}CK (AVG)	Reserved		Reserved		ns	2, 3
CL = 7 CWL = 5	^{t}CK (AVG)	Reserved		Reserved		ns	3
CWL = 6	^{t}CK (AVG)	1.875	< 2.5	Reserved		ns	2, 3
CL = 8 CWL = 5	^{t}CK (AVG)	Reserved		Reserved		ns	3
CWL = 6	^{t}CK (AVG)	1.875	<2.5	1.875	< 2.5	ns	2
Supported CL settings		5, 6, 7, 8		5, 6, 8		CK	
Supported CWL settings		5, 6		5, 6		CK	

Notes:
1. ^{t}REFI depends on T$_{OPER}$.
2. The CL and CWL settings result in ^{t}CK requirements. When selecting ^{t}CK, both CL and CWL requirement settings need to be fulfilled.
3. Reserved settings are not allowed.

SPD Field #14 and #15: "CAS Latencies Supported" Example from Micron MT41J256M8 Datasheet

SPD Field 0×10: CAS Latency Time (tAAmin or tCL)

This field must also be extracted from the datasheet and divided by the Medium Time-base Divisor. Although the SPD specification calls out this abbreviation as tAA, I've found that it is usually abbreviated tCL or just "CL" in the various SDRAM datasheets (as shown above).

In our example:
1. The tCL value found in the Micron MT41J256M8 datasheet for our specific SDRAM chip gives 13.1 ns.
2. This number must be divided by the Medium Timebase Divisor, the value in 0×0B. In our example this is 0.125 ns.
3. 13.1 ns / 0.125 ns = 104.8 (round up) = 0×69.

Byte (Dec)	Byte (Hex)	Field Name	Typ. Value	Definition
16	0×10	CAS Latency Time (t$_{AA}$min or t$_{CL}$)	0×69	13.125ns

Byte 16: Minimum CAS Latency Time (tAAmin)
This byte defines the minimum CAS Latency in Medium Timebase (MTB) units. Software can use this information, along with the CAS Latencies supported (found in bytes 14 and 15) to determine the optimal cycle time for a particular module. This value comes from the DDR3 SDRAM datasheet.

Bits 7:0
Minimum SDRAM CAS Latency Time (t$_{AA}$min) MTB Units
Values defined from 1 to 255

If tAAmin cannot be divided evenly by the MTB, this byte must be rounded up to the next larger integer and the Fine Offset for tAAmin (SPD byte 35) used for correction to get the actual value.

Examples:

tAAmin MTB units)		MTB (ns)	tAAmin Offset (FTB units)1	FTB (ns)	tAAmin Result (ns)	Use
100	0×64	0.125	0	0	0.001	12.5	DDR3-800D
120	0×78	0.125	0	0	0.001	15	DDR3-800E
90	0×5A	0.125	0	0	0.001	11.25	DDR3-1066E

tAAmin (MTB units)		MTB (ns)	tAAmin Offset (FTB units)[1]		FTB (ns)	tAAmin Result (ns)	Use
105	0×69	0.125	0	0	0.001	13.125	DDR3-1066F
120	0×78	0.125	0	0	0.001	15	DDR3-1066G
84	0×54	0.125	0	0	0.001	10.5	DDR3-1333F
96	0×60	0.125	0	0	0.001	12	DDR3-1333G
108	0×6C	0.125	0	0	0.001	13.5	DDR3-1333H[2]
105	0×69	0.125	0	0	0.001	13.125	DDR3-1333H downbin[2]
120	0×78	0.125	0	0	0.001	15	DDR3-1333J
80	0×50	0.125	0	0	0.001	10	DDR3-1600G
90	0×5A	0.125	0	0	0.001	11.25	DDR3-1600H
100	0×64	0.125	0	0	0.001	12.5	DDR3-1600J
110	0×6E	0.125	0	0	0.001	13.75	DDR3-1600K[2]
105	0×69	0.125	0	0	0.001	13.125	DDR3-1600K downbin[2]
86	0×56	0.125	-50	0×CE	0.001	10.7	DDR3-1866J
95	0×5F	0.125	-105	0×97	0.001	11.77	DDR3-1866K
103	0×67	0.125	-35	0×DD	0.001	12.84	DDR3-1866L
112	0×70	0.125	-90	0×A6	0.001	13.91	DDR3-1866M[2]
105	0×69	0.125	0	0	0.001	13.125	DDR3-1866M downbin[2]
83	0×53	0.125	-90	0×A6	0.001	10.285	DDR3-2133K
90	0×5A	0.125	-30	0×E2	0.001	11.22	DDR3-2133L
98	0×62	0.125	-95	0×A1	0.001	12.155	DDR3-2133M
105	0×69	0.125	-35	0×DD	0.001	13.09	DDR3-2133N

Notes:
1. See SPD byte 35.
2. Refer to device datasheet for downbin support details.

SPD Field #16: "Minimum CAS Latency Time (t$_{AA}$min)" Definition from JEDEC DDR3 SPD Specification

Table 1 Key Timing Parameters

Speed Grade	Data Rate (MT/s)	Target tRCD- ^{t}RP- CL	^{t}RCD (ns)	^{t}RP (ns)	CL (ns)
-125[1,2]	1600	11-11-11	13.75	13.75	13.75
-125E[1,2]	1600	10-10-10	12.5	12.5	12.5
-153	1333	10-10-10	15	15	15
15E1	1333	9-9-9	13.5	13.5	13.5
-187	1066	8-8-8	15	15	15
-187E	1066	7-7-7	13.1	13.1	13.1

Notes:
1. Backward compatible to 1066, CL = 7 (-187E).
2. Backward compatible to 1333, CL = 9 (-15E).
3. Backward compatible to 1066, CL = 8 (-187).

SPD Field #16: "Minimum CAS Latency Time (t_{AA}min)" Example from Micron MT41J256M8 Datasheet

SPD Field 0×11: Write Recovery Time (twrmin)

This is another field that must be extracted from the datasheet and divided by the Medium Timebase Divisor.

In our example:
1. The tWR value found in the Micron MT41J256M8 datasheet for our specific SDRAM chip gives 15 ns.
2. This number must be divided by the Medium Timebase Divisor, the value in 0×0B. In our example this is 0.125 ns.
3. 15 ns / 0.125 ns = 120 = 0×78.

Byte (Dec)	Byte (Hex)	Field Name	Typ. Value	Definition
17	0×11	Write Recovery Time (t_{WR}min)	0×78	15ns

From the JEDEC Specification: Byte 17: Minimum Write Recovery Time (tWRmin)
This byte defines the minimum SDRAM write recovery time in Medium Timebase (MTB) units. This value comes from the DDR3 SDRAM datasheet.

Bits 7–0
Minimum Write Recovery Time (tWR) MTB Units
Values defined from 1 to 255

Example:

tWRmin (MTB units)	Timebase (ns)	tWR Result (ns)	Use
120	0.125	15	All DDR3 speed grades

Steps:
1. The BIOS first determines the common operating frequency of all modules in the system, ensuring that the corresponding value of tCK (tCKactual) falls

between tCKmin (Bytes 12 and 34) and tCKmax. If tCKactual is not a JEDEC standard value, the next smaller standard tCKmin value is used for calculating Write Recovery.

2. The BIOS then calculates the "desired" Write Recovery (WRdesired):

WRdesired = ceiling (tWRmin/tCKactual)

where tWRmin is defined in Byte 17. The ceiling function requires that the quotient be rounded up always.

3. The BIOS then determines the "actual" Write Recovery (WRactual):

WRactual = max (WRdesired, min WR supported)

where min WR is the lowest Write Recovery supported by the DDR3 SDRAM. Note that not all WR values supported by DDR3 SDRAMs are sequential, so the next higher supported WR value must be used in some cases. Usage example for DDR3-1333G operating at DDR3-1333:

tCKactual = 1.5 ns
WRdesired = 15 / 1.5 = 10
WRactual = max(10, 10) = 10

Table 56 Electrical Characteristics and AC Operating Conditions (Continued)
Notes 1–8 apply to the entire table

Parameter		Symbol	DDR3-800		DDR3-1066		DDR3-1333		DDR3-1600		Units
			Min	Max	Min	Max	Min	Max	Min	Max	
DQS, DQS # differential READ postamble		^{t}RPST	0.3	Note 27	0.3	Note 27	0.3	Note 27	0.3	Note 27	CK
Command and Address Timings											
DLL locking time		^{t}DLLK	512	–	512	–	512	–	512	–	CK
CTRL, CMD, ADDR setup to CK, CK#	Base (Specification) V_{REF}@1 V/ns	^{t}IS AC175	200 375	– –	125 300	– –	65 240	– –	45 220	– –	ps ps
CTRL, CMD, ADDR setup to CK, CK#	Base (Specification) V_{REF}@1 V/ns	^{t}IS AC150	350 500	– –	425	– –	340	– –	320	– –	ps p
CTRL, CMD, ADDR setup to CK, CK#	Base (Specification) V_{REF}@1 V/ns	^{t}IH DC100	275 375	– –	200 300	– –	140 240	– –	120 220	– –	ps ps
Minimum CTRL, CMD, ADDR pulse width		^{t}IPW	900	–	780	–	620	–	560	–	ps
ACTIVATE to internal READ or WRITE delay		^{t}RCD	See Speed Bin Tables (page 72) for ^{t}RCD								ns

Parameter		Symbol					Unit
PRECHARGE command period		^tRP	See Speed Bin Tables (page 72) for ^tRP				ns
ACTIVATE-to-PRECHARGE command period		^tRAS	See Speed Bin Tables (page 72) for ^tRAS				ns
ACTIVATE-to-ACTIVATE command		^tRC	See Speed Bin Tables (page 72) for ^tRC				ns
ACTIVATE- to- ACTIVATE minium command period	1KB page size	^tRRD	MIN= greater of 4CK or 10ns	MIN= greater of 4CK or 7.5ns	MIN= greater of 4CK or 6ns	MIN= greater of 4CK or 6ns	CK
	2KB page size		MIN= greater of 4CK or 10ns		MIN= greater of 4CK or 7.5ns		CK
Four ACTIVATE windows	1KB page size	^tFAW	40 – 37.5 – 30 – 30 –				ns
	2KB page size		50 – 50 – 45 – 40 –				ns
Write recovery time		^tWR	MIN = 15ns; MAX = n/a				ns
Delay from start of internal WRITE transaction to internal READ command		^tWTR	MIN = greater of 4CK or 7.5ns; MAX = n/a				CK
READ-to-PRECHARGE time		^tRTP	MIN = greater of 4CK or 7.5ns; MAX = n/a				CK
CAS# to CAS# command delay		^tCCD	MIN = 4CK; MAX = n/a				CK
Auto precharge write recovery + precharge time		^tDAL	MIN = WR+$^tRP/^tCK$ (AVG); MAX = n/a				CK
MODE REGISTER SET command cycle time		^tMRD	MIN = 4CK; MAX = n/a				CK
MODE REGISTER SET command update delay		^tMOD	MIN = greater of 12CK or 15ns; MAX = n/a				CK

SPD Field #17: "Minimum Write Recovery Time (t$_{WR}$min)" Example from Micron MT41J256M8 Datasheet

SPD Field 0×12 RAS# to CAS# Delay (tRCDmin)

This field must also be extracted from the datasheet and divided by the Medium Timebase Divisor.

In our example:
1. The t$_{RCD}$ value found in the Micron MT41J256M8 datasheet for our specific SDRAM chip gives 13.1 ns.
2. This number must be divided by the Medium Timebase Divisor, the value in 0×0B. In our example this is 0.125 ns.
3. 13.1 ns / 0.12 5ns = 104.8 (round up) = 0×69.

Byte (Dec)	Byte (Hex)	Field Name	Typ. Value	Definition
18	0×12	RAS# to CAS# Delay (t_{RCD}min)	0×69	13.125ns

Byte 18: Minimum RAS# to CAS# Delay Time (tRCDmin)
This byte defines the minimum SDRAM RAS# to CAS# Delay in Medium Timebase (MTB) units. This value comes from the DDR3 SDRAM datasheet.

Bits 7–0
Minimum RAS# to CAS# Delay (tRCD) MTB Units
Values defined from 1 to 255

If tRCDmin cannot be divided evenly by the MTB, this byte must be rounded up to the next larger integer and the Fine Offset for tRCDmin (SPD byte 36) used for correction to get the actual value.

Examples:

tRCD (MTB units)		MTB (ns)	tRCD Offset (FTB units)1	FTB (ns)	tRCD Result (ns)	Use
100	0×64	0.125	0	0	0.001	12.5	DDR3-800D
120	0×78	0.125	0	0	0.001	15	DDR3-800E
90	0×5A	0.125	0	0	0.001	11.25	DDR3-1066E
105	0×69	0.125	0	0	0.001	13.125	DDR3-1066F
120	0×78	0.125	0	0	0.001	15	DDR3-1066G
84	0×54	0.125	0	0	0.001	10.5	DDR3-1333F
96	0×60	0.125	0	0	0.001	12	DDR3-1333G
108	0×6C	0.125	0	0	0.001	13.5	DDR3-1333H2
105	0×69	0.125	0	0	0.001	13.125	DDR3-1333H downbin2
120	0×78	0.125	0	0	0.001	15	DDR3-1333J
80	0×50	0.125	0	0	0.001	10	DDR3-1600G
90	0×5A	0.125	0	0	0.001	11.25	DDR3-1600H
100	0×64	0.125	0	0	0.001	12.5	DDR3-1600J
110	0×6E	0.125	0	0	0.001	13.75	DDR3-1600K2
105	0×69	0.125	0	0	0.001	13.125	DDR3-1600K downbin2
86	0×56	0.125	-50	0×CE	0.001	10.7	DDR3-1866J
95	0×5F	0.125	-105	0×97	0.001	11.77	DDR3-1866K

tRCD (MTB units)		MTB (ns)	tRCD Offset (FTB units)1		FTB (ns)	tRCD Result (ns)	Use
103	0×67	0.125	-35	0×DD	0.001	12.84	DDR3-1866L
112	0×70	0.125	-90	0×A6	0.001	13.91	DDR3-1866M[2]
105	0×69	0.125	0	0	0.001	13.125	DDR3-1866M downbin[2]
83	0×53	0.125	-90	0×A6	0.001	10.285	DDR3-2133K
90	0×5A	0.125	-30	0×E2	0.001	11.22	DDR3-2133L
98	0×62	0.125	-95	0×A1	0.001	12.155	DDR3-2133M
105	0×69	0.125	-35	0×DD	0.001	13.09	DDR3-2133N

Notes:
1. 1. See SPD byte 36.
2. Refer to device datasheet for downbin support details.

SPD Field #18: "Minimum RAS# to CAS# Delay Time (t_{RCD}min)" Definition from JEDEC DDR3 SPD Specification

Table 1 Key Timing Parameters

Speed Grade	Data Rate (MT/s)	Target tRCD- tRP- CL	tRCD (ns)	tRP (ns)	CL (ns)
-125[1,2]	1600	11-11-11	13.75	13.75	13.75
-125E[1,2]	1600	10-10-10	12.5	12.5	12.5
-153	1333	10-10-10	15	15	15
-15E1	1333	9-9-9	13.5	13.5	13.5
-187	1066	8-8-8	15	15	15
-187E	1066	7-7-7	13.1	13.1	13.1

Notes:
1. Backward compatible to 1066, CL = 7 (-187E).
2. Backward compatible to 1333, CL = 9 (-15E).
3. Backward compatible to 1066, CL = 8 (-187).

SPD Field #18: "Minimum RAS# to CAS# Delay Time (t_{RCD}min)"
Example from Micron MT41J256M8 Datasheet

SPD Field 0x13: Min. Row Active to Row Active Delay (t_{RRD}min)

This field must also be extracted from the datasheet and divided by the Medium Timebase Divisor. In our example:

1. The t_{RRD} value found in the Micron MT41J256M8 datasheet for our specific SDRAM chip gives 7.5 ns.
2. This number must be divided by the Medium Timebase Divisor, the value in 0×0B. In our example this is 0.125 ns.
3. 7.5 ns / 0.125 ns = 60 = 0×3C.

Byte (Dec)	Byte (Hex)	Field Name	Typ. Value	Definition
19	**0×13**	Min. Row Active to Row Active Delay (t_{RRD}min)	0×3C	7.5ns

Byte 19: Minimum Row Active to Row Active Delay Time (tRRDmin)
This byte defines the minimum SDRAM Row Active to Row Active Delay Time in Medium Timebase units. This value comes from the DDR3 SDRAM datasheet. The value of this number may be dependent on the SDRAM page size; please refer to the DDR3 SDRAM datasheet section on Addressing to determine the page size for these devices. Controller designers must also note that at some frequencies, a minimum number of clocks may be required, resulting in a larger tRRDmin value than indicated in the SPD. For example, tRRDmin for DDR3-800 must be 4 clocks.

Bits 7–0
Min. Row Active to Row Active Delay (t_{RRD}min)
Values defined from 1 to 255

tRRD (MTB units)	Timebase (ns)	tRRD Result (ns)	Use
48	0.125	6.0	Example: DDR3-1333, 1KB page size
60	0.125	7.5	Example: DDR3-1333, 2KB page size
80	0.125	10	Example: DDR3-800, 1KB page size

Note: tRRD is at least 4 nCK independent of operating frequency.

Table 56 Electrical Characteristics and AC Operating Conditions (Continued)
Notes 1–8 apply to the entire table

Parameter	Symbol	DDR3-800		DDR3-1066		DDR3-1333		DDR3-1600		Units
		Min	Max	Min	Max	Min	Max	Min	Max	
DQS, DQS # differential READ postamble	^{t}RPST	0.3	Note 27	0.3	Note 27	0.3	Note 27	0.3	Note 27	CK
Command and Address Timings										
DLL locking time	^{t}DLLK	512	–	512	–	512	–	512	–	CK

Parameter		Symbol									Unit
CTRL, CMD, ADDR setup to CK, CK#	Base (Specification) V_{REF}@1 V/ns	^tIS AC175	200	–	125	–	65	–	45	–	ps
			375	–	300	–	240	–	220	–	ps
CTRL, CMD, ADDR setup to CK, CK#	Base (Specification) V_{REF}@1 V/ns	^tIS AC150	350	–		–		–		–	ps
			500	–	425	–	340	–	320	–	p
CTRL, CMD, ADDR setup to CK, CK#	Base (Specification) V_{REF}@1 V/ns	^tIH DC100	275	–	200	–	140	–	120	–	ps
			375	–	300	–	240	–	220	–	ps
Minimum CTRL, CMD, ADDR pulse width		^tIPW	900	–	780	–	620	–	560	–	ps
ACTIVATE to internal READ or WRITE delay		^tRCD	See Speed Bin Tables (page 72) for ^tRCD								ns
PRECHARGE command period		^tRP	See Speed Bin Tables (page 72) for ^tRP								ns
ACTIVATE-to-PRECHARGE command period		^tRAS	See Speed Bin Tables (page 72) for ^tRAS								ns
ACTIVATE-to-ACTIVATE command		^tRC	See Speed Bin Tables (page 72) for ^tRC								ns
ACTIVATE- to-ACTIVATE minium command period	1KB page size	^tRRD	MIN= greater of 4CK or 10ns		MIN= greater of 4CK or 7.5ns		MIN= greater of 4CK or 6ns		MIN= greater of 4CK or 6ns		CK
	2KB page size		MIN= greater of 4CK or 10ns				MIN= greater of 4CK or 7.5ns				CK
Four ACTIVATE windows	1KB page size	^tFAW	40	–	37.5	–	30	–	30	–	ns
	2KB page size		50	–	50	–	45	–	40	–	ns
Write recovery time		^tWR	MIN = 15ns; MAX = n/a								ns
Delay from start of internal WRITE transaction to internal READ command		^tWTR	MIN = greater of 4CK or 7.5ns; MAX = n/a								CK
READ-to-PRECHARGE time		^tRTP	MIN = greater of 4CK or 7.5ns; MAX = n/a								CK
CAS# to CAS# command delay		^tCCD	MIN = 4CK; MAX = n/a								CK
Auto precharge write recovery + precharge time		^tDAL	MIN = WR+^tRP/^tCK (AVG); MAX = n/a								CK
MODE REGISTER SET command cycle time		^tMRD	MIN = 4CK; MAX = n/a								CK
MODE REGISTER SET command update delay		^tMOD	MIN = greater of 12CK or 15ns; MAX = n/a								CK

SPD Field #19: "Minimum Row Active to Row Active Delay Time (t_{RRD}min)" Example from Micron MT41J256M8 Datasheet

SPD Field 0×14: Min. Row Precharge Delay (t$_{RP}$min)

This is another field that must be extracted from the datasheet and divided by the Medium Timebase Divisor.

In our example:
1. The t$_{RP}$ value found in the Micron MT41J256M8 datasheet for our specific SDRAM chip gives 13.125 ns.
2. This number must be divided by the Medium Timebase Divisor, the value in 0×0B. In our example this is 0.125 ns.
3. 13.125 ns / 0.125 ns = 105 = 0×69.

Byte (Dec)	Byte (Hex)	Field Name	Typ. Value	Definition
20	0×14	Min. Row Precharge Delay (t$_{RP}$min)	0×69	13.125ns

Byte 20: Minimum Row Precharge Delay Time (tRPmin)
This byte defines the minimum SDRAM Row Precharge Delay Time in Medium Timebase (MTB) units. This value comes from the DDR3 SDRAM datasheet.

Bits 7–0
Min. Row Active to Row Active Delay (t$_{RRD}$min)
Values defined from 1 to 255

If tRPmin cannot be divided evenly by the MTB, this byte must be rounded up to the next larger integer and the Fine Offset for tRPmin (SPD byte 37) used for correction to get the actual value.

tRP (MTB units)		MTB (ns)	tRP Offset (FTB units)1	FTB (ns)	tRP Result (ns)	Use
100	0×64	0.125	0	0	0.001	12.5	DDR3-800D
120	0×78	0.125	0	0	0.001	15	DDR3-800E
90	0×5A	0.125	0	0	0.001	11.25	DDR3-1066E
105	0×69	0.125	0	0	0.001	13.125	DDR3-1066F
120	0×78	0.125	0	0	0.001	15	DDR3-1066G
84	0×54	0.125	0	0	0.001	10.5	DDR3-1333F
96	0×60	0.125	0	0	0.001	12	DDR3-1333G
108	0×6C	0.125	0	0	0.001	13.5	DDR3-1333H$_2$

tRP (MTB units)		MTB (ns)	tRP Offset (FTB units)[1]		FTB (ns)	tRP Result (ns)	Use
105	0×69	0.125	0	0	0.001	13.125	DDR3-1333H downbin[2]
120	0×78	0.125	0	0	0.001	15	DDR3-1333J
80	0×50	0.125	0	0	0.001	10	DDR3-1600G
90	0×5A	0.125	0	0	0.001	11.25	DDR3-1600H
100	0×64	0.125	0	0	0.001	12.5	DDR3-1600J
110	0×6E	0.125	0	0	0.001	13.75	DDR3-1600K[2]
105	0×69	0.125	0	0	0.001	13.125	DDR3-1600K downbin[2]
86	0×56	0.125	-50	0×CE	0.001	10.7	DDR3-1866J
95	0×5F	0.125	-105	0×97	0.001	11.77	DDR3-1866K
103	0×67	0.125	-35	0×DD	0.001	12.84	DDR3-1866L
112	0×70	0.125	-90	0×A6	0.001	13.91	DDR3-1866M[2]
105	0×69	0.125	0	0	0.001	13.125	DDR3-1866M downbin[2]
83	0×53	0.125	-90	0×A6	0.001	10.285	DDR3-2133K
90	0×5A	0.125	-30	0×E2	0.001	11.22	DDR3-2133L
98	0×62	0.125	-95	0×A1	0.001	12.155	DDR3-2133M
105	0×69	0.125	-35	0×DD	0.001	13.09	DDR3-2133N

Notes:

1. See SPD byte 37.
2. Refer to device datasheet for downbin support details.

Table 53 DDR3-1066 Speed Bins

DDR3-1066 Speed Bin		-187E		-187			
CL-tRCD-tRP		7-7-7		8-8-8			
Parameter	Symbol	Min	Max	Min	Max	Units	Notes
ACTIVATE to internal READ or WRITE delay time	tRCD	13.125	-	15	-	ns	
PRECHARGE command period	tRP	13.125	-	15	-	ns	
ACTIVATE-to- ACTIVATE or Refresh command period	tRC	50.625	-	52.5	-	ns	

DDR3-1066 Speed Bin			-187E		-187			
CL-^{t}RCD-^{t}RP			7-7-7		8-8-8			
Parameter		Symbol	Min	Max	Min	Max	Units	Notes
ACTIVATE-to-PRECHARGE command period		^{t}RAS	37.5	9 × tREFI	37.5	9 × tREFI	ns	1
CL = 5	CWL = 5	^{t}CK (AVG)	3.0	3.3	3.0	3.3	ns	2, 3
	CWL = 6	^{t}CK (AVG)	Reserved		Reserved		ns	3
CL = 6	CWL = 5	^{t}CK (AVG)	2.5	3.3	2.5	3.3	ns	2
	CWL = 6	^{t}CK (AVG)	Reserved		Reserved		ns	2, 3
CL = 7	CWL = 5	^{t}CK (AVG)	Reserved		Reserved		ns	3
	CWL = 6	^{t}CK (AVG)	1.875	< 2.5	Reserved		ns	2, 3
CL = 8	CWL = 5	^{t}CK (AVG)	Reserved		Reserved		ns	3
	CWL = 6	^{t}CK (AVG)	1.875	<2.5	1.875	< 2.5	ns	2
Supported CL settings			5, 6, 7, 8		5, 6, 8		CK	
Supported CWL settings			5, 6		5, 6		CK	

Notes:
1. ^{t}REFI depends on T_{OPER}.
2. The CL and CWL settings result in ^{t}CK requirements. When selecting ^{t}CK, both CL and CWL requirement settings need to be fulfilled.
3. Reserved settings are not allowed.

SPD Field #20: "Minimum Row Precharge Delay Time (t_{RP}min)" Micron MT41J256M8 Datasheet

SPD Field 0×15: Upper Nibble of t_{RAS} & t_{RC}

This field is the Most Significant nibble (4 bits) for both the Active to Precharge Delay (tRASmin) and Active to Active/Refresh delay (tRCmin). See the next two sections for how to determine the tRASmin and tRCmin values and put the upper nibble of those results into this field.

Byte (Dec)	Byte (Hex)	Field Name	Typ. Value	Definition
21	0×15	Upper Nibble of t_{RAS} & t_{RC}	0×11	---

Byte 21: Upper Nibbles for tRAS and tRC
This byte defines the most significant nibbles for the values of tRAS (byte 22) and tRC (byte 23). These values come from the DDR3 SDRAM datasheet.

Bits 7–4	Bits 3–0
tRC Most Significant Nibble	tRAS Most Significant Nibble
See Byte 23 description	See Byte 22 description

SPD Field #21: "Upper Nibbles for t_{RAS} and t_{RC}" Definition from JEDEC DDR3 SPD Specification

SPD Field 0×16: Min. Active to Precharge Delay (t_{RAS}min) LSB

This is another field that must be extracted from the datasheet and divided by the Medium Timebase Divisor. In our example:

1. The tRAS value found in the Micron MT41J256M8-187E datasheet for our specific SDRAM chip gives 37.5 ns.
2. This number must be divided by the Medium Timebase Divisor, the value in 0×0B. In our example this is 0.125 ns.
3. 37.5 ns / 0.125 ns = 300 = 0×012C.
4. The LSB, 0×2C, goes into SPD field #22 (0×16).
5. The lower nibble of the MSB, 0×01, goes into bits [3:0] of SPD field #21 (0×15)

Byte (Dec)	Byte (Hex)	Field Name	Typ. Value	Definition
22	**0×16**	Min. Active to Precharge Delay (t_{RAS}min) LSB	0×2C	37.5ns

Byte 22: Minimum Active to Precharge Delay Time (tRASmin), Least Significant Byte
The lower nibble of Byte 21 and the contents of Byte 22 combined create a 12-bit value that defines the minimum SDRAM Active to Precharge Delay Time in Medium Timebase (MTB) units. The most significant bit is Bit 3 of Byte 21, and the least significant bit is Bit 0 of Byte 22. This value comes from the DDR3 SDRAM datasheet.

Byte 21 Bits 3–0, Byte 22 Bits 7–0
Minimum Active to Precharge Time (tRAS) MTB Units
Values defined from 1 to 4095

Examples:

tRAS (MTB units)		MTB (ns)	tRAS Result (ns)	Use
300	0×12C	0.125	37.5	DDR3-800D
300	0×12C	0.125	37.5	DDR3-800E

tRAS (MTB units)		MTB (ns)	tRAS Result (ns)	Use
300	0×12C	0.125	37.5	DDR3-1066E
300	0×12C	0.125	37.5	DDR3-1066F
300	0×12C	0.125	37.5	DDR3-1066G
288	0×120	0.125	36	DDR3-1333F
288	0×120	0.125	36	DDR3-1333G
288	0×120	0.125	36	DDR3-1333H
288	0×120	0.125	36	DDR3-1333J
280	0×118	0.125	35	DDR3-1600G
280	0×118	0.125	35	DDR3-1600H
280	0×118	0.125	35	DDR3-1600J
280	0×118	0.125	35	DDR3-1600K
272	0×110	0.125	34	DDR3-1866J
272	0×110	0.125	34	DDR3-1866K
272	0×110	0.125	34	DDR3-1866L
272	0×110	0.125	34	DDR3-1866M
264	0×108	0.125	33	DDR3-2133K
264	0×108	0.125	33	DDR3-2133L
264	0×108	0.125	33	DDR3-2133M
264	0×108	0.125	33	DDR3-2133N

SPD Field #22: "Minimum Active to Precharge Delay Time (tRASmin)" Definition from JEDEC DDR3 SPD Specification

Table 53 DDR3-1066 Speed Bins

DDR3-1066 Speed Bin		-187E		-187			
CI-^{t}RCD-^{t}RP		7-7-7		8-8-8			
Parameter	Symbol	Min	Max	Min	Max	Units	Notes
ACTIVATE to internal READ or WRITE delay time	^{t}RCD	13.125	-	15	-	ns	
PRECHARGE command period	^{t}RP	13.125	-	15	-	ns	
ACTIVATE-to-ACTIVATE or Refresh command period	^{t}RC	50.625	-	52.5	-	ns	
ACTIVATE-to-PRECHARGE command period	^{t}RAS	37.5	9 × tREFI	37.5	9 × tREFI	ns	1

DDR3-1066 Speed Bin			-187E		-187			
Cl-^{t}RCD-^{t}RP			7-7-7		8-8-8			
Parameter		Symbol	Min	Max	Min	Max	Units	Notes
CL = 5	CWL = 5	^{t}CK (AVG)	3.0	3.3	3.0	3.3	ns	2, 3
	CWL = 6	^{t}CK (AVG)	Reserved		Reserved		ns	3
CL = 6	CWL = 5	^{t}CK (AVG)	2.5	3.3	2.5	3.3	ns	2
	CWL = 6	^{t}CK (AVG)	Reserved		Reserved		ns	2, 3
CL = 7	CWL = 5	^{t}CK (AVG)	Reserved		Reserved		ns	3
	CWL = 6	^{t}CK (AVG)	1.875	< 2.5	Reserved		ns	2, 3
CL = 8	CWL = 5	^{t}CK (AVG)	Reserved		Reserved		ns	3
	CWL = 6	^{t}CK (AVG)	1.875	<2.5	1.875	< 2.5	ns	2
Supported CL settings			5, 6, 7, 8		5, 6, 8		CK	
Supported CWL settings			5, 6		5, 6		CK	

Notes:

1. ^{t}REFI depends on T_{OPER}.
2. The CL and CWL settings result in ^{t}CK requirements. When selecting ^{t}CK, both CL and CWL requirement settings need to be fulfilled.
3. Reserved settings are not allowed.

SPD Field #22: "Minimum Active to Precharge Delay Time (t_{RAS}min)" Example from Micron MT41J256M8 Datasheet

SPD Field 0×17: Min. Active to Active Refresh Delay (t_{RC}min) LSB

This is another field that must be extracted from the datasheet and divided by the Medium Timebase Divisor. In our example:

1. The t_{RC} value found in the Micron MT41J256M8-187E datasheet for our specific SDRAM chip gives 50.625 ns.
2. This number must be divided by the Medium Timebase Divisor, the value in 0×0B. In our example this is 0.125 ns.
3. 50.625 ns / 0.125 ns = 405 = 0×0195.
4. The LSB, 0×95, goes into SPD field #23 (0×17).
5. The lower nibble of the MSB, 0x01, goes into bits [7:4] of SPD field #21 (0×15).

Byte (Dec)	Byte (Hex)	Field Name	Typ. Value	Definition
23	**0×17**	Min. Active to Active Refresh Delay (t_{RC}min) LSB	0×95	50.625

Byte 23: Minimum Active to Active/Refresh Delay Time (tRCmin),
Least Significant Byte

The upper nibble of Byte 21 and the contents of Byte 23 combined create a 12-bit value that defines the minimum SDRAM Active to Active/Refresh Delay Time in Medium Timebase (MTB) units. The most significant bit is Bit 7 of Byte 21, and the least significant bit is Bit 0 of Byte 23. This value comes from the DDR3 SDRAM datasheet.

Byte 21 Bits 7–4, Byte 23 Bits 7–0

Minimum Active to Active/Refresh Time (tRAS) MTB Units

Values defined from 1 to 4095

tRC (MTB units)		MTB (ns)	tRC Offset (FTB units)1		FTB (ns)	tRC Result (ns)	Use
400	0×190	0.125	0	0	0.001	50	DDR3-800D
420	0×1A4	0.125	0	0	0.001	52.5	DDR3-800E
390	0×186	0.125	0	0	0.001	48.75	DDR3-1066E
405	0×195	0.125	0	0	0.001	50.625	DDR3-1066F
420	0×1A4	0.125	0	0	0.001	52.5	DDR3-1066G
372	0×174	0.125	0	0	0.001	46.5	DDR3-1333F
384	0×180	0.125	0	0	0.001	48	DDR3-1333G
396	0×18C	0.125	0	0	0.001	49.5	DDR3-1333H2
393	0×189	0.125	0	0	0.001	49.125	DDR3-1333H downbin2
408	0×198	0.125	0	0	0.001	51	DDR3-1333J
360	0×168	0.125	0	0	0.001	45	DDR3-1600G
370	0×172	0.125	0	0	0.001	46.25	DDR3-1600H
380	0×17C	0.125	0	0	0.001	47.5	DDR3-1600J
390	0×186	0.125	0	0	0.001	48.75	DDR3-1600K2
385	0×181	0.125	0	0	0.001	48.125	DDR3-1600K downbin2
358	0×166	0.125	-50	0×CE	0.001	44.7	DDR3-1866J
367	0×16F	0.125	-105	0×97	0.001	45.77	DDR3-1866K
375	0×177	0.125	-35	0×DD	0.001	46.84	DDR3-1866L
384	0×180	0.125	-90	0×A6	0.001	47.91	DDR3-1866M2
377	0×179	0.125	0	0	0.001	47.125	DDR3-1866M downbin2
347	0×15B	0.125	-90	0×A6	0.001	43.285	DDR3-2133K
354	0×162	0.125	-30	0×E2	0.001	44.22	DDR3-2133L
362	0×16A	0.125	-95	0×A1	0.001	45.155	DDR3-2133M
369	0×171	0.125	-35	0×DD	0.001	46.09	DDR3-2133N

Notes:
1. See SPD byte 38.
2. Refer to device datasheet for downbin support details.

SPD Field #23: "Minimum Active to Active/Refresh Delay Time ($t_{RC}min$)" Definition from JEDEC DDR3 SPD Specification

Table 53 DDR3-1066 Speed Bins

DDR3-1066 Speed Bin		-187E		-187			
CL-tRCD-tRP		7-7-7		8-8-8			
Parameter	Symbol	Min	Max	Min	Max	Units	Notes
ACTIVATE to internal READ or WRITE delay time	tRCD	13.125	-	15	-	ns	
PRECHARGE command period	tRP	13.125	-	15	-	ns	
ACTIVATE-to-ACTIVATE or Refresh command period	tRC	50.625	-	52.5	-	ns	
ACTIVATE-to-PRECHARGE command period	tRAS	37.5	9 × tREFI	37.5	9 × tREFI	ns	1
CL = 5	CWL = 5	tCK (AVG)	3.0	3.3	3.0	3.3	ns	2, 3
	CWL = 6	tCK (AVG)	Reserved		Reserved		ns	3
CL = 6	CWL = 5	tCK (AVG)	2.5	3.3	2.5	3.3	ns	2
	CWL = 6	tCK (AVG)	Reserved		Reserved		ns	2, 3
CL = 7	CWL = 5	tCK (AVG)	Reserved		Reserved		ns	3
	CWL = 6	tCK (AVG)	1.875	< 2.5	Reserved		ns	2, 3
CL = 8	CWL = 5	tCK (AVG)	Reserved		Reserved		ns	3
	CWL = 6	tCK (AVG)	1.875	<2.5	1.875	< 2.5	ns	2
Supported CL settings		5, 6, 7, 8		5, 6, 8		CK	
Supported CWL settings		5, 6		5, 6		CK	

Notes:
1. tREFI depends on T$_{OPER}$.
2. The CL and CWL settings result in tCK requirements. When selecting tCK, both CL and CWL requirement settings need to be fulfilled.
3. Reserved settings are not allowed.

SPD Field #23: "Minimum Active to Active/Refresh Delay Time ($t_{RC}min$)" Example from Micron MT41J256M8 Datasheet

SPD Field 0×18 and 0×19: Min. Refresh Recovery Delay (t$_{RFC}$min)

This is another field that must be extracted from the datasheet and divided by the Medium Timebase Divisor. In our example:

1. The t$_{RFC}$ value found in the Micron MT41J256M8-187E datasheet for our specific SDRAM chip gives 160 ns. Note that the MT41J256M8- 187E is a 2 Gb part.
2. This number must be divided by the Medium Timebase Divisor, the value in 0×0B. In our example this is 0.125 ns.
3. 50.625 ns / 0.125 ns = 1280 = 0×0500.
4. The LSB, 0×00, goes into SPD field #24 (0×18).
5. The MSB, 05, goes into SPD field #25 (0×19).

Byte (Dec)	Byte (Hex)	Field Name	Typ. Value	Definition
24	0×18 (LSB)	Min. Refresh Recovery Delay	0×00	160ns
25	0×19 (MSB)	(t$_{RFC}$min)	0×05	

Byte 24: Minimum Refresh Recovery Delay Time (tRFCmin), Least Significant Byte
Byte 25: Minimum Refresh Recovery Delay Time (tRFCmin), Most Significant Byte
The contents of Byte 24 and the contents of Byte 25 combined create a 16-bit value that defines the minimum SDRAM Refresh Recovery Time Delay in Medium Timebase (MTB) units. The most significant bit is Bit 7 of Byte 25, and the least significant bit is Bit 0 of Byte 24. These values come from the DDR3 SDRAM datasheet.

Byte 25 Bits 7–0, Byte 24 Bits 7–0
Minimum Refresh Recover Time Delay (tRFC) MTB Units
Values defined from 1 to 65535

Examples:

tRFC (MTB units)		Timebase (ns)	tRFC Result (ns)	Use
720	0×2D0	0.125	90	512 Mb
880	0×370	0.125	110	1 Gb
1280	0×500	0.125	160	2 Gb
2400	0×960	0.125	300	4 Gb
2800	0×AF0	0.125	350	8 Gb

SPD Field #24 and #25: "Minimum Refresh Recovery Delay Time (t$_{RFC}$min), LSB"
Definition from JEDEC DDR3 SPD Specification

Table 56 Electrical Characteristics and AC Operating Conditions (Continued)
Notes 1–8 apply to the entire table

Parameter		Symbol	DDR3-800		DDR3-1066		DDR3-1333		DDR3-1600		Units
			Min	Max	Min	Max	Min	Max	Min	Max	s
MULTIPURPOSE REGISTER burst end to mode register exit		^{t}MPRR	MIN = 1CK; MAX = n/a								CK
Calibration Timing											
ZQCL command: Long calibration time	POWER-UP and RESET operation	^{t}ZQinit	512	–	512	–	512	–	512	–	CK
	Normal operation	^{t}ZQoper	256	–	256	–	256	–	256	–	ck
ZQCS command: short calibration		^{t}ZQcs	64	–	64	–	64	–	64	–	CK
Initialization and Reset Timing											
Exit reset from CKE HIGH to a valid command		^{t}XRP	MIN = greater of 5CK or ^{t}RFC + 10ns; MAX = n/q								CK
Begin power supply ramp to power supplies stable		^{t}Vddpr	MIN = n/a; Max = 200								ms
RESET # LOW to power supplies stable		^{t}RPS	MIN = 0; Max = 200								ms
RESET # LOW to I/O and R_{TT} High = Z		^{t}IOz	MIN = n/a; Max = 20								ns
Refresh Timing											
REFRESH-to-ACTIVATE or REFRESH command period		^{t}RFC–1Gb	MIN = 110; MAX = 70,200								ns
		^{t}RFC–2Gb	MIN = 160; MAX = 70,200								
		^{t}RFC–4Gb	MIN = 3000; MAX = 70,200								
Maximum refresh period	Tc £ + 85°C	–	64 (1X)								ms
	Tc > + 85°C		32 (1X)								ms
Maximum average periodic refresh	Tc £ + 85°C	^{t}REFI	7.8 (64ms/8,19240								µs
	Tc > + 85°C		3.9 (32ms/8,19240								µs
Write recovery time		^{t}WR	MIN = 15ns; MAX = n/a								ns
Delay from start of internal WRITE transaction to internal READ command		^{t}WTR	MIN = greater of 4CK or 7.5ns; MAX = n/a								CK
Self-Refresh Timing											
Exit self-refresh to commands not requiring a locked DLL		^{t}XS	MIN = Greater of 5CK or ^{t}RFC + 10ns; MAX = n/a								CK
Exit self-refresh to commands requiring a locked DLL		^{t}X SDLL	MIN = ^{t}DLLK (MIN); MAX = n/a								CK
Minimum CKE low pulse width for self-refresh exit timing		^{t}CKESR	MIN = ^{t}CKE + CK, Max = n/a								CK
Valid clocks after self-refresh entry or power down entry		^{t}CK SRE	MIN = greater of SCK or 15ns; MAX = n/a								CK

SPD Field #24 and #25: "Minimum Refresh Recovery Delay Time (t$_{RFC}$min), LSB"
Micron MT41J256M8 Datasheet

SPD Field 0×1A: Min. Write to Read Command Delay (t$_{WTR}$min)

This is another field that must be extracted from the datasheet and divided by the Medium Timebase Divisor. In our example:

1. The t$_{WTR}$ value found in the Micron MT41J256M8 datasheet for our specific SDRAM chip gives 7.5 ns.
2. This number must be divided by the Medium Timebase Divisor, the value in 0×0B. In our example this is 0.125 ns.
3. 75 ns / 0.125 ns = 60 = 0×3C.

Byte (Dec)	Byte (Hex)	Field Name	Typ. Value	Definition
26	0×1A	Min. Write to Read Command Delay (t$_{WTR}$min)	0×3C	7.5ns

Byte 26: Minimum Internal Write to Read Command Delay Time (tWTRmin)
This byte defines the minimum SDRAM Internal Write to Read Delay Time in Medium Timebase (MTB) units. This value comes from the DDR3 SDRAM datasheet. The value of this number may be dependent on the SDRAM page size; please refer to the DDR3 SDRAM datasheet section on Addressing to determine the page size for these devices. Controller designers must also note that at some frequencies, a minimum number of clocks may be required, resulting in a larger tWTRmin value than indicated in the SPD. For example, tWTRmin for DDR3-800 must be 4 clocks.

Bits 7–0
Internal Write to Read Delay Time (tWTR) MTB Units
Values defined from 1 to 255

Example:

tWTR (MTB units)		Timebase (ns)	tWTR Result (ns)	Use
60	0×3C	0.125	7.5	All DDR3 SDRAM speed bins

Note: tRTP is at least 4 nCK independent of operating frequency.

SPD Field #26: "Minimum Internal Write to Read Command Delay Time (t$_{WTR}$min)" Definition from JEDEC DDR3 SPD Specification

Table 56 Electrical Characteristics and AC Operating Conditions (Continued)
Notes 1–8 apply to the entire table

Parameter		Symbol	DDR3-800		DDR3-1066		DDR3-1333		DDR3-1600		Units
			Min	Max	Min	Max	Min	Max	Min	Max	
DQS, DQS # differential READ postamble		^{t}RPST	0.3	Note 27	0.3	Note 27	0.3	Note 27	0.3	Note 27	CK
Command and Address Timings											
DLL locking time		^{t}DLLK	512	–	512	–	512	–	512	–	CK
CTRL, CMD, ADDR setup to CK, CK#	Base (Specification) V$_{REF}$@1 V/ns	^{t}IS	200	–	125	–	65	–	45	–	ps
		AC175	375	–	300	–	240	–	220	–	ps
CTRL, CMD, ADDR setup to CK, CK#	Base (Specification) V$_{REF}$@1 V/ns	^{t}IS	350	–		–		–		–	ps
		AC150	500	–	425	–	340	–	320	–	p
CTRL, CMD, ADDR setup to CK, CK#	Base (Specification) V$_{REF}$@1 V/ns	^{t}IH	275	–	200	–	140	–	120	–	ps
		DC100	375	–	300	–	240	–	220	–	ps
Minimum CTRL, CMD, ADDR pulse width		^{t}IPW	900	–	780	–	620	–	560	–	ps
ACTIVATE to internal READ or WRITE delay		^{t}RCD	See Speed Bin Tables (page 72) for ^{t}RCD								ns
PRECHARGE command period		^{t}RP	See Speed Bin Tables (page 72) for ^{t}RP								ns
ACTIVATE-to-PRECHARGE command period		^{t}RAS	See Speed Bin Tables (page 72) for ^{t}RAS								ns
ACTIVATE-to-ACTIVATE command		^{t}RC	See Speed Bin Tables (page 72) for ^{t}RC								ns
ACTIVATE- to- ACTIVATE minium command period	1KB page size	^{t}RRD	MIN= greater of 4CK or 10ns		MIN= greater of 4CK or 7.5ns		MIN= greater of 4CK or 6ns		MIN= greater of 4CK or 6ns		CK
	2KB page size		MIN= greater of 4CK or 10ns				MIN= greater of 4CK or 7.5ns				CK
Four ACTIVATE windows	1KB page size	^{t}FAW	40	–	37.5	–	30	–	30	–	ns
	2KB page size		50	–	50	–	45	–	40	–	ns
Write recovery time		^{t}WR	MIN = 15ns; MAX = n/a								ns
Delay from start of internal WRITE transaction to internal READ command		^{t}WTR	MIN = greater of 4CK or 7.5ns; MAX = n/a								CK
READ-to-PRECHARGE time		^{t}RTP	MIN = greater of 4CK or 7.5ns; MAX = n/a								CK
CAS# to CAS# command delay		^{t}CCD	MIN = 4CK; MAX = n/a								CK
Auto precharge write recovery + precharge time		^{t}DAL	MIN = WR+tRP/^{t}CK (AVG); MAX = n/a								CK
MODE REGISTER SET command cycle time		^{t}MRD	MIN = 4CK; MAX = n/a								CK

| MODE REGISTER SET | ᵗMOD | MIN = greater of 12CK or 15ns; MAX = n/a | CK |
| command update delay | | | |

SPD Field #26: "Minimum Internal Write to Read Command Delay Time (t_{WTR}min)" Example from Micron MT41J256M8 Datasheet

SPD Field 0×1B: Min. Read to Precharge Command Delay (t_{RTP}min)

This is another field that must be extracted from the datasheet and divided by the Medium Timebase Divisor.

In our example:
1. The t_{RTP} value found in the Micron MT41J256M8 datasheet for our specific SDRAM chip gives 7.5 ns.
2. This number must be divided by the Medium Timebase Divisor, the value in 0×0B. In our example this is 0.125 ns.
3. 75 ns / 0.125 ns = 60 = 0×3C.

Byte (Dec)	Byte (Hex)	Field Name	Typ. Value	Definition
27	0×1B	Min. Read to Precharge Command Delay (t_{RTP}min)	0×3C	7.5ns

Byte 27: Minimum Internal Read to Precharge Command Delay Time (tRTPmin)
This byte defines the minimum SDRAM Internal Read to Precharge Delay Time in Medium Timebase (MTB) units. This value comes from the DDR3 SDRAM datasheet. The value of this number may depend on the SDRAM page size; please refer to the DDR3 SDRAM datasheet section on Addressing to determine the page size for these devices. Controller designers must also note that at some frequencies, a minimum number of clocks may be required, resulting in a larger tRTPmin value than indicated in the SPD. For example, tRTPmin for DDR3-800 must be 4 clocks.

Bits 7–0
Internal Read to Precharge Delay Time (tRTP) MTB Units
Values defined from 1 to 255

Examples:

tRTP (MTB units)		Timebase (ns)	tRTP Result (ns)	Use
60	0×3C	0.125	7.5	All DDR3 SDRAM speed bins

Note: tRTP is at least 4 nCK independent of operating frequency.

SPD Field #27: "Minimum Internal Read to Precharge Command Delay Time (t$_{RTP}$min)" Definition from JEDEC DDR3 SPD Specification

Table 56 Electrical Characteristics and AC Operating Conditions (Continued)
Notes 1–8 apply to the entire table

Parameter		Symbol	DDR3-800		DDR3-1066		DDR3-1333		DDR3-1600		Units
			Min	Max	Min	Max	Min	Max	Min	Max	
DQS, DQS # differential READ postamble		^{t}RPST	0.3	Note 27	0.3	Note 27	0.3	Note 27	0.3	Note 27	CK
Command and Address Timings											
DLL locking time		^{t}DLLK	512	–	512	–	512	–	512	–	CK
CTRL, CMD, ADDR setup to CK, CK#	Base (Specification)	^{t}IS	200	–	125	–	65	–	45	–	ps
	V$_{REF}$@1 V/ns	AC175	375	–	300	–	240	–	220	–	ps
CTRL, CMD, ADDR setup to CK, CK#	Base (Specification)	^{t}IS	350	–		–		–		–	ps
	V$_{REF}$@1 V/ns	AC150	500	–	425	–	340	–	320	–	p
CTRL, CMD, ADDR hold from CK, CK#	Base (Specification)	^{t}IH	275	–	200	–	140	–	120	–	ps
	V$_{REF}$@1 V/ns	DC100	375	–	300	–	240	–	220	–	ps
Minimum CTRL, CMD, ADDR pulse width		^{t}IPW	900	–	780	–	620	–	560	–	ps
ACTIVATE to internal READ or WRITE delay		^{t}RCD	See Speed Bin Tables (page 72) for ^{t}RCD								ns
PRECHARGE command period		^{t}RP	See Speed Bin Tables (page 72) for ^{t}RP								ns
ACTIVATE-to-PRECHARGE command period		^{t}RAS	See Speed Bin Tables (page 72) for ^{t}RAS								ns
ACTIVATE-to-ACTIVATE command		^{t}RC	See Speed Bin Tables (page 72) for ^{t}RC								ns
ACTIVATE- to- ACTIVATE minium command period	1KB page size	^{t}RRD	MIN= greater of 4CK or 10ns		MIN= greater of 4CK or 7.5ns		MIN= greater of 4CK or 6ns		MIN= greater of 4CK or 6ns		CK
	2KB page size		MIN= greater of 4CK or 10ns				MIN= greater of 4CK or 7.5ns				CK
Four ACTIVATE windows	1KB page size	^{t}FAW	40	–	37.5	–	30	–	30	–	ns
	2KB page size		50	–	50	–	45	–	40	–	ns

Write recovery time	^{t}WR	MIN = 15ns; MAX = n/a	ns
Delay from start of internal WRITE transaction to internal READ command	^{t}WTR	MIN = greater of 4CK or 7.5ns; MAX = n/a	CK
READ-to-PRECHARGE time	^{t}RTP	MIN = greater of 4CK or 7.5ns; MAX = n/a	CK
CAS# to CAS# command delay	^{t}CCD	MIN = 4CK; MAX = n/a	CK
Auto precharge write recovery + precharge time	^{t}DAL	MIN = WR+^{t}RP/^{t}CK (AVG); MAX = n/a	CK
MODE REGISTER SET command cycle time	^{t}MRD	MIN = 4CK; MAX = n/a	CK
MODE REGISTER SET command update delay	^{t}MOD	MIN = greater of 12CK or 15ns; MAX = n/a	CK

SPD Field #27: "Minimum Internal Read to Precharge Command Delay Time (t_{RTP}min)" Example from Micron MT41J256M8 Datasheet

SPD Field 0×1C: t_{FAW} Upper Nibble

This is the upper nibble for the t_{FAW} SDRAM timing parameter. See the next section for how to calculate this value, and put the upper nibble into SPD Field #28, bits [3:0].

Byte (Dec)	Byte (Hex)	Field Name	Typ. Value	Definition
28	0×1C	t_{FAW} Upper Nibble	0×01	---

Byte 28: Upper Nibble for tFAW
This byte defines the most significant nibble for the value of tFAW (SPD byte 29). This value comes from the DDR3 SDRAM datasheet.

Bits 7–4	Bits 3–0
Reserved	t_{faw} **Most Significant Nibble**
Reserved	See Byte 29 description

SPD Field #28: "Upper Nibble for t_{FAW}" Definition from JEDEC DDR3 SPD Specification

SPD Field 0×1D: Min. Four Activate Window Delay (t_{FAW}min) LSB

This is another field that must be extracted from the datasheet and divided by the Medium Timebase Divisor. In our example:
1. The t_{FAW} value found in the Micron MT41J256M8 datasheet for our specific SDRAM chip gives 37.5 ns. Note that in the case of this SDRAM part, the number varies,

depending on the part's page size. In the case of the MT41J256M8, the page size is 1K as shown.

2. This number must be divided by the Medium Timebase Divisor, the value in 0×0B. In our example this is 0.125 ns.
3. 37.5 ns / 0.125 ns = 300 = 0×12C.
4. The upper nibble, 0×1, is put into SPD field #28, bits [3:0].
5. The LSB, 0×2C, is put into SPD field #29.

Byte (Dec)	Byte (Hex)	Field Name	Typ. Value	Definition
29	0×1D Min.	Four Activate Window Delay (t$_{FAW}$min) LSB	0×2C	37.5ns

Byte 29: Minimum Four Activate Window Delay Time (tFAWmin), Least Significant Byte
The lower nibble of Byte 28 and the contents of Byte 29 combined create a 12-bit value that defines the minimum SDRAM Four Activate Window Delay Time in Medium Timebase (MTB) units. This value comes from the DDR3 SDRAM datasheet. The value of this number may depend on the SDRAM page size; please refer to the DDR3 SDRAM datasheet section on Addressing to determine the page size for these devices.

Byte 28 Bits 3–0, Byte 29 Bits 7–0
Minimum Four Activate Window Delay Time (t$_{faw}$) MTB Units
Values defined from 1 to 4095

Examples:

tFAW (MTB units)		Timebase (ns)	tFAW Result (ns)	Use
320	0×140	0.125	40	Example: DDR3-800 1 KB page size
400	0×190	0.125	50	Example: DDR3-800 2 KB page size
300	0×12C	0.125	37.5	Example: DDR3-1066 1 KB page size
400	0×190	0.125	50	Example: DDR3-1066 2 KB page size
240	0×0F0	0.125	30	Example: DDR3-1333 1 KB page size
360	0×168	0.125	45	Example: DDR3-1333 2 KB page size
240	0×0F0	0.125	30	Example: DDR3-1600 1 KB page size
320	0×140	0.125	40	Example: DDR3-1600 2 KB page size
216	0×0D8	0.125	27	Example: DDR3-1866 1 KB page size
280	0×118	0.125	35	Example: DDR3-1866 2 KB page size
200	0×0C8	0.125	25	Example: DDR3-2133 1 KB page size

tFAW (MTB units)		Timebase (ns)	tFAW Result (ns)	Use
280	0×118	0.125	35	Example: DDR3-2133 2 KB page size

SPD Field #29: "Minimum Four Activate Window Delay Time (tFAWmin) LSB" Definition from JEDEC DDR3 SPD Specification

Table 56 Electrical Characteristics and AC Operating Conditions (Continued)
Notes 1–8 apply to the entire table

Parameter		Symbol	DDR3-800		DDR3-1066		DDR3-1333		DDR3-1600		Units
			Min	Max	Min	Max	Min	Max	Min	Max	
DQS, DQS # differential READ postamble		ᵗRPST	0.3	Note 27	0.3	Note 27	0.3	Note 27	0.3	Note 27	CK
Command and Address Timings											
DLL locking time		ᵗDLLK	512	–	512	–	512	–	512	–	CK
CTRL, CMD, ADDR setup to CK, CK#	Base (Specification) V_{REF}@1 V/ns	ᵗIS AC175	200 375	– –	125 300	– –	65 240	– –	45 220	– –	ps ps
CTRL, CMD, ADDR setup to CK, CK#	Base (Specification) V_{REF}@1 V/ns	ᵗIS AC150	350 500	– –	– 425	– –	– 340	– –	– 320	– –	ps p
CTRL, CMD, ADDR setup to CK, CK#	Base (Specification) V_{REF}@1 V/ns	ᵗIH DC100	275 375	– –	200 300	– –	140 240	– –	120 220	– –	ps ps
Minimum CTRL, CMD, ADDR pulse width		ᵗIPW	900	–	780	–	620	–	560	–	ps
ACTIVATE to internal READ or WRITE delay		ᵗRCD	See Speed Bin Tables (page 72) for ᵗRCD								ns
PRECHARGE command period		ᵗRP	See Speed Bin Tables (page 72) for ᵗRP								ns
ACTIVATE-to-PRECHARGE command period		ᵗRAS	See Speed Bin Tables (page 72) for ᵗRAS								ns
ACTIVATE-to-ACTIVATE command		ᵗRC	See Speed Bin Tables (page 72) for ᵗRC								ns
ACTIVATE- to- ACTIVATE minium command period	1KB page size	ᵗRRD	MIN= greater of 4CK or 10ns		MIN= greater of 4CK or 7.5ns		MIN= greater of 4CK or 6ns		MIN= greater of 4CK or 6ns		CK
	2KB page size		MIN= greater of 4CK or 10ns				MIN= greater of 4CK or 7.5ns				CK
Four ACTIVATE windows	1KB page size	ᵗFAW	40	–	37.5	–	30	–	30	–	ns
	2KB page size		50	–	50	–	45	–	40	–	ns
Write recovery time		ᵗWR	MIN = 15ns; MAX = n/a								ns

Delay from start of internal WRITE transaction to internal READ command	ᵗWTR	MIN = greater of 4CK or 7.5ns; MAX = n/a	CK
READ-to-PRECHARGE time	ᵗRTP	MIN = greater of 4CK or 7.5ns; MAX = n/a	CK
CAS# to CAS# command delay	ᵗCCD	MIN = 4CK; MAX = n/a	CK
Auto precharge write recovery + precharge time	ᵗDAL	MIN = WR+ᵗRP/ᵗCK (AVG); MAX = n/a	CK
MODE REGISTER SET command cycle time	ᵗMRD	MIN = 4CK; MAX = n/a	CK
MODE REGISTER SET command update delay	ᵗMOD	MIN = greater of 12CK or 15ns; MAX = n/a	CK

Table 2 Addressing

Parameter	512 Meg × 4	256 Meg × 8	128 Meg × 16
Configuration	64 Meg × 4 × 8 banks	32 Meg × 8 × 8 banks	16 Meg × 16 × 8 banks
Refresh count	8K	8K	8K
Row addressing	32K (A[14:0])	32K (A[14:0])	16K (A[13:0])
Bank addressing	8 (BA[2:0])	8 (BA[2:0])	8 (BA[2:0])
Column addressing	2K(A[11,9:0])	1K(A[9:0])	1K(A[9:0])

SPD Field #29: "Minimum Four Activate Window Delay Time (tFAWmin) LSB" Example from Micron MT41J256M8 Datasheet

SPD Field 0x1E: SDRAM Optional Features

These three bits need to be set if the SDRAM device supports the respective feature. Included above is an example from the MT41J256M8 datasheet that shows it supports all three features.

Byte (Dec)	Byte (Hex)	Field Name	Typ. Value	Definition
30	0×1E	SDRAM Optional Features	0×83	RZQ/7, RZQ/6, and DLL-Off Mode Support

Byte 30: SDRAM Optional Features
This byte defines support for certain SDRAM features and the optional drive strengths supported by the SDRAMs on this module. This value comes from the DDR3 SDRAM datasheet.

Bit 7	Bits 6–2	Bit 1	Bit 0
DLL-Off Mode Support	**Reserved**	**RZQ / 7**	**RZQ / 6**
0 = Not Supported 1 = Supported		0 = Not Supported 1 = Supported	0 = Not Supported 1 = Supported

SPD Field #30: "SDRAM Optional Features" Definition from JEDEC DDR3 SPD Specification

SPD Field 0×1F: SDRAM Thermal and Refresh Options

These bits need to be set if the SDRAM component supports the specific thermal property. As shown above, the MT41J256M8 supports the extended temperature and extended temperature refresh rates, along with the ability to do Auto Self Refresh (SPD field #33=0×07).

Byte (Dec)	Byte (Hex)	Field Name	Typ. Value	Definition
31	0×1F	SDRAM Thermal and Refresh options	0×07	Extended Temp. Ranges and Auto Self Refresh (ASR)

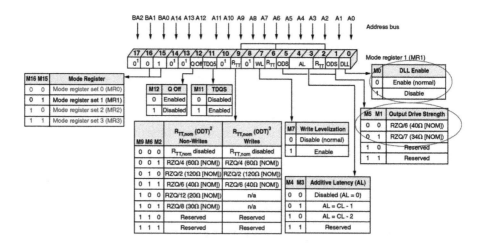

Figure 53 Mode Register 1(MR1) Definition

SPD Field #30: "SDRAM Optional Features" Example from Micron MT41J256M8 Datasheet

Byte 31: SDRAM Thermal and Refresh Options

This byte describes the module's supported operating temperature ranges and refresh options. These values come from the DDR3 SDRAM datasheet. Use of self-refresh in the Extended Temperature Range, ASR, or ODTS require appropriate SDRAM Mode Register programming (MR2 bits A6, A7, and MR3 bit A3). Please refer to the DDR3 SDRAM datasheet (JESD79-3 or supplier datasheet) for a complete description of these options.

Bit 7	Bits 6–4	Bit 3	Bit 2	Bit 1	Bit 0
Partial Array Self- Refresh (PASR)	Reserved	On-Die Thermal Sensor (ODTS)	Readout Auto Self Refresh (ASR)	Extended Temperature Refresh Rate	Extended Temperature Range
1 = Supported 0 = Not supported		1 = On-die thermal sensor readout is supported 0 = On-die thermal sensor readout is not supported (pending ballot of ODTS)	1 = ASR is supported and the SDRAM will determine the proper refresh rate for any supported temperature 0 = ASR is not supported	1 = Extended operating temperature range from 85–95° C supported with standard 1X refresh rate 0 = Use in extended operating temperature range from 85–95° C requires 2X refresh rate	1 = Normal and extended operating temperature range 0–95° C supported 0 = Normal operating temperature range 0–85° C supported

SPD Field #31: "SDRAM Thermal and Refresh Options" Definition from JEDEC DDR3 SPD Specification

SPD Field 0×20: Module Thermal Sensor

If the memory-down-on-board design has a dedicated thermal sensor for the SDRAM components, then this field should be set to 0×80, otherwise to 0×00.

Byte (Dec)	Byte (Hex)	Field Name	Typ. Value	Definition
32	0×20	Module Thermal Sensor	0×00	None

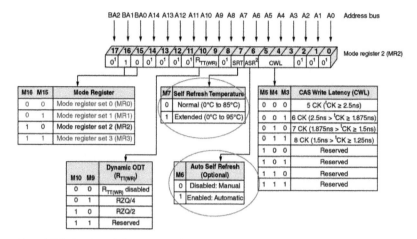

Notes: 1. MR2[17, 14:11, 8, and 2:0] are reserved for future use and must all be programmed to 0.
2. On die revision A, ASR is not available; MR2[6] must be programmed to a "0," and if operating self refresh mode above 85°C, use SRT, MR2[7].

Extended Temperature Usage

Micron's DDR3 SDRAM supports the optional extended temperature range of 0°C to +95°C, Tc. Thus, the SRT and ASR options must be used at a minimum.

Figure 55 Mode Register 2 (MR2) Definition

SPD Field #31: "SDRAM Thermal and Refresh Options" Example from Micron MT41J256M8 Datasheet

Byte 32: Module Thermal Sensor
This byte describes the module's supported thermal options.

Bit 7	Bits 6–0
Thermal Sensor1	Thermal Sensor Accuracy
0 = Thermal sensor not incorporated onto this assembly 1 = Thermal sensor incorporated onto this assembly	0 = Undefined All others settings to be defined.

Note: 1. Thermal sensor compliant with TSE2002 specifications.

SPD Field #32: "Module Thermal Sensor" Definition from JEDEC DDR3 SPD Specification

SPD Field 0x21: SDRAM Device Type

Set this field to 0×00.

Byte (Dec)	Byte (Hex)	Field Name	Typ. Value	Definition
33	0×21	SDRAM Device Type	0×00	Normal DRAM

Byte 33: SDRAM Device Type

This byte describes the type of SDRAM Device on the module.

Bit~7	Bits 6~4	Bits 3~2	Bit 1~0	
SDRAM Device Type		**Die Count**	**Reserved**	**Signal Loading2**
0 = Standard Monolithic DRAM Device 1 = Non-Standard Device1		000 = Not specified 001 = Single die 010 = 2 die 011 = 4 die 100 = 8 die All others settings reserved	0 = Undefined	00 = Not specified 01 = Multiload stack 10 = Single load stack 11 = Reserved

SPD Field #33: "SDRAM Device Type" Definition from JEDEC DDR3 SPD Specification

SPD Field 0×22–0×3B: Reserved

For JEDEC SPD Specification v1.0, these fields are reserved and should be set to 0×00. For JEDEC SPD Specification v1.1, some of these fields are defined.

Byte (Dec)	Byte (Hex)	Field Name	Typ. Value	Definition
34–59	0×22–0×3B	Reserved	0×00	V1.0

For v1.1 of the specification, the following bytes may be programmed.

Byte 34: Fine Offset for SDRAM Minimum Cycle Time (tCKmin)

This byte modifies the calculation of SPD Byte 12 (MTB units) with a fine correction using FTB units. The value of tCKmin comes from the SDRAM datasheet. This value is a Two's Complement multiplier for FTB units, ranging from +127 to -128. Examples: See SPD byte 12. For Two's Complement encoding, see *Relating the MTB and FTB*.

Byte 35: Fine Offset for Minimum CAS Latency Time (tAAmin)

This byte modifies the calculation of SPD Byte 16 (MTB units) with a fine correction using FTB units. The value of tAAmin comes from the SDRAM datasheet. This value is a Two's Complement multiplier for FTB units, ranging from +127 to -128. Examples: See SPD Byte 16. For Two's Complement encoding, see *Relating the MTB and FTB.*

Byte 36: Fine Offset for Minimum RAS# to CAS# Delay Time (tRCDmin)
This byte modifies the calculation of SPD Byte 18 (MTB units) with a fine correction using FTB units. The value of tRCDmin comes from the SDRAM datasheet. This value is a Two's Complement multiplier for FTB units, ranging from +127 to -128. Examples: See SPD byte 18. For Two's Complement encoding, see *Relating the MTB and FTB.*

Byte 37: Minimum Row Precharge Delay Time (tRPmin)
This byte modifies the calculation of SPD Byte 20 (MTB units) with a fine correction using FTB units. The value of tRPmin comes from the SDRAM datasheet. This value is a Two's Complement multiplier for FTB units, ranging from +127 to -128. Examples: See SPD byte 20. For Two's Complement encoding, see *Relating the MTB and FTB.*

Byte 38: Fine Offset for Minimum Active to Active/Refresh Delay Time (tRCmin)
This byte modifies the calculation of SPD Bytes 21 and 23 (MTB units) with a fine correction using FTB units. The value of tRCmin comes from the SDRAM datasheet. This value is a Two's Complement multiplier for FTB units, ranging from +127 to -128. Examples: See SPD byte 21 and 23. For Two's Complement encoding, see *Relating the MTB and FTB.*

Module-Specific Section: Bytes 60–116

This section contains SPD bytes specific to DDR3 module families. Module Type Key Byte 3 is used as an index for the encoding of bytes 60–116. The content of bytes 60–116 are described in multiple appendices, one for each memory module family.

SPD Field #60: "Module Nominal Height" Definition from JEDEC DDR3 SPD Specification

SPD Field 0×3C: (Unbuffered): Module Nominal Height

Down-on-board memory designs should set this field to 0×00.

Byte (Dec)	Byte (Hex)	Field Name	Typ. Value	Definition
60	0×3C	(Unbuffered): Module Nominal Height	0×00	Height<15 mm

Byte 60 (Unbuffered): Module Nominal Height

This byte defines the nominal height (A dimension) in millimeters of the fully assembled module, including heat spreaders or other added components. Refer to the relevant JEDEC JC-11 module outline (MO) documents for dimension definitions.

Bits 7–5	Bits 4–0
Reserved	Module Nominal Height max in mm (baseline height = 15 mm)
Reserved	00000 = height≤15 mm
	00001 = 15 < height≤16 mm
	00010 = 16 < height≤17 mm
	00011 = 17 < height≤18 mm
	00100 = 18 < height≤19 mm
	...
	01010 = 24 < height≤25 mm
	01011 = 25 < height≤26 mm
	...
	01111 = 29 < height≤30 mm
	10000 = 30 < height≤31 mm
	...
	11111 = 45 mm<height

SPD Field 0×3D: (Unbuffered): Module Max. Thickness

Down-on-board memory designs should set this field to 0×00.

Byte (Dec)	Byte (Hex)	Field Name	Typ. Value	Definition
61	0×3D	(Unbuffered): Module Max. Thickness	0×00	Thickness<1mm

Byte 61 (Unbuffered): Module Maximum Thickness

This byte defines the maximum thickness (E dimension) in millimeters of the fully assembled module, including heat spreaders or other added components above the module circuit board surface. Thickness of the front of the module is calculated as the E1 dimension minus the PCB thickness. Thickness of the back of the module is calculated as the E dimension minus the E1 dimension. Refer to the relevant JEDEC JC-11 module outline (MO) documents for dimension definitions.

Bits 7–4	Bits 3–0
Module Maximum Thickness max, Back, in mm (baseline thickness = 1 mm)	Module Maximum Thickness max, Front, in mm (baseline thickness = 1 mm)
0000 = thickness≤1 mm	0000 = thickness≤1 mm

Bits 7–4	Bits 3–0
Module Maximum Thickness max, Back, in mm (baseline thickness = 1 mm)	**Module Maximum Thickness max, Front, in mm (baseline thickness = 1 mm)**
0001 = 1 < thickness≤2 mm	0001 = 1 < thickness≤2 mm
0010 = 2 < thickness≤3 mm	0010 = 2 < thickness≤3 mm
0011 = 3 < thickness≤4 mm	0011 = 3 < thickness≤4 mm
...	...
1110 = 14 < thickness≤15 mm	1110 = 14 < thickness≤5 mm
1111 = 15 < thickness	1111 = 15 < thickness
Note: Thickness = E - E1	Note: Thickness = E1 - PCB

SPD Field #61: "(Unbuffered): Module Maximum Thickness" Definition from JEDEC DDR3 SPD Specification

SPD Field 0x3E: (Unbuffered): Reference Raw Card Used

Each DIMM equivalent consists of a single rank of ×8 SDRAM devices, no ECC. This corresponds to RAW Card Version A, ×64, which would make SPD field #62=0×00.

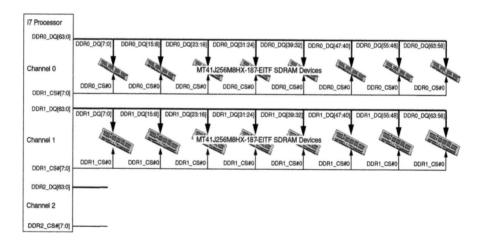

The various Reference Raw Card Enumerators are described in this document: JEDEC Standard No. 21C: 240-Pin PC3-6400/PC3-8500/PC3- 10600/PC3-12800 DDR3 SDRAM Unbuffered DIMM Design Specification, Revision 1.01, November 2009, http://www.jedec.org/ (requires account).

Byte (Dec)	Byte (Hex)	Field Name	Typ. Value	Definition
62	**0×3E**	(Unbuffered): Reference Raw Card Used	0×00	Raw Card A, ×64

Byte 62 (Unbuffered): Reference Raw Card Used

This byte indicates which JEDEC reference design raw card was used as the basis for the module assembly, if any. Bits 4–0 describe the raw card and bits 6–5 describe the revision level of that raw card. Special reference raw card indicator, ZZ, is used when no JEDEC standard raw card reference design was used as the basis for the module design. Preproduction modules should be encoded as revision 0 in bits 6–5.

The JEDEC committee defines a specific "Reference Raw Card" enumerator for a given DIMM topology. The DIMM equivalents used in the design must be analyzed (number of ranks, ×4, ×8, ×16 components, ECC, and so on) and matched to the appropriate JEDEC Reference Raw Card. The matching Reference Raw Card number is put into this SPD field.

In our example topology shown below:

Bit 7	Bits 6–5	Bits 4–0
Reference Raw Card Extension	**Reference Raw Card Revision**	**Reference Raw Card**
0 = Reference raw cards A through AL	00 = revision 001 = revision 1 10 = revision 2 11 = revision 3	When bit 7 = 0, 00000 = Reference raw card A 00001 = Reference raw card B 00010 = Reference raw card C 00011 = Reference raw card D 00100 = Reference raw card E 00101 = Reference raw card F 00110 = Reference raw card G 00111 = Reference raw card H 01000 = Reference raw card J 01001 = Reference raw card K 01010 = Reference raw card L 01011 = Reference raw card M 01100 = Reference raw card N 01101 = Reference raw card P 01110 = Reference raw card R 01111 = Reference raw card T 10000 = Reference raw card U 10001 = Reference raw card V 10010 = Reference raw card W 10011 = Reference raw card Y 10100 = Reference raw card AA

Bit 7	Bits 6–5	Bits 4–0
Reference Raw Card Extension	Reference Raw Card Revision	Reference Raw Card
		10101 = Reference raw card AB
		10110 = Reference raw card AC
		10111 = Reference raw card AD
		11000 = Reference raw card AE
		11001 = Reference raw card AF
		11010 = Reference raw card AG
		11011 = Reference raw card AH
		11100 = Reference raw card AJ
		11101 = Reference raw card AK
		11110 = Reference raw card AL
		11111 = ZZ (no JEDEC reference raw card design used)

Bit 7	Bits 6–5	Bits 4–0	
Reference Raw Card Extension		Reference Raw Card Revision	Reference Raw Card
1 = Reference raw cards AM through CB		00 = revision 0	When bit 7 = 1,
		01 = revision 1	00000 = Reference raw card AM
		10 = revision 2	00001 = Reference raw card AN
		11 = revision 3	00010 = Reference raw card AP
			00011 = Reference raw card AR
			00100 = Reference raw card AT
			00101 = Reference raw card AU
			00110 = Reference raw card AV
			00111 = Reference raw card AW
			01000 = Reference raw card AY
			01001 = Reference raw card BA
			01010 = Reference raw card BB
			01011 = Reference raw card BC
			01100 = Reference raw card BD
			01101 = Reference raw card BE
			01110 = Reference raw card BF
			01111 = Reference raw card BG
			10000 = Reference raw card BH
			10001 = Reference raw card BJ
			10010 = Reference raw card BK
			10011 = Reference raw card BL
			10100 = Reference raw card BM
			10101 = Reference raw card BN
			10110 = Reference raw card BP
			10111 = Reference raw card BR
			11000 = Reference raw card BT

Bit 7	Bits 6–5	Bits 4–0	
Reference Raw Card Extension	Reference Raw Card Revision	Reference Raw Card	
		11001 = Reference raw card BU	
		11010 = Reference raw card BV	
		11011 = Reference raw card BW	
		11100 = Reference raw card BY	
		11101 = Reference raw card CA	
		11110 = Reference raw card CB	
		11111 = ZZ (no JEDEC reference raw card design used)	

SPD Field #62: "(Unbuffered): Reference Card Used" Definition from JEDEC DDR3 SPD Specification

SPD Field 0×3F: Unbuff Addr. Mapping from Edge Connector to DRAM

If the motherboard has mirrored the address lines, set to 1. The typical values assume the board address mapping is standard.

Byte (Dec)	Byte (Hex)	Field Name	Typ. Value	Definition
63	0×3F	Unbuff Addr. Mapping from Edge Connector to DRAM	0×00	Standard

Byte 63: Address Mapping from Edge Connector to DRAM

This byte describes the connection of edge connector pins for address bits to the corresponding input pins of the DDR3 SDRAMs for rank 1 only; rank 0 is always assumed to use standard mapping. Only two connection types are supported, standard or mirrored, as described in the mapping table below. System software must compensate for this mapping when issuing mode register set commands to the ranks of DDR3 SDRAMs on this module.

Bits 7–1	Bit 0
Reserved	Rank 1 Mapping
Reserved	0 = standard 1 = mirrored

The definition of standard and mirrored address connection mapping is detailed below; highlighted rows in the table indicate which signals change between mappings.

Edge Connector Signal	DRAM Pin Standard	DRAM Pin Mirrored
A0	A0	A0
A1	A1	A1
A2	A2	A2
A3	A3	A4
A4	A4	A3
A5	A5	A6
A6	A6	A5
A7	A7	A8
A8	A8	A7
A9	A9	A9
A10/AP	A10/AP	A10/AP
A11	A11	A11
A12/BC	A12/BC	A12/BC
A13	A13	A13
A14	A14	A14
A15/BA3	A15/BA3	A15/BA3
BA0	BA0	BA1
BA1	BA1	BA0
BA2	BA2	BA2

SPD Field #63: "Address Mapping from Edge Connector to DRAM" Definition from JEDEC DDR3 SPD Specification

SPD Field 0×40-0×74: Reserved

All reserved fields should be set to 0×00.

Byte (Dec)	Byte (Hex)	Field Name	Typ. Value	Definition
64–116	0×40–0×74	Unbuffered RESERVED	0×00	---

SPD Field 0×75 and 0×76: Module Manufacturer ID Code, LSB

Although a module is "technically" the DIMM manufacturer, it is recommended to put in the ID for the SDRAM vendor. The JEDEC specification JEP-106 contains the list of module vendors. The code for Micron Technology is 0×802C.

Byte (Dec)	Byte (Hex)	Field Name	Typ. Value	Definition
117–118	0×75–0×76	Module Manufacturer ID Code, LSB	0×80 0×2C	Micron Technology

Byte 117: Module Manufacturer ID Code, Least Significant Byte
Byte 118: Module Manufacturer ID Code, Most Significant Byte
This two-byte field indicates the manufacturer of the module, encoded as follows: the first byte is the number of continuation bytes indicated in JEP- 106; the second byte is the last nonzero byte of the manufacturer's ID code, again as indicated in JEP-106.

Byte 118 Bits 7–0	Byte 117 Bit 7	Byte 117 Bits 6–0
Last Nonzero Byte Module Manufacturer	Odd Parity for Byte 117 bits 6–0	Number of Continuation Codes Module Manufacturer
See JEP-106		See JEP-106

Examples:

Company	JEP-106		# Continuation Codes	SPD	
	Bank	Code		Byte 117	Byte 118
Fujitsu	1	04	0	0×80	0×04
US Modular	5	A8	4	0×04	0×A8

SPD Field #117 and #118: "Module Manufacture ID Code" Definition from JEDEC DDR3 SPD Specification

SPD Field 0×77: Module Manufacturer Location

Byte (Dec)	Byte (Hex)	Field Name	Typ. Value	Definition
119	0×77	Module Manufacturer Location	0×00	---

Byte 119: Module Manufacturing Location
The module manufacturer includes an identifier that uniquely defines the manufacturing location of the memory module. While the SPD specification will not attempt to present a decode table for manufacturing sites, the individual manufacturer may keep track of manufacturing location and its appropriate decode represented in this byte.

SPD Field 0×78 and 0×79: Module Manufacturing Date

The current week number should be inserted into the lower byte. The last two years of the year number should be inserted into the upper byte. Make sure to use Binary Coded Decimal for the two numbers.

Byte (Dec)	Byte (Hex)	Field Name	Typ. Value	Definition
120–121	0×78–0×79	Module Manufacturing Date	0×1004	Week 4, 2010

Bytes 120–121: Module Manufacturing Date
The module manufacturer includes a date code for the module. The JEDEC definitions for bytes 120 and 121 are year and week, respectively. These bytes must be represented in Binary Coded Decimal (BCD). For example, week 47 in year 2003 would be coded as 0×03 (0000 0011) in byte 120 and 0×47 (01000111) in byte 121.

SPD Field 0x7A–0x7D: Module Serial Number

Since there isn't a module (DIMM) physically present, this field is a "not care." However, it should be programmed for BIOS algorithms to be able to tell "if the DIMM has changed," which is a trigger for fast or slow boot paths.

Byte (Dec)	Byte (Hex)	Field Name	Typ. Value	Definition
122–125	0×7A–0×7D	Module Serial Number	20534846	"SHF"

Bytes 122–125: Module Serial Number
The supplier must include a unique serial number for the module. The supplier may use whatever decode method desired to maintain a unique serial number for each module. One method of achieving this is by assigning a byte in the field from 122–125 as a tester ID byte and using the remaining bytes as a sequential serial number. Bytes 117–125 will then result in a 9-byte unique module identifier. Note that part number is not included in this identifier: the supplier may not give the same value for bytes 119–125 to more than one DIMM even if the DIMMs have different part numbers.

SPD Field 0×7E and 0×7F: CRC Bytes

The CRC bytes must be calculated for bytes 0–125 using the formula above. Note that CRC needs to be checked for bytes 0–116 if bit 7 in SPD field #0 was set to 1b (which I don't recommend). This site is very useful for calculating the CRC-16 values: http://www.lammertbies.nl/comm/info/crc-calculation.html.

The result is shown in the CRC-16 field. Make sure to remove all spaces between the bytes, and make sure to select the "Hex" option, not "ASCII."

Byte (Dec)	Byte (Hex)	Field Name	Typ. Value	Definition
126–127	0×7E–0×7F	CRC Bytes	0×B227	---

Bytes 126–127: SPD Cyclical Redundancy Code (CRC)

This 2-byte field contains the calculated CRC for previous bytes in the SPD. The following algorithm and data structures (shown in C) are to be followed in calculating and checking the code. Bit 7 of byte 0 indicates which bytes are covered by the CRC.

```
int Crc16  (char *ptr, int  count)
{
int rc, i; crc = 0;
while  (--count  >=  0) {
crc = crc ^ (int)*ptr++ << 8; for  (i =  0;  i <  8; ++i)
if (crc  &  0x8000)
crc = crc << 1 ^ 0x1021; else
crc  =  crc  << 1;
}
return  (crc  &  0xFFFF);
}
char spdBytes[] = { SPD_byte_0, SPD_byte_1, ..., SPD_ byte_N-1 };
int data16;

data16  =  Crc16  (spdBytes,  sizeof(spdBytes));  SPD_byte_126  =
(char) (data16 & 0xFF); SPD_byte_127  =  (char)  (data16  >> 8);
```

SPD Field #126 and #127: "CRC Bytes" Definition from JEDEC DDR3 SPD Specification

SPD Field 0×80–0×91

Since there isn't a physical DIMM, I tend to use the SDRAM component name in lieu of the Module Part number. Also, this site is very useful for converting ASCII strings to hex values: http://easycalculation.com/ascii-hex.php.

Ensure to use the "Equivalent Hex Value" result.

Byte (Dec)	Byte (Hex)	Field Name	Typ. Value	Definition
128–145	0×80–0×91	Module Part Number (ASCII)	---	"MT41J256M8HX-187"

Bytes 128–145: Module Part Number
The manufacturer's part number is written in ASCII format within these bytes. Unused digits are coded as ASCII blanks (0×20).

SPD Field 0×92 and 0×93: Module Revision Code

Down-on-board memory designs should set these bytes to 0×00.

Byte (Dec)	Byte (Hex)	Field Name	Typ. Value	Definition
146–147	0×92–0×93	Module Revision Code	0×0000	---

Bytes 146–147: Module Revision Code
This refers to the module revision code. While the SPD specification will not attempt to define the format for this information, the individual manufacturer may keep track of the revision code and its appropriate decode represented in this byte.

SPD Field 0×94 and 0×95: DRAM Manufacturer ID Code

Use the same value used for fields 0×75–0×76 (the SDRAM component manufacturer ID extracted from the JEP-106 JEDEC specification).

Byte (Dec)	Byte (Hex)	Field Name	Typ. Value	Definition
148–149	0×94–0×95	DRAM Manufacturer IDCode	0×802C	Micron Technology

Byte 148: DRAM Manufacturer ID Code, Least Significant Byte
Byte 149: DRAM Manufacturer ID Code, Most Significant Byte
This two-byte field indicates the manufacturer of the DRAM on the module, encoded as follows: the first byte is the number of continuation bytes indicated in JEP-106; the second byte is the last non-zero byte of the manufacturer's ID code, again as indicated in JEP-106.

Byte 149, Bits 7–0	Byte 148 Bit 7	Byte 148 Bits 6–0
Last Nonzero Byte, DRAM Manufacturer	Odd Parity for Byte 148 bits 6–0	Number of Continuation Codes DRAM Manufacturer
See JEP-106		See JEP-106

SPD Field 0×96–0×AF: Manufacturer's Specific Data

Down-on-board memory designs should set these bytes to 0×00.

Byte (Dec)	Byte (Hex)	Field Name	Typ. Value	Definition
150–175	0×96–0×AF	Manufacturer's Specific Data	0×00	---

Bytes 150–175: Manufacturer's Specific Data
The module manufacturer may include any additional information desired into the module within these locations.

SPD Field 0×B0–0×FF: Open for Customer Use

Down-on-board memory designs should set these bytes to 0×00.

Byte (Dec)	Byte (Hex)	Field Name	Typ. Value	Definition
176–255	0×B0–0×FF	Open for Customer Use	0×00	---

Bytes 176–255: Open for Customer Use
These bytes are unused by the manufacturer and are open for customer use.

References for Appendix A

JEDEC Standard No. 21C: 240-Pin PC3-6400/PC3-8500/PC3-10600/PC3-
12800 DDR3 SDRAM Unbuffered DIMM Design Specification, Revision 1.01,
November 2009 http://www.jedec.org/ (requires account)
Standard Manufacturer's Identification Code JEP106-I (Revision of JEP-106-H)
JULY 2000 http://www.jedec.org/ (requires account)
Annex K: Serial Presence Detect (SPD) for DDR3 SDRAM Modules SPD Revision
1.0 Release 18 JEDEC Standard No. 21-C http://www.jedec.org/ (requires account)

MT41J256M8 Datasheet

http://download.micron.com/pdf/datasheets/dram/ddr3/2Gb_DDR3_SDRAM.pdf

All data from the JEDEC DDR3 SPD Specification is Copyright © JEDEC. All Rights Reserved. Reproduced with permission.

Information on JEDEC standards is current as of the date of this publication. For the most up-to-date version of JEDEC standards, visit www.jedec.org.

Index